ACCOUNTING FOR TRANSSEXUALISM

AND

TRANSHOMOSEXUALITY

ACCOUNTING FOR TRANSSEXUALISM

AND

TRANSHOMOSEXUALITY

THE GENDER IDENTITY CAREERS OF OVER 200
MEN AND WOMEN WHO HAVE PETITIONED FOR
SURGICAL REASSIGNMENT OF THEIR SEXUAL IDENTITY

Bryan Tully

w&b

Whiting & Birch Ltd
London
MCMXCII

Published by Whiting & Birch Ltd,
PO Box 872, Forest Hill, London SE23 3HL. United Kingdom.

London 1992

British Library Cataloguing in Publication Data
A CIP catalogue record is available on request from the British Library

ISBN 1 871177 04 9 (pbk)
ISBN 1 871177 08 1 (cased)

Printed in England by Short Run Press, Exeter

For my beloved parents

Jim and Pat Tully

CONTENTS

Bryan Tully

SUMMARY

This study reports the systematic collection of account from 204 transsexual subjects, most of whom attended the Gender Identity clinic at Charing Cross Hospital (Fulham).

A review of the literature covers cross gender behaviour in other societies, recent biological, social and psychological studies on gendered and cross gendered behaviour, a medical history of transsexualism and 'sex reassignment surgery'. Psychological 'frames' for the study of cross gendered careers are derived from attributional theories and symbolic interactionist approaches to the construction of sexual categories of behaviour and experiences.

The collection of accounts follows a methodology derived from Harré and his associates' ethogenic approach to the study of social behaviour and the principles of generating 'grounded (sociological) theory' propounded by Glaser and Strauss.

There is a short statistical section on the population of research subjects as a whole.

Transsexuals' accounts, some 500 excerpts, are marshalled under nearly 200 headings and subheadings. These cover almost all areas of relevant life experience.

The conclusions argue that there is a fundamental weakness in the imposition of psychiatric 'syndromes' on gender dysphoric phenomena. Rather, 'gender dysphoric careers' are proposed as fluctuating enterprises in the construction of meanings, some meanings being more fateful and workable than others. an attributional - 'imaginative involvement' model to account for transsexualism in explicated. The implications which can be drawn form this, for the way the management of these unfortunate people could be improved, completes the text.

INTRODUCTION

Jean Raymond in her book *The Transsexual Empire*, begins her articulate and polemical critique of the clinical world which 'manages' transsexuals, by pointing out that in about a quarter of a century only, transsexualism has become a household word. In that twenty five years or so, a steadily growing number of people, tens of thousands now, have presented themselves worldwide for radical surgery to be performed on their usually healthy bodies, so they can look and live as a member of the sex opposite to that which biology and society has originally assigned them. Although paradoxically, surgery cannot change genetic sex, nor indeed directly can a knife carve gender role or identity, which are psychological constructs, still these operations are generally referred to as 'sex reassignment surgery'.

Some transsexuals have achieved sensationalist public interest. Most ache for quiet 'undercover' lives. In this quarter century, thousands of studies have been carried out; interviews, questionnaires, psychological tests, chemical and physiological monitoring too. It is not clear whether all this has brought us much further along the road than was the case when Harry Benjamin published has careful and perceptive milestone classic *The Transsexual Phenomenon* in 1966. An imperfect overview of these studies is provided in Chapter One.

Something has been missing from these studies to date. This is the natural history of experience, the accounts transsexuals give of themselves, their voice. Their sayings are sometimes published as anecdotal examples of 'case material' to illustrate what the clinical researcher is referring to. Otherwise the responses of transsexual people are channelled to answering multiple choice questions devised by clinical researchers or are categorised under psychiatric headings which help the examiner to make sense of the answers to his or her questions. This of course is a completely defensible and effective scientific method when hypotheses are being 'explored' or tested. But hypotheses should surely arise out of an intimate acquaintance with that-which-is-to be- explained. for transsexuals, that is what they say they feel, what they say they need. That is the differentiating essence of the phenomenon. No person , no matter how he or she looks, or functions behaviourally or physiologically, will be diagnosed as 'transsexual', let alone prescribed sex reassignment surgery, unless what that person says he or she feels and says he or she needs, bears some resemblance to the ' transsexual phenomenon'.

This work is a detailed study of 'what they say'. It is claimed therefore to provide an archive or natural history of accounts, concerning which, theories, theses, explanations and so on can be built . It may be questioned as to why a special study is required when over a score of transsexuals have had published their life 'stories'. The reason is straightforward. Unfortunately these stories and apologias have been put together with the overriding purposes of justifying the transsexual status. Events and thoughts are marshalled together to demonstrate, to convince. They are a form of rhetoric, which unexamined and unchallenged as they are produced, after few glimpses of how such extraordinary tales came to develop, and what function they serve.

The Charing Cross Hospital study provided an opportunity for the writer, a psychologist who knew little of transsexual experience when he started, and over two hundred transexual subjects who knew little of the methods and means of psychological examination when they started to collaborate in a systematic, sympathetic yet sceptical 'interrogation' (from the Latin *interrogare* 'asking between'). The principles of this are described in Chapter Two.

To some extent, rather like archeology, the significance and the 'place' of matter so collected, depends on what other matter has been found and understood. Initial understandings have to be revised as the systematic comparative process goes on. The range of comparative experience made available by so many subjects has been unprecedented and unpredictable. Although the samples organised and tabled in Chapters Three, Four and Five represent only some ten per cent of the material collected, it will be clear that the unpackaged meanings of transsexual life experience are not easily recompressed into short generalisations or clichés.

Some of the subjects in this study were intellectually gifted, having studied and worked at prestigious universities in the UK and the USA. Professional accomplishments were common in many fields, including the humanities, science, the arts, medicine, architecture, the law, clinical psychology, music and mathematics. Many humbler occupations were highly represented in the numbers. So too were individuals who were petty criminals, prostitutes, drug addicts and alcoholics. Some subjects had major psychiatric problems on top of their transsexualism, and others had physical problems to overcome. These included multiple orthopaedic problems, being deaf and dumb, paraplegic, suffering from epilepsy, cerebral palsy, diabetes, haemophilia, etc. A special group are the mentally handicapped. Not specifically studied before, from them came some of the most striking and raw eloquence. They lack the mental wherewithal to gloss over discrepancies with sophisticated rationales. Their 'disturbances' and unmanageability present the most difficult of clinical challenges. Statistical data on the research population as a whole is to be found in the appendix.

BT

Bryan Tully

ACKNOWLEDGEMENTS

The late Dr. John B. Randall
formerly Consultant Psychiatrist
Charing Cross Hospital (Fulham)

who took care of over 2,000 patients with gender
identity problems over a period of twenty five years, and
without whom this study would have been impossible.

Professor Steven Hirsch
Head of Department of Psychiatry
Charing Cross and Westminster Hospital Medical School
(University of London)

who has maintained and sustained the existence and work
of the major gender identity clinic in the United Kingdom.

Professor Liam Hudson
Department of Psychology
Brunel University

who sustained the writer by encouragement and
challenge concerning this study over many years.

The research subjects
(listed on the following page)

who worked hard to make this study a success.

*This study was completed with the assistance of a grant from the North West
Thames Regional Health Authority through the 'locally organised research scheme'.*

THE RESEARCH SUBJECTS

Adele	William	Nina	Adam	Jamie
Tai-yan	John	Susan	Jennifer	Alex
Anne-Marie	Harry	Mandy	David	Carol
Tony	Carise	David	Katherine	Nina
Andrew	Adam	Wendy	Jack	Bob
Yana	Adrian	Julia	Martin	Sally
Janet	Tricia	James	Keith	Helen
John	Siew-ching	Bob	Stephen	Roger
Alan	Anthony	Philamena	Kevin	Clare
Matt	Patrick	Jennie	Carole	Ivan
Susan	David	Nick	Anthea	Denis
Alan	Diana	James	Rachel	Jan
Geoff	Marian	Brian	Christopher	Kate
Andrew	Matthew	Adrienne	Keith	George
Justine	Barry	Terence	Michaela	Grazana
Anthony	Chris	David	Carry	Owen
Sharn	Thomas	Brian	Auriol	Anna
Andrew	Kenneth	Angela	Trevor	Eric
Beatrice	Mark	Ellis	Moria	Matthew
Paula	Andrew	Andy	Keith	Derrick
Michelle	Saffendi	Kerry	Abdul	Ron
Susan	Marion	Herbert	Sandra	Elizabeth
Michael	Ronald	Catherine	Tu-yee	Glen
Marion	Timothy	Joan	Rebecca	Reginald
Jackie	George	Paul	Robert	Stanley
Jackqueline	Richard	Louise	John	Steven
Arthur	Susan	Chris	Collette	Donald
Sien-hoe	Bryan	David	Terri	Barbara
Rachel	Patricia	Ricky	Simon	Clifford
Anthea	Keith	Shirley	Maurice	Kim
Jule	Adrian	David	William	Vicky
Paul	Kenneth	Ronald	Letitia	Nicolas
Nina	Antonia	Clare	Henry	Robert
Arlene	Kevin	Joan	Ronnie	Michella
Peter	Angela	Ivy	Richard	Brian
Tony	Daren	Colin	Toni	Melanie
Davuid	Marion	Nedda	Joe	Angela
John	Jean	Anne	Joan	Vivienne
Peta	Burton	Stevie	'J'	Sara
Patrick	Michele	Nicholas	Phoebe	Becky
Phillip	Bruce	Charles	Arnold	

Bryan Tully

TRANSSEXUAL RAGE AND DESPAIR

'To anyone willing to listen'

'I will kill myself if I don;t become a girl. I don't want to die really, but if I don't become a woman, I will have to. Otherwise I will mentally tear myself apart and go mad ... what stupid, big headed, pompous and insensitive people professionals are. I thought doctors were supposed to make people better. I am being made into a nervous, frightened, confused, bitter and desperate wreck, making me worse and worse. I have so much to say but I just can' t get through to anyone. No one yet has ever understood me or had the time for me. This is why I write these notes because people don't ask the right questions. No one asks me what my qualifications are in, although they are biochemistry and physiology ... no one has ever started to find out what kind of person I am ... I have tried suicide before and considered that after the last attempt by exposure. I left my bedroom windows open with no clothes on and the heating turned off. It was minus two degrees centigrade that night. I have some explosives at home and a gun and flick knife. I have been responsible for some sabotage. I don't want anybody released from gaol, not 100, not a 1,000.. All I want is my rightful quota of female sex hormone which I have been deprived of since the age of 11. If I don't get it, I might do something silly. I am becoming that desperate. I may come armed next time. I am a very sensitive person, usually very gentle and not violent and to have had to come to this is a crime caused by my doctor. It is a good job that I wrote Immaculate Heart of Mary on my dashboard, otherwise there is no telling what I could do in my car ... It is absolutely fruitless delaying it as it has been a life long aim and I am going to get it anyway by fair means or foul.'

A young male transsexual, 1978

'Untreated transsexuals are among the most miserable people I have met. They rarely find any sympathy or understanding.'

Dr. Harry Benjamin, 1967

TRANSSEXUAL RHETORIC

'What (Dr. Harry Benjamin) did know was that no true transsexual has yet been persuaded, bullied, drugged, analysed, shame, ridiculed, or electrically shocked into an acceptance of his psyche ...
... It is only in writing this book that I have delved so deeply into my own emotions. Yet nothing I have discovered there has shaken my conviction, and if I were trapped in that cage again nothing would keep me from my goal, however fearful the prospects, however hopeless the odds. I would search the earth for surgeons, I would bribe barbers or abortionists, I would take a knife and do it myself without fear, without qualms, without a second thought.'

Jan Morris, Conundrum, 1974

CHAPTER ONE

THE PROBLEM OF TRANSSEXUALISM

Historical and Cross Cultural Variation and Meaning of Cross Gender Expression

The biological differences between men and women are the foundation for the most obvious and important division in human societies. Upon this basic sexual dimorphism has been built a much more extended set of gender norms which govern the role and conduct of men and women in all areas of social life. All societies have in common strong forms of divergent gender appropriate conduct. These forms, however, vary enormously across different societies, and across different periods of their histories (Davenport 1976).

The regulation and following of divergent gender appropriate conduct has never been perfect. First, fundamental differences of behaviour and ability determined by biological sexual dimorphism seem to be very limited (Maccoby & Jacklin 1974). Second, few rules and roles in society are absolute, permitting little or no variation in personal expression. More or less complete counter conformity in gender expression, *i.e.* transgender enactments, have been a persistent and puzzling feature in most societies. In Antiquity, Hippocrates considered transvestism in men to be an illness sent by the Gods. During the Puritan Commonwealth in England, such disordered behaviour was interpreted as a sinister and diabolical challenge to God's natural order, aligned to witchcraft (Ackroyd 1979). Among more contemporary societies, *e.g.* certain North American Indians, 'third gender' or transvestite status might be accorded to males who failed to pass muster as warriors, or indeed they might be honoured as shamans (Devereaux 1937). In various Eastern societies, the sacred and the profane were institutionalised together. The *hsiang ku* or 'mock women' of China's Sung Dynasty were organised into venerated prostitute guilds. In European late medieval societies, festive improprieties, including cross-dressing, were sanctioned as highlighting just what social proprieties were. In many societies, both east and west, there have been strong theatrical traditions of men dressing as women. The function of this has varied from protecting respectable women from acting to offensive misogynist mockery (Ackroyd 1979). Transgender activity then is not necessarily simple or singular in its motivation or meaning.

History of the Diagnosis of Transsexualism

According to Hoenig (1982) the phenomenon of transsexualism first entered the medical literature in 1853. Dr Frankel described a case of 'homomollia', *viz* a man who masqueraded as a women and had many sexual involvements with soldiers and sailors. He was eventually arrested, disease-ridden, and committed suicide. In 1930 a Danish painter Eingar Wegemar underwent castration surgery in Dresden, and a book was published in English in 1933, Man into Woman. Earlier, in 1925 Hirshfield had been the first to classify transvestite behaviour in males as distinctive from homosexuality *per se*. In 1949 Cauldwell first coined the term 'psychopathia transsexualis', and a few years later the world read of the first widely publicised case of the transformation of George Jorgensson to Christine Jorgensen. Danish surgeons carried out this castration in the belief it would help their patient overcome overriding sexual impulses.

The modern approach and study of transsexualism as a recognisable medical phenomenon can be dated to an early paper by Benjamin (1953).

It was not until 1963, however, that the first book was published reporting findings from some 50 cases mostly from the previous decade. This study by Georgina Turtle in the U.K.

has been largely overlooked, but the echoes this historical work has with the most up-to-date findings are most striking. The statistical data on age, occupation, and previous marital status for males anyhow are very similar to current findings. Turtle provided an interesting picture of the development of the transsex desire in individuals who were uncomfortable in a strictly divided and complementary scheme of heterosexuality. The role of the dream world of fantasy, shifting sexual desires, the believed availability of newly synthesised hormones and so-called sex change surgery are all shown to play a part in the transsex enterprise. Turtle also provided the first detailed picture of the enormous and confusing practical task of making a full-time gender change. In addressing the issue of what was the 'real answer', Turtle identified the real dangers of both seekers and surgeons taking an over medicalised and technical approach to this extraordinary form of human suffering. It has taken over a quarter of a century for some people to realise this.

It was, however, Harry Benjamin's book *The Transsexual Phenomenon* published three years later which put transsexualism on the map as a condition to be recognised and diagnosed. Benjamin believed transsexualism was an incurable endocrinological condition. He believed that the palliative treatment of 'sex reassignment surgery' (altering bodies to conform more closely in appearance to the desired other gender) was life-saving for people who he stated were among the most miserable he had met.

Tens of thousands of patients have now undergone various procedures worldwide. Transsexualism is nowadays included in most medical psychiatric classification systems. It has been grouped with a whole range of 'gender dysphoric syndromes' which include, for example, heterosexual transvestism and effeminate homosexuality. Transsexualism as a syndrome itself has been subdivided into 'primary' (early, assumed at least partly constitutional) and 'secondary' (appearing later, assumed somehow acquired).

Difficulties in the Diagnostic Classification of Transsexualism

The attempt to classify transsexualism as a medical syndrome, or set of sub-syndromes, is fraught with difficulty because such a task requires the discovery of a reasonable degree of regularity in the presenting diagnostic features, and in history and outcome or response to treatment.

Psychometric studies have generally failed to come up with any significant and consistent psychopathology associated with transsexualism (Lothstein 1984). Psychodynamic clinicians do claim to 'trace' severe psychopathology arising from the first few years of life, through projective tests and the like, but quite often all there is to be found is a mild or moderate difficulty in adjustment (Buhrich 1981). This is not related to strength of cross-gender expression as such. Langevin has found some male cross-gender expression associated with tendencies towards sadistic violence.

Sexual responsivity is mixed among male transvestites who become transsexuals (Bancroft 1972). Perhaps the most reliable sub-grouping which can be made is that of fetishistic transvestites who are usually heterosexual with weak cross-gender identities, and strong cross-gender identified transsexuals with little or no history of fetishistic arousal and with biologically homosexual orientations. Since the correlation of measures of biological sexual arousal, and subjective experience of arousal (modest anyhow for most people) are particularly low for transsexuals (Winzce & Steinman 1981), it should not be surprising that even the most enthusiastic of classifiers can only accommodate the mixed pattern of features by inventing various 'marginal' and 'borderline' groups (Buhrich & McConaghy 1977; Freund, Steiner & Chan 1982).

Perhaps the most precarious of all the diagnostic sub-classifications is that of primary *vs* secondary transsexualism. Primary transsexuals are sometimes referred to as 'real', 'nuclear', 'true' or 'core' transsexuals, and their condition is often considered to be partly due to a 'biological force', and/or a disordered development in the first few years of life when the bedrock of gender identity is supposedly established. This is a commonly held view by American psychiatrists who are more influenced by psychoanalytically derived theories of gender and personality development (Stoller 1968). In addition, some very young cross-gender identified males look so effeminate and seem so extremely cross-gendered, that it is hard for the examining physician not to feel that this must be constitutional, and to have any expectation that this youngster could live as a male is impossible. The fact remains that these views are not substantiated by evidence of an underlying constitutional disorder, or that the physical appearance is any more than the effeminate extreme of the range of masculine presentation at that age. Further evidential objections to this formulation will be presented in the sections examining the susceptibilities of gender socialisation and the progress of strongly cross-gendered individuals, notwithstanding what age this expression came to crystallise and appear 'natural'.

Difficulties in the Diagnostic Classification of Children Exhibiting Cross-Gender Identity and Behaviour

Most presenting adult transsexuals claim a marked cross-gendered self during childhood. Notwithstanding this, there is usually neither claim nor confirmation of any professional referral at that time. Professional referrals for strong and persistent cross-gender expressions in childhood are extremely uncommon (Zucker 1985). However, there are some children who make a clear statement of dislike for their own sex and/or genitalia. In addition they may exhibit sex-typed mannerisms and activity preferences more commonly associated with the opposite sex. Understandably, psychiatric diagnosticians such as Green (1974) have considered such children 'at risk' for adult transsexualism. *The Diagnostic and Statistical Manual (III)* of the American Psychiatric Association has recently included a syndrome of 'gender identity disorder of children' to assist medical diagnosis. The criteria comprise permutations of various degrees of cross-gender identity expression and cross-gendered behaviour. Rosen, Rekers & Friar (1977) tried to discriminate distinct syndromes of predominantly gender identity or gender role disorder. The overall correlations of their measures was in the order of 0.7. This was not low enough to support their two syndromes hypothesis, but neither was it strong enough to establish that all cases were examples of the one and same syndrome.

There is much evidence now that, for boys especially, cross-gender behaviour occurs in association with other psychological problems. These include their having generally poorer social interaction skills (Klein & Bates 1980), being less active, more introverted and possessing poorer general motor coordination (Bates, Bentler & Thompson 1973), and being more passive, harm avoidant and compulsively neat (Bates, Skilbeck, Smith & Bentler 1974). In over a third of Zuger's (1974) sample, there was a history of nocturnal enuresis, and a similar number had suffered from some form of language delay or speech impediment. Sreenivason (1981) reported a very interesting study from the opposite perspective so to speak. She reviewed a sample of boys attending a Newfoundland psychiatric clinic. They had been diagnosed as exhibiting neurotic disorders of all types, other than a gender identity disorder. Boys with higher ratings of neurotic psychopathology, exhibited much higher levels of cross-gendered sex-typed behaviour. The confounding of neurotic difficulties with cross-gender expressions has a parallel in the examination of studies of 'antecedent variables' of homosexuality. Green (1979) has pointed out that if effeminacy is partialled out of the childhood histories of homosexuals and heterosexuals, so are the neurotic differences. If the neurotic differences are partialled out, so are those differences in the data concerning close-bonding to a more intimate mother and having a more detached father.

With cross-gendered girls, childhood histories are almost the converse. Green, Williams & Harper (1979) found the majority of masculine girls to be good mixers, and many of them popular leaders among their peers.

The above findings do not fit well into a model of a specific cross-gender syndrome in children, which has its own distinctive symptomology and course. Various factors may be associated with cross-gender expression. The forms of that expression are varied. Psychoanalytic theory notwithstanding, there is little evidence that the problems seen in childhood are usually the outcome of particular faults or deficits in gender identity development.

Difficulties of Diagnostic Classification Associated with Prognosis and Therapeutic Outcome

Once a true syndrome has been established and recognised, then there should be some predictable course, albeit with normal variation. Contrary to what a theory of primary trans-sexualism might predict, most successful transsexuals are not diagnosed as gender-disordered in childhood. Zucker (1984) reviewed 94 cases of children who were so diagnosed, however, and where there was adequate follow-up. Around five per cent became adult transsexuals.

Generally, sex reassignment surgery is granted on the basis of the success of a trial period of a year or so full-time in the cross-gender role. Reviews of various clinic follow-ups (*e.g.* Pauly 1981) indicate that usually some 75 per cent of men and women are regarded as doing well, whilst six to eight per cent are classified as exhibiting clearly unsatisfactory outcomes. An early finding from the Stanford University group (Laub & Fisk 1974) indicated that once this cross-gender trial period was accomplished, then post-surgical adjustment was independent of any original diagnosis of 'true' transsexualism, transvestism, effeminate homosexuality or anything else. Lundstom (1981) found that the great majority of his patient series, who were denied surgery, continued to have strong gender dysphoric feelings three to five years later. In an admittedly controversial study, Meyer & Reter (1979) found no superior objective rehabilitation outcome for operated *vs* unoperated patients in their programme. Some kind of ceiling of adjustment had been accomplished before surgery. In addition, what were considered objective measures of adjustment, to be expected following a palliative medical treatment of a maladjustment syndrome, are considered something rather different by transsexuals. In many cases, the loss of well-paid jobs or certain relationships, or the burden of some bodily discomfort or inconvenience, or the restriction of certain aspects of sexual life are seen as a price willingly paid for a subjective satisfaction of great worth. The meaning of both the 'features' of transsexualism and reassignment surgery (which has effects even in advance of it being undertaken) cannot be partialled out of the evaluation of an individual.

Cases where individuals are 'reassigned' by surgeons, and then later revert back to their original gender role, are usually reported as tragic mistakes of original clinical assessment (Money & Wolfe 1973; Lothstein 1982). In the former case for example a man tried living as a male, 'neuter' and female, but none satisfactorily. Only after he had proved he could not fully accomplish the cross-gender role, after reassignment, did reversion take place. For the first time he settled down to a stable gender role and follow-up indicated he was functioning 'unexpectedly well', in spite of the lack of a penis. An alternative interpretation to that of this man being mistaken for a real transsexual when he wasn't, would accept the fact of genuine gender fluctuation and experiment as a gender career process.

Difficulties of Diagnostic Classification Associated with Psychological Theories of Gender Development and Socialisation

A major influence on the formulation of primary transsexualism as a disorder of the 'bedrock' of gender identity, has been psychoanalysis. Psychoanalytic theory posits gender identity and its disorders as arising out of the 'oedipal stage' of development, *i.e.* around the second year of life. Stoller (1975), the major authority, gives this account of how a mother makes a boy transsexual:

> ... mother felt a supreme oneness with the boy and ... did everything possible ... never to allow that blissful feeling to be interrupted ... Having created this beautiful phallus for which she had yearned (being latently bisexual) ... she could not let go of her cure.

Stoller offers no hard data to support these assertions, but the power of the interpretative imagination of the psychoanalyst is revealed by this quote from the mother's speech, which Stoller claims shows her 'latent bisexuality':

> I rarely have pants - I wear a dress, but before I got married and after I married I wore pants. I was really smart, top of my class you know. Nobody whipped me in grades.

Stoller's interpretations do not compel agreement. Even Person & Ovesey (1974a), who subscribe to the pre-oedipal development of transsexualism, searched in vain in the histories of ten primary transsexuals for anything consonant with Stoller's 'blissful closeness'. Another analytic writer, Lothstein (1983) made a major study of female transsexualism and asserted that, during the second year of life, the female transsexual-to-be is targeted by parents to change her gender to male because of its destructive and threatening potential. Out of all the histories of 53 females, Lothstein made not one reference to any empirical data linking family activity to the child's two-year-old gender identity.

Empirical studies by cognitive developmental theorists (Kohlberg 1966; Slaby & Frey 1975; Lewis & Weinraub 1979) indicate that a form of gender identity is established between the ages of two and three years. Children regularly refer to themselves in the correct gender. Gender 'stability' is recognised in the following year, *i.e.* the child acknowledges normal continuity in gender of infant, child and adult. True gender 'constancy' (*i.e.* that gender cannot be changed by wishes or appearance) emerges during the Piagetian 'concrete operational' phase of cognitive development, roughly from the fourth to seventh year. Even then, the cues used for assignment may be hairstyle and body shape, rather than the genitalia. McConaghy (1983) found some children to assert the constancy of gender as linked to sex role concepts. That is girls could not become men in the same way they could not become generals. A normal child may be nine years old before a complete genital basis for gender is fully established.

The staging of sex role prescriptions is not symmetrical across the sexes. Archer (1984) found that boys are brought up to avoid girls' activities, far more than the other way around. Failure to achieve the masculine stereotype far more readily prompts concern or hostility. After adolescence this strictness as to role expression is almost reversed. This illuminates why masculine-failing boys are seen so much more frequently than feminine-failing girls. Where erotic drives occur unusually early, the initial sexual attachments are far more likely to be with the homosocial peer group (Storms 1981). Boys who are masculine 'failures' may fail at the stage of heterosexual dating or they may have some success and develop bisexual attachments. Girls who have been tomboys have been able to behave much more freely. If they develop lesbian attachments, this conflicts with the new suddenly much more restricted adult female role (sweetheart, wife, mother) so that a crisis is likely to occur. This fits the general finding that female transsexual awareness emerges at adolescence rather than before, and almost all female transsexuals are biologically homosexual. Boy transsexuals and transsexuals-to-be have a more mixed range of sexual orientations.

A number of studies have failed to find specific transgenderising features in mother-son relations of transsexuals or homosexuals (Bell, Weinberg & Kiefer-Hammersmith 1981; Parker & Barr 1981). However absence, or distance, or overprotectiveness, or sex anxiety or psychiatric disturbances in fathers have all been found to have some association with boys' effeminacy and other problems (Green 1974). The general circumstances have been such as to undermine boys' confidence and fail to provide adequate masculine role models and support. The tolerance of extreme feminine behaviour in boys is the one extraordinary and specific contribution to an established cross-gender problem. Successful treatment of cross-gendered boys is based on remedying these circumstances (Rekers 1977). Overall, the current evidence is less consistent with gender identity and disorder being rooted in psychoanalytic bedrock than in a more developmental clay.

Difficulties of Diagnostic Classification Associated with 'Biological Dispositions'

The search for the underlying disorder of transsexualism has often involved the consideration of biological dispositions. It is known that temporal lobe damage can strikingly affect sexual behaviour (Hoenig 1985). There are often other associated changes in mood state, appetitive and other instinctive behaviours, and altered states of consciousness. However, the great majority of transsexuals do not exhibit such differentiated abnormalities, and patients who do are not usually transsexual.

The hypothalamic sex centres in lower animals have been found to differ in anatomical organisation, and to have specific control over divergent sexual fixed action patterns. By suitable surgical and hormonal interventions, it is possible, for example, to prepare a male rat which attempts to behave as a female in the sex act, and *vice versa* (Dörner 1976). Dörner's findings of dimorphic anatomical structure and fixed action patterns have not been found in humans. The range and diversity of sexual activity in humans belies such a simple control mechanism.

There are, however, a number of hormonal developmental disorders in humans which affect secondary sexual characteristics and behaviour. For example, andrenogenital hermaphroditism in girls appears to have some prenatal androgenising effects on central structures, in that even when individuals are diagnosed and treated at birth, there is subsequently a more masculine style in behaviour *i.e.* a greater preference for vigorous physical activity, less concern for self adornment and less strong responsivity to helpless infants. Notwithstanding this, such individuals still identify themselves as girls and usually have conventional relationships. Where the condition is missed at birth, and the child is raised as a male, then these behavioural traits can and are easily worked into a male identity. (Money & Ehrhardt 1972). Money and his associates have followed up scores of hermaphrodites and have concluded that individuals of the same hermaphroditic diagnosis, if reared in completely opposite gender roles, differentiate a gender identity in agreement with their biography, *irrespective* of chromasomal, gonadal and hormonal sex. Money, at least in his earlier work, insisted on important caveats to this generalisation. One was that imposed gender identities must be established during a critical period (roughly up to 3 years of age) so as not to conflict with an earlier developing identity. Second, the medical and social treatment of the individual had as far as possible to minimise incongruities. Many writers criticised Money's strong position on this, and cited cases where late gender switches or reversals had occurred, (*e.g.* Diamond 1982). Generally these were cases where physical or social incongruities existed and caused marked distress. Money himself (1980) published discussions of cases where the presence of these incongruities led to 'unfinished' or undermined gender identities. Under these circumstances, a gender career may still have stages through which to progress.

Whilst it is hard to find direct biological fixers of gender identity, it seems reasonable that biological constitutions, especially involving problems, defects, or incongruities in childhood or adolescence, can give rise to crises where gender identity is spoiled or reworked. Green (1974) reported identical twins where one was repeatedly hospitalised and otherwise brought up in a highly protected passive way, and became strongly feminine. The other brother spent most of his time with the father in rough and tumble games and activities; he exhibited no such traits. Thus everyone must be some *body*. The development of gender identity and role appears to depend on the perceived adequacy and salience of physical robustness and attractiveness, behavioural traits, erotic sensibility and readiness. When these biologically grounded experiences disrupt the integrity of assigned gender, this may lead to a reworking of that identity.

'Imaginative Involvements', Alternative Personifications, and Other Dissociative Experiences

Green, Williams & Harper (1979) found that many cross-gendered boys often spent time alone. This was partly due to their timidity, lack of social skill and the rejection of others, but for at least 32 per cent this was definitely their choice too. One aspect of this, which has been given comparatively little attention, is the extraordinarily high levels of imaginative play-acting found in such boys, as compared with normal boys. This was often linked to 'exquisite sensitivity' to colours, sounds and textures, and included extensive and highly developed role-play often with imaginary companions.

Overt make-believe play seems to peak in American children at around the age of five (Singer 1980). Ordinary children who show the greatest predispositions tend to be those who take up reading most enthusiastically (Singer 1981), and they too are more likely to have spent more time alone. Daydreaming (internal make-believe) develops through childhood and peaks around adolescence, and Singer's research indicates that much of it is involved in exploring future possibilities, and how significant relationships should work. Sexual fantasies, which go beyond the conventional, may develop unusual storylines or scripts and involve a degree of aggression, violence or masochistic and fetishistic themes. Very deviant and complex fantasies are generally found in males where significant guilt or anxiety is associated with sexual activity *per se*.

In her study of hypnotic susceptibility, Josephine Hilgard (1979) found good subjects to be high on 'imaginative involvement'. They demonstrated lifelong propensities to become absorbed in reading, drama, religious experience and the like, and could enjoy the most vivid sense of actually 'being there' say in a novel or a play. Hypnosis seemed to capitalise on a capacity to allow free play of the imagination which could set aside reality. Childhood imaginary playmates were reported very frequently and played a major role. She cites one case where a girl 'tomboy' wished she had been a boy. She played with, or substituted herself by, an imaginary twin brother. Even as an adult she would take on the personality of this imaginary companion. This finding of extraordinary capabilities to 'be' an imaginary companion was confirmed by Wilson & Barber's (1980) study of 'excellent' hypnotic subjects. Again, this 'resource' was found to be a means of escape from a bad environment, and it was often associated with long periods of isolation and loneliness. As adults these subjects reported 'addiction' to fantasy, hallucinatory images, make-believe alternative personalities, and psychic experiences.

Misattributions concerning erotic arousal have often been demonstrated. Cantor, Zielman & Bryant (1975) manipulated subjects to enhance their erotic 'perception' of a film, depending on their stage of recovery from previous strong physical activity. Cox & Aroaz (1977) used hypnosis to recover orgasmic memories for disabled sexually anaesthetic patients. Much of the training used nowadays to assist non-orgasmic women is fantasy based and directed to help the subject 'let go', and disattend to interfering monitoring of self-arousal. These procedures are used to manoeuvre around monitoring or performance anxiety, but other kinds of sex related anxieties may also lead to fantasy-based manoeuvres to dissociate that anxiety from once removed sexual stimuli. This is the function, Gosselin & Wilson (1980) argue, of the need fetishists, transvestites and sado-masochists have to create crude theatrical scenarios and roles, along with appropriate 'props' (whips, ropes, underwear, rubber *etc.*). The 'scripts' for these rituals usually start at a young age and become increasingly elaborated through life, through creative association. They report one interesting finding, that as this fantasy sex drive increases, so does the elaboration of submissive fantasies. They speculate this is possibly the result of early conditioning when sexual arousal may have been experienced under conditions of restraint *e.g.* whilst being punished.

Under conditions of long-term highly rehearsed, vivid imagery, 'reality monitoring' of the boundary of fantasy and reality may fail (Johnson & Rage 1981). Many of the most brutal multiple or lust killers have been shown to have indulged very extensively in fantasy life, to the point where actually torturing a person to death is but an extension of that fantasy life (Hazelwood & Douglas 1980). Langevin (1985) has made a special study of the Erotic Violence Syndrome in such men. A number have been found unexpectedly to have transvestite interests, and many do exhibit right temporal lobe abnormalities. Money (1979) has pointed out that the fantasy and rituals involved help establish a trance-like altered state of consciousness, necessary for satisfaction. These subjects, like transsexuals, often have memory difficulties in their alternative personas concerning their feelings and actions, if they are interviewed in their conventional roles. These amnesic barriers have often been reported in cases of multiple personality (Hilgard 1977), and are also reported in mood mediated state-dependent learning or recall *e.g.* depression *vs* euphoria (Bower 1981). This organising, and therefore dividing, principle of memory has been drawn on by Hilgard to develop his neo-dissociationist theory of these phenomena. Cognitive sub-systems may be activated for one activity and not another. Central monitors usually activated by danger, pain, novelty *etc.* may fail to be so if imaginative involvements or highly rehearsed fantasy or rituals encode memories in terms of the special affect and script memory (Tulving & Thomson 1973) associated specifically with one sub-system, or domain of mental life.

Conclusion

The purpose of this first chapter has been to make a critical examination of the notion 'transsexualism' as a medical condition of which increasing numbers of people report themselves to be a victim. This sets the scene for an alternative approach, the examination of biographical courses where both biologically-grounded and socially-derived experience constitute the powers and resources brought to bear on the task of constructing and maintaining a gender identity.

This approach is primarily concerned with the symbolic enterprise of framing private meanings of experience, and public categories which underpin emergent gender identity.

It should be possible to delineate moral careers, sequences of crucial turning points, progressions which fatefully converge on the clinical syndrome of transsexualism, and also divergencies, retreats, relapses, and droppings out.

The examination of what is entailed by acts, intentions, judgements and justifications and so on should be revealing of the crucial cognitive, emotional and imaginative processes necessary for the final crystallization of the transgender commitment. It will be expected that these fateful crystallizations can be found to have common attributional dimensions. This approach although leading to certain generalisations is expected to reveal highly idiosyncratic autobiographical legends with significant individual differences in dissociative consciousness, self serving biased or self deceptive attributions, areas of hypersensitivity or glossings over and so on.

From what is known of the different developmental pathways of gender normative socialization in males and females, then differences should be found between male and female transsexualism in relation to such relevant issues as perceived adequacy and salience of physical robustness, behavioural 'traits', group membership, sexual style preferences and other erotic sensibilities and anatomical endowments. In contrast with theories which locate the cause of transsexualism in the earliest years, the cognitive-developmental grasp of gender identity, stability, and constancy would not be expected to be disordered. In other words as children there should be clear evidence of established appropriate gender identities which are therefore pre-transsexual.

Sex reassignment surgery is part of this moral career and its symbolic significance and effect should be shown to be serious and far reaching well before such surgery actually takes place for the individual. Objective satisfaction will be considered alongside a search for the appropriate vocabulary used to account for the psychic and physical cost involved in order to achieve a legitimately acknowledged sense of gendered self which would hopefully be a firm enough defence against external invalidation and internal doubt.

This kind of examination of transsexuals' accounts is expected to establish how transsexualism is a practical symbolic problem, why commitments to this identity work, as opposed to other alternatives, and what the limitations are of the undertaking of a transsexual passage.

CHAPTER TWO

STUDYING ACCOUNTS:
THE CHARING CROSS PROJECT

Accounts as Data

The 'ethogenic' approach to the understanding of human behaviour has been developed in its modern form primarily by Harré and his associates (Harré & Secord 1972; Harré 1976; Harré & De Waele 1977). Central to this approach is that individuals are authorities on themselves, and can be called to account for actions which have specific social meanings. This is distinguished conceptually and methodologically from the study of behaviour as 'movements' or physiological mechanisms. The progressive revealing of the reasons for actions cannot provide a final, efficient cause which a physical science might seek. Nonetheless, the study of authentic reasons is undisregardable for the study of persons.

The competency to create meaningful acts, make plans, experience emotion, hold certain values, be subject to prejudicial influences and so on, all constitute the personality, that is to say the powers and resources available for acting, and expressing personas and roles under different socially understood circumstances. No one can know all the influences which bear on his (or others') conduct, and so no account can reveal completely or perfectly the powers and resources expressed by any act. Neither is this necessary for the practical tasks of understanding personal and social life. An account can reveal enough to 'warrant' a behaviour called into question. Insofar as it does, it is honoured and satisfactory. Insofar as it does not, it is discounted and not considered authentic. The authenticity of accounts is a different issue from that of the 'correctness' of objective explanations of physical phenomena. Whether accounts are warranted or not depends on the context. For example, a robber explaining that he robbed a certain bank, because he knew the safe mechanism was defective, will not have that considered a satisfactory explanation in court. In a pub with his fellow villains, there would be no further questions. In court a less discountable account, in terms of the norms of the court, might be that he and his family needed money desperately to prevent a mortgage foreclosure on their home. The test of authenticity is not the historical truth, but whether in a particular context, an act is considered warranted by the account. Accounts therefore reflect both the special authority that an individual is on his own behaviour, and the interlacing context in which it is rendered (Shotter 1978).

Accounts are gathered for the purpose of scholastic study, by negotiation, in order to satisfy appropriate tests of credibility. Revelations of what underlies acts is achieved by exploration of what was entailed by those acts, intentions, excuses, justifications and so on. Fundamental statements of motivation involving loving or desiring another person, for example, have a promissory character. They reflect an undertaking, and the test of acceptance is not whether the current antecedent conditions can be identified, but whether, through the monitoring of that undertaking, it can be inferred that he or she meant what he or she said, or had something else 'in mind'.

Where it is difficult to persuade audiences, examiners, judges *etc* to accept very deviant behaviour, then in that context, special 'vocabularies of motive' (Mills 1940) may be employed to achieve a false negotiated concordance with the thinking and value systems of those powerful authorities. Thus child molesters provide excusing accounts centred on the difficulties of controlling sexual feelings, the seductiveness of children and so on (McCaghy 1979). Strong avowals may be made to satisfy potential discounting, for excuses and justifications 'throw bridges between the promised and the performed' (Scott & Lyman 1968). A current situation may be so difficult that fake accounts may be honestly reworked from earlier perspectives and come to be believed by the individual; an instance of self-deception. Many psychiatric patients struggle to regain authority over their acts and deny their illness as a cause of behaviour, but where psychiatric disorder is presented to account for *e.g.* transsexualism, special care must be exercised. This account renders to the doctor the appropriate patient status, a victim of a condition, a product of an aetiology of disorder, impairments, lacking of will and ability, altogether the 'sad tale' necessary to qualify for receiving the 'medical treatment' of sex reassignment surgery.

Principles and Methods of Gathering Accounts in the Charing Cross Project

Biographies of subjects were built up through a series of interviews over a number of years. 'Topics' were developed out of emergent accounts of experiences, understandings, doubts, views of the past and future destinies, implications, puzzles, confusions and conflicts. Also examined were special pleadings, excuses, justifications, exaggerations and glossings-over. The grounds for action and belief would be called for, especially those where they had not been called for hitherto. Managing problems, conflicts and dilemmas in real life and especially 'changes of mind' provided opportunities for penetrating assumptions and assisting the revelation of powers and resources, or the lack of them. This progressive revealing of 'what is in mind' was of course interlaced with the plans, judgements and actions of other people, including crucially 'treatment' from the gender identity clinic. This interlacing was not fixed over time, and retrospective frames of avowal could be moved back and forth from different points in real time. This reminding process was used to search for discrepancies, unarticulated qualifications, self-serving 'vocabularies of motive', and to provoke half-used or discarded perspectives. Persistent and consistent self-serving constructions are likely to be incorporated into psychic structures, and it is not always possible to 'uncover' a history. However, since so many subjects were interviewed at length at different stages in their lives, a sufficient discovering of developmental dynamics proved possible to accomplish. Hudson (1978) has commented on this sort of method of inquiry as,

> ... the hermeneutic reading of .... accounts does require a contributing leap from the inquiring psychologist. Neither data nor belief are adequate in themselves, nor is the relationship between them... simple... The active reading of a person's account is an attempt to grasp the structure of meaning with which his thought gives rise, and which contributes to organizing the context of action. ... The relationship between the investigator and data base is an intimate one which can be an access or an obstacle to his examination of human nature. There is an eloquent traffic between account giver and gatherer that is genuinely heuristic.

The 'topics' emerged initially at whatever analytic level fitted the account givers' expressions. They were constantly compared (Glaser & Strauss 1967), cross-referenced, revised and refined, until finally they could be ordered in such a way as to constitute an appropriate framework for understanding what it is to be transsexual. The subheadings in chapters three, four and five, all concerning transsexuals accounts, are the final outcome of this process, and they are related together through their different conceptual levels.

Subject Groups and Interviewing Schedule

The gender identity clinic at Charing Cross Hospital was the gateway to the research project for all subjects diagnosed as transsexual. Subjects fell into one of five of the following cohorts:

Cohort 1: new beginners

107 individuals - 67 males, 40 females
This cohort was made up of patients who attended the gender identity clinic for the first time at the beginning of the research project. This recruitment took just over one year to be completed. At the end of the study, 23 individuals achieved sex reassignment surgery; 25 individuals had ceased attending; 40 individuals still attended the clinic.

Cohort 2: already attending

27 individuals - 23 males, 4 females
These patients were already attending the clinic when the research project started. Since it was a longitudinal 'follow through' study, it was hoped more of these would have reached sex reassignment surgery than the new beginners. It turned out in due course, however, that this was not the case. At the end of the study 4 individuals achieved sex reassignment surgery; 8 individuals still attended the clinic; 15 individuals had ceased attending.

Cohort 3: post-reassignment surgery

33 individuals - 22 males, 11 females
This cohort comprised patients who had all achieved sex reassignment surgery, and were being followed up.

Cohort 4: special cases

37 individuals - 31 males, 6 females
This cohort comprised patients who reported some extraordinary feature of history or current presentation.

Cohort 5: transhomosexuals

12 individuals - 6 males, 6 females
This cohort comprised a special group of referrals from a research project into transhomosexuality, conducted by Dorothy Clare at the London Hospital. Transhomosexuality has been defined by Clare (1984) as a special 'penchant' for, identification with, or attraction to homosexual persons of the opposite sex. A subject may exhibit varying degrees of identification with the desired sex object. An expanded note on transhomosexuality is to be found in the Appendix.

On average, subjects were seen for in-depth interviews every six months or so, but this varied depending on how their 'career' was going and how easy it was for them to get to the clinic from various parts of the UK. Some individuals were only seen once a year, and some 'special cases' only once or twice. The 'new beginners' of cohort 1 were the most extensively interviewed over the data collection phase of the study 1979-83. The total number of extended interviews conducted for each cohort were as follows:

Cohort 1:	New beginners	423
Cohort 2:	Already attending	62
Cohort 3:	Post-reassignment surgery	73
Cohort 4:	Special cases	53
Cohort 5:	Transhomosexuals	17

Judging the Credibility of Accounts Rendered

Where research data are examined for the purposes of the verification or refutation of specific hypotheses, then strongly parsimonious uniformities will be required of that data. 'Grounded' data, on the other hand, of a kind necessary for the generation of theory is likely to involve a diversity of topics and analytic levels (Glaser & Strauss 1967).

The ethogenic test of accounts as to whether they can be 'warranted' as authentic, is that of whether they satisfy a particular 'calling into question' of words or behaviour. At the very least there must be seen to be a sensitivity and aptness of language in the transformed accounts, not 'out of place' with a plausible background context. For the finally rendered research account to be judged credible, there must be sufficient transparency in its construction for several matters to be resistible to the process of their attempted discounting. The scheme of the accounts must be seen to be coherent and non parochial, *i.e.* to reflect a proper range of informants and their experiences. The degree of involvement of those who render accounts to the research enterprise must be clearly adequate, casual or unthinking comments will not be good grounds for future conclusions. A basic competence to meet the research objectives must be demonstrated. Motivation underlying the account-giving, and the function of avowals concerning conduct must be sufficiently manifest to resist the discounting of that account.

The contribution of expertise in the collection of accounts should be perceptible. This refers clearly to special knowledge. This covers the intensive knowledge of individuals whose experience is being examined, and the extensive knowledge of the examiner beyond the boundary of the individual subject concerned. Genuine collaboration should reflect the researcher's developing expertise in cross examination and ability to test for internal consistency. According to Brown and her associates (Brown & Sime 1977; Canter & Brown 1981), attestability of this kind of qualitative data is 'built in', insofar as they allow outside judges to make the above kinds of 'authenticity checks'.

Two qualifications in particular need to be made concerning any faith put in transsexuals' accounts. One concerns the recognition of deliberate and skilful deception contrived to achieve hormones and surgery. It is very difficult to sustain complex cover stories over a long time in the face of extended cross-examination. As police and espionage interrogators know full well, some 'leakage' of what is being covered up is almost impossible to prevent. The topics most prone to such distortion are well known as are the types of distortion and gloss (Walker 1981). Uncovering cover-ups is usually not resisted when subjects come to believe they will not suffer a disadvantage.

The question of self-deception is more problematic. Rorty (1972) has made a rare but useful attempt to explore the philosophical implications of what this amounts to. Basically, it needs to be recognised that there are mighty forces marshalling the memories of past experience in order to sustain a present and future direction of gender identity. There are reasons to believe matters where good grounds for that belief are lacking. There are always unacknowledged sources of behaviour, but substantial self-deception is likely to be manifest as a general affirmation or avowal somewhat dissociated from expected entailments for action other than the particular entailments the self-deception is self-serving. In practice, this means that where there is a major motivational bias in the recollection of memories, then this entails behaviours and identity statements which are excessively strong, broad and 'neat'. What is not so entailed is dislocated so to speak from its place in an account. It is glossed, minimised, disowned. In its extreme form, genuine dissociative experience may be the result. This involves barriers or divisions in consciousness and memory. Special attention has been given to this process, and its role in transgender career developments.

Statistical Findings Concerning the Research Population

A number of statistical findings were extracted from subjects' interviews and medical records, and these have been tabulated in the Appendix.

Some 29 per cent of the total sample of 204 transsexual subjects achieved sex reassignment surgery (Table 1 refers). However the rate of achievement for those who had not been operated on when the study started was just over 20 per cent. This is comparable to many other gender identity clinics internationally, but probably somewhat above average.

There was a clear tendency for females to present at an earlier age than males (Table 14 refers). Females usually came during or before their early twenties. Males were mostly in their twenties and thirties, some were in their forties and fifties, and a few in their sixties and seventies. Our oldest customer was a veteran of the Spanish Civil War. Generally, subjects presenting after their forties were much less likely to be granted reassignment surgery.

Generally, patients stayed on the books for two or three years during which time they could be expected to be accepted for reassignment if they ever were to be (Table 15 refers). There was a very wide variation in attending periods, from less than a year, to almost a decade.

The occupational accomplishments of transsexual subjects were hugely varied, with many having reached high levels within their professions. This reflected the equally wide-range of intellectual resources available to various subjects (Tables 2 and 3 refer).

Nearly a third of males who achieved surgery, and half of those who did not, had been married. A small number had been married more than once. This has important implications for any theory of transgender development in males. It must take into account that at certain times as adults, serious beliefs and attempts to live in the original assigned gender role have existed. By contrast, marriage among female transsexuals is uncommon (Table 4 refers).

When males have fathered children in their original gender role, their chances of being successful candidates for reassignment surgery is significantly lowered. Only half a dozen males did so. Females bear children far less commonly, and this reflects their consistent lack of desire for sexual relations with men under any circumstances (Table 4 refers).

About a third of all transsexuals reported severe family problems in their family of origin. These included histories of violence, crime, drug or alcohol abuse, severe psychiatric illness, family breakups including unhappy wartime evacuations and circumstances leading to adoption. Assessments were indicative rather than definitive. Subjects' evaluations were a guide as were the involvement of medical, social service or court agencies. In general, this kind of background lowers significantly the chances of achieving sex reassignment surgery as it affects both psychological stability and social resourcefulness (Table 7 refers).

Almost half of all males who achieved sex reassignment surgery, and two thirds of those who had not, had received some form of psychiatric treatment other than for gender dysphoria. These treatments were mostly for depression. About a fifth of males had been hospitalised at some time for in-patient treatment, and that history weighed very heavily against their chances of achieving sex reassignment surgery. This is probably a joint product of the lack of stable resourcefulness needed by any individual to successfully change gender life-style permanently, and the wariness of medical practitioners in granting potentially disturbing treatment to such persons. About a third of females who achieved sex reassignment, and about half of those who had not, had received other psychiatric treatment. In-patient treatment was uncommon (Table 6 refers).

A major distinction between males and females concerned the incidence of childhood 'nervous timidity'. Four out of five presenting males reported such a history, including significant fear of peers, an overriding sense of personal weakness, marked shyness, a loathing of physical activity and so on. This was reported rarely among females, and not at all among those granted reassignment surgery (Table 13 refers).

Over half of all males also reported conditions or appearances during childhood, about which they were significantly anxious and self-conscious. Among those reported were a huge range of both objectively serious defects such as paraplegia, or being deaf and dumb, to matters where psychological reactions were extremely marked to small genitals, stuttering, obesity *etc*. Just over 10 per cent of females reported any such thing from childhood.

These self-conscious conditions do not include those which would be part of gender dysphoria *e.g.* a boy hating an ordinary penis, or a female her pubescent breasts (Tables 8, 9 and 10 refer).

About half of all males, and a third of all females got involved in criminal activities at some time or other. This was usually petty crime, but sometimes included more serious theft and drug offences. This reflected one of the hazards of living in 'marginal' or socially deviant worlds, as well as perhaps of making a practical habit of dissimulation. In turn, about half of all transsexual subjects had been victims of violence at some time (Tables 11 and 12 refer).

A final statistical footnote concerns the total number of patients attending the gender identity clinic at Charing Cross Hospital. From 1960-1979 there was virtually a linear trend upward, doubling the number of new cases twice over the two decades. The early 1980s showed a fairly stable 'recruitment' of over 200 new patients each year.

CHAPTER THREE

TRANSSEXUAL ACCOUNTS: CHILDHOOD AND ADOLESCENCE

Note on the Use of Verbatim Material by Research Subjects

The methods by which topics are identified and addressed, and recollections and perceptions examined, has been described in Chapter Two. The segments quoted constitute the actual words spoken by research subjects. They are however, edited passages, arranged with other passages so as to make manifest some point or argument. The publication of raw transcript would of course be unassimilable. The reader should read the passages with this in mind.

In some early parts, the passages speak for themselves, and have required only a skeletal set of links or commentary. In later parts the meaning of quoted statements is embedded much more in existing contexts of foundation knowledge and theory discussed in Chapter One.

Indexation Code for Subjects

MF	male to female transsexual who has not undertaken sex reassignment surgery
FM	female to male transsexual who has not undertaken sex reassignment surgery
MF-PR	male to female transsexual, post-Reassignment
FM-PR	female to male transsexual, post-Reassignment
M-THO	male transhomosexual
F-THO	female transhomosexual

Childhood Nature

Male to female transsexuals

Physical impairments and stuttering

In the statistical survey of the project's transsexual population, it was found that 60 per cent of male children suffered some condition in childhood which they were significantly anxious or self conscious about (Table 10 refers). The association of these experiences and other basic feelings about how such a child felt about itself are indicated in the following quotations:

> Before I was twenty, I felt strongly that I didn't like anything to do with my body, but since then, I have had these feelings only about my genitalia. As a child I was small and had rheumatism in my ankles, wrists, forearms and chin (MF 176).

> In my early years I was known as a dear little child. I ran away from primary school repeatedly to be with my mother. I was more frail than other children because of a chronic tapeworm illness. I had treatments, including starvation, between the ages of two and five years (MF 111).

> As a child I spent a lot of time in hospital undergoing orthopaedic surgeries, and I have had various operations on my left hip and right knee, and both my feet have had abnormalities. After I came out of hospital, my mother died and I started cross-dressing (MF 102).

> I was timid, wet the bed, bit my nails, feared the dark, and thunder. I was small and had a strangulated testicle when I got pushed against some machine by accident. The doctor said I didn't have the right physique (MF 100).

> When I was seven years old I got sleeping sickness and never went to school afterwards. I was always flaked out and exhausted, and a nervous thing. I was so frightened my mother

had to accompany me to the toilet ... other children used to laugh at me (MF 49).

I have always been afraid of dogs. I was frightened at school and bullied, although ... I was particularly intelligent ... I was taunted when I had to strip for P.E. At age 12, a diagnosis of undescended testicle was made. I knew then I was becoming anxious about becoming a man and the teachers considered me as a dead loss (MF 34).

I had a history of fits and convulsions ... was of very tender build ... was afraid of the dark and animals and was bullied at school (MF 145).

Reactions of children to a spoiled appearance can be very strong, even when the deficits are not objectively severe:

I was considered a sissy at school, having very gentle behaviour ... I was envious of my sister's hair. My nose seemed very big and I told myself I wanted it changed. I continued to have these feelings and ... once I had to pose in an art class and I felt my nose would annoy good artists. I felt worse and thought others believed that I had a pudgy fat nose. I was referred to as a 'queer looking bugger' (MF 31).

I may have been a little self conscious because my ears stuck out ... and I had acne ... I stopped talking to people and took a lot of time off school. I was ugly and looked like a monkey (MF 53).

Many males reported stuttering as well as other things:

I was sent to a special boarding school, and I was shy, timid, nervous, scared of the dark and a bed wetter until the age of ten. At the age of five or six, I had a speech problem and had to go to a speech therapist. It comes out if my mother or father have a go at me. It hurts so much that my words get jumbled and now (as an adult) my false teeth come loose at times. As a child I walked different from other boys, and my nose was not right (MF 130).

I was often beaten up at school. I stuttered very badly right through school until the age of 17 or 18 (MF 94).

The following subject had many problems, and subscribes to the psychoanalytic view of child development:

As a child I was nervous and tearful and cared for by many nannies. I was backward at lessons, and not allowed to mix with other children. I suffered from poor co-ordination and double vision due to ocular palsy caused by birth trauma. I also suffered rheumatic fever. I was sent to an orphanage, and when my mother left me there I had a strong sense of inferiority. I was excluded and victimised by pupils and staff. I had to learn to love my mother and believe that she cared for me. The oral stage of development remained with me and I found myself always hungry for food, love, and later for knowledge (MF-PR 30).

Physical appearances linked to gender

Although most males in this category did not explicitly link their perceived deficits to gender, during childhood, some did, and thus their gender dysphoria had an earlier start. This following subject is clearly describing a spoiled male identity:

I was teased about my curly hair and people said my eye lashes were wasted on a boy. My voice was late breaking, and my body hair was sparse. (When younger) I was circumcised and made to feel a freak because I mixed this up with castration ... and I thought they had cut half of me off. I always was more lightly endowed with muscles, co-ordination, and stamina than other people. It upset my father that I could not whistle, and he was an accomplished whistler himself. I used to walk in an odd way ... Mother used to work on textile machines and used to pick soft coloured fabrics ... which made the boys tease me, I have a recollection of trying on my father's clothes ... at the age of seven or eight, and I remember thinking 'what on earth has this got to do with me?'. I felt clumsy, and there was an overall feeling of incorrectness (MF 198).

This next subject makes a specific cross-gender link:

> When I was seven or eight, I had some kind of podginess on my chest and I identified that with what was on my mother's chest. At school, I was teased when I had to undress for gymnastics (MF-PR 136).

Some children had deficient genital organs:

> At the time he was examined, it was discovered that his penis was extremely small, barely protruding from the body, and his testicles were absolutely minimal (Medical Report on MF-PR 69).

Childhood fears

For some children, childhood fears were extreme, and contributed towards their general timidity and difficulties with their peers:

> As a child I had a great fear of birds and moths, in fact, anything that fluttered. If I was in a room with a bird, I felt I would have to kill myself. Other children made fun of me ... There were days when I engaged in no conversation with anyone. This might be three or four days a week. My mother didn't want me to go out and play with other children because it was too rough (MF 192).

The introverted reader

Many children especially those with higher levels of intelligence found imaginative escapes from their misery in reading:

> I was always nervous and never mixed with most of the pupils. I was very timid, introverted and emotional. I was most uncomfortable at public school, and was bullied and ostracised. Later I began to do well academically, I was an advanced reader, and loved to read Wordsworth and write my own poetry (MF 109).

The child's sense of failure as a male

For many children, the sense of failure as a male, is the most striking component of their recollections:

> In my late teenage years, I developed ulcerative colitis. I was disappointing to my father as he thought I was a weakling. I had hardly any friends as a young lad, and I used to observe boys carefully to learn how to act, in order to please my father. Later on, I always felt awkward in the company of men, and inferior and always had to ask their opinion, even when I knew I was correct (MF 189).

> I must have had problems to be picked on all the time. I didn't feel I wanted to be a female, but I was pushed around so much I became a loner, and got into music which other boys didn't like. I was quiet and introverted and have been bitter and resentful all my life (MF 143).

> I was so afraid of boys I would not go into the toilets if any were there. One time that made me ill. I used to sit in class and cry because I didn't have any little boys as friends at all (MF-PR 98).

This child stumbled on an interesting idea:

> As a child I was rather timid and was called a sissy. If only I had been a girl, I wouldn't have been called sissy (MF 104).

Most of a male child's sense of isolation, loneliness and sense of failure is experienced among his peers. For a few boys, the family dynamics also contributed to this:

> I was always a loner at primary school, and would always take a back seat and be a non-entity. My mother was always very strict and made me stay in the house. She was always very short-tempered and hated men, because of the way her father treated her. I was going to write a book all about this when I was about six or seven. (MF 122).

Sexual aspects of childhood experiences

Very few males recollected explicit childhood sexual experiences, but for a small number these played a part in their developing attitude concerning their future relationships with men. One precocious subject recollected at around the age of six, the following:

> I had already developed sexual orientations towards certain boys, and had fantasies in which they were doing things to me as men. I was treated as a surrogate female in drama classes, and homosexual approaches were made to me. I didn't want to be attractive because of my maleness, I wanted more warmth, and to be taken care of (MF-PR 97).

The following subject, having been terrified of bigger boys throughout early childhood, found himself at around the age of 11 or 12:

> ... getting attracted to those boys. I was attracted to tough boys who would have frightened me before, and I used to like to watch them as a spectator (MF-PR 98).

Atypical childhoods

According to the statistical survey of the project's 143 male to female transsexuals, 80 per cent had strong histories of 'nervous timidity' of the types described above. For some subjects, what started off as a less severely impaired childhood sense of self, became worse with the approach of adolescence. Two quoted examples illustrate this:

> In my primary school I could beat anyone up, and I was head of a little clique. No-one ever took advantage of me. As I got older I was a little disappointed I wasn't taller. I was serious minded, and later this turned into me becoming oversensitive to remarks. When I was about eight or nine, my parents started arguing. There was a teacher who always supported me for outstanding achievements, one day she made me stand

in front of the whole class and from that moment, my whole world collapsed. Suddenly I wasn't being identified as an angel and that feeling made me worse than anything else. My spirits collapsed, and home life deteriorated although I still did well in sports (MF 40).

I enjoyed primary school and was happy in games, indeed I was popular. I was a bit shy, and stuttered, and was afraid of men. I had begun cross-dressing from the age of six or seven, but things began to go wrong because I suffered from delayed puberty. I was seen by a child psychiatrist and given testosterone and aversion therapy for my cross-dressing (MF 142).

For other male children, there was almost nothing recollected from childhood that would have predicted their final transsexual status.

Atypical, aggressive and disturbed childhoods

This minority group of children differed markedly from the majority 'nervous timidity' cases. There were high rates of gross emotional disturbance, antisocial and aggressive behaviour. These children did get taken for psychiatric evaluations. In more than half of these cases (nine overall), there was an association with mental retardation:

At the age of five I got beaten for defecating in my pants, then I kept wetting my bed and I couldn't help it. I had to fight them back the only way I could, that's my parents, and that was with force. I did everything I could to keep my parents together, but when they did part, I started cross-dressing. I didn't like leaving home and I cried. When I went to the other place, at Barnardo's, there was trouble there too. I just couldn't shake it off. My face didn't fit. I can't trust anyone (MF 140).

A medical report on this man contains the following:

P. has been in the care of Kent County Council during his childhood. He was assessed as retarded and sent to a special residential school. There were behaviour problems, he was unable to communicate, and was so violent he had to be withdrawn from the school. He was given Largactil at age nine or ten.

A medical report on another similar case includes the following:

History of antisocial behaviour, homosexuality (passive), violence against father because 'fed up' being male. History of school refusal because pupils treated him 'horribly'. In the care of social services. History of stealing, long periods of headaches, restlessness, clumsiness and stuttering when anxious. Unpopular and no friends except small girls (MF 176).

The following case turned out eventually to be quite a successful sex reassignment. A medical report on childhood psychiatric problems stated:

Boy who always disliked school and considered to have emotional disorder since early childhood. Attended child guidance and special school. Considerably shy and school phobic. Also phobic of snakes, spiders, fire, water, sight of blood, the dark, pointed instruments *etc*. There was nothing to indicate his troubles would take the specific forms they have (MF-PR 78).

A most important point to be understood from these reports is that although these histories of nervous timidity can present as sissy or even as effeminate behaviour and, indeed, some more specific cross-gender experiences and behaviour may be reported, the overwhelming nature of the childhood self for male to female transsexuals-to-be is that of a spoiled (in Goffman's sense of the word), neurotic failing personality.

Female to male transsexuals
Happy, independent childhoods

By contrast to males, the majority of female to male transsexuals report happy autonomous childhoods, generally from their point of view unspoiled by gender discriminations. Typical examples are these:

> I was always a rough little girl, always up to mischief and climbing trees ... there was a lot of dare-devil in me, as opposed to my cousins, one of whom was very sissy. I couldn't do embroidery as well as her, so I knew I was different. I couldn't be the dainty girl my mother wanted, and I was forever getting my dresses torn. My father let me help him in the chicken house, and I always played with the boys at school and thought the girls were silly. However, I didn't have any special thoughts about being a boy or a girl (FM-PR 35).

> Before the age of 14 I was a tomboy and did not have any distinctive idea of being the other gender, but I felt there was something different which had not come to the surface. Even this was not true as a young child, for I got on with everyone and was good at games. I was quiet, confident and very happy (FM 71).

Sometimes an initial seed of resentment or resistance is expressed:

> I was always a happy, inquisitive energetic infant, very different from my younger brother who arrived 18 months later as a sickly feeble child. I used to get into fights and often win them. At school I generally enjoyed myself, but I became unhappy because I was very bright, and it was resented when I came first. My primary school was all girls, and I did not have too many friends. From the age of six, I learned to play the piano and it was thought I was naturally gifted (FM-PR 56).

Sometimes this sense of success or mastery comes later, as not every girl is naturally a tomboy:

As a young child, I was extremely shy and had a bad stammer. When I went to grammar school, I did reasonably well. I was idolised and elected to everything going. I was games captain and head girl. I did well, later at education college, but I had a feeling of barrenness and emptiness (FM 32).

The constraints of gender socialisation for females

It seems that the more female gender role expectations are used as constraints on the natural inclinations of these strong-minded girls, the more likely is alienation from that gender identity, rather than the gradual accommodation which is the outcome for most 'tomboys'. The following girl clearly began to see a convergence between being able to do what she wanted and being 'one of the boys':

I was a mischievous adventurous little girl, and couldn't see the reasons for doing things I was told to. I was left out, and lonely, and hated everything and knocked everything down. I wasn't allowed to play in the sand, but rather had to go and play with the girls' house. I began to hate girls and fought with them because they were not like me and I was too rough for them and made them cry. The boys didn't cry when things didn't work out for them, and they were more adventurous ... Some children looked at me funny and laughed. That rejection made me feel alone. Between the ages of eight and 11, in my junior school, I had a lot of problems with teachers because they said I was so rebellious and wouldn't do what they said. I couldn't understand, and they kept on saying it's because you are a little girl. I wanted to do all the things the boys did. Up until I went to school, my brother and I were the same, you see. Then we were in separate playgrounds and in their playground, you could play football and cricket. I had to masturbate very hard so I wouldn't be asked to show I was a boy without a penis, I was left out when all the lads were showing their penises to each other. I had nothing to show. This made my desire for male identity, and a penis, very strong (FM-PR 194).

37

Once this sense of difference is felt acutely, and is genderised, a girl may find herself separated from the society in which she longs to be triumphant. A stage of isolation may be crucially important for the fashioning of magic dreams - to be a man:

> I was a solitary child, though not altogether shy. I had no real friends, but became quite self-sufficient and neat and tidy. I dressed in boys' clothes whenever I could from the age of six (FM-PR 114).

> I was different from other children because I preferred to be on my own and play football with the boys. I was always a bit of a loner, and didn't want to talk. I felt insecure but my difficulties have reduced over time (FM-PR 179).

Sometimes something very particular may occur to spoil a girl's full sense of adequacy or of being valued for what she is, for example:

> I was adopted and when my adopted parents had a girl of their own, when I was about seven, everything went wrong (FM-PR 125).

Responses to a spoiled sense of 'self'

A common response to the spoiling of sense of self in girls who become female to male transsexuals is a gritty determination to overcome:

> My earliest memories are about myself being strong willed and adamant. When I was seven or eight, I realised other boys were rougher than me, and I had a sense of a risk of dirt, and used to wash myself four or five times a day. I had depressive moods, and resented my stepfather coming into my life and telling me what to do. I was adopted at age six, but I rejected it, I didn't feel whole. My adoptive father was a drunkard and abused my adoptive mother. I thought girls silly cry babies. Eventually I was just as rough as other boys, and could outdo them in climbing trees, and using pen-knives (FM-PR 81).

The common finding of female to male transsexuals to be, *i.e.* their being the strong protector of an abused or downtrodden mother, exists here along with other factors pushing the child to prove herself, not with girls (they are dismissed), but with 'other' boys. When this 'proving' is frustrated or fails, it frequently leads to strong and hostile resentment which turns some of these individuals into highly chauvinist adults.

There are atypical histories which, as in the case of boys, lead to atypical outcomes. The following individual presented with a request for reassignment surgery, but was not committed to it. Gender dysphoric feelings were strong, but as an adult she was ambivalent about the full implications of reassignment. In some ways her history has some similarities with that of a boy transsexual-to-be:

I was nervous, timid, and highly strung as a child. I loathed games and could not see very well. I had been happy as a small child, but rather isolated, and got on better with adults. I resented my adolescence and became introverted. I had few friends. I was ill a lot between the ages of five and eight, and I remember I really wanted a brother to play with. I remember thinking girls were a bad thing, second best. I became very jealous and nasty about my new sister, as I was no longer the centre of attention. Also I was bullied by particularly horrible, bossy and spiteful little girls at school. My parents wanted me to achieve a lot, and I got nervous when I couldn't and felt 'out of gear'. My mother used to read to me a lot of fantasy stories when I was sick. I remember praying to be a boy and would drink the bath water to achieve this with magic. I would have strange dreams in which I was a boy inside a prickly suit or skin, which was a bit like a conker skin, all prickly and green. It was me, a good looking boy trying to get out of a prickly Angela ... I developed a boy's daydream world when I was about eight onwards ... Later I saw another boy undressed and I realized what a physical difference there was, I had real penis envy. A lot of my feelings antedated my knowledge of physical differences. In those years, between five and eight I did play with a doll's house, but also a clockwork train, and toy animals. I had a lot of imaginary games in my head with the dolls and animals. I have visual imagery which is very vivid (FM 121).

Childhood Behaviour

Male to female transsexuals
Childhood 'nervous timidity'

In the section on 'Childhood Nature', mention is made of behaviour and of course its separation under this particular heading is simply a convenience of presentation. The statistical survey of our sample of 115 male to female transsexuals, indicated that 80 per cent exhibited a history of significant nervous timidity, fear of peers, marked shyness, loathing of physical activities and so on. Below is a very typical statement concerning activity associated with this 'nature':

> My first day at school I screamed because I didn't want to be parted from my mother. I was miserable being on my own. I tried to avoid the boys that tried to beat me up, and I joined a group of timid boys I was friendly with. I made no close friends. I used to play with the girls and they would accept me. I didn't like any rough and tumble and in any fight I would come off the worst (MF 14).

Some individual experience of victimisation was very intense. An example:

> I was treated mercilessly because of my clumsiness and I had no friends ... My brother was always bullying me and he tried to kill me on several occasions, even my mother too. Once he tried to strangle me, once he tried to drown me and once tried to use a hatchet on me. At some time, between the ages of six to eight, I was brought home dazed and crying, and a doctor examined me and stated that an object of very substantial size had been forced into my anus, which was bleeding, and tender ... On another occasion, three boys aged about eight, took me

into a back yard, and whilst two of them held me, the third cut my hands and fingers with a razor blade. When each boy had cut me I was allowed to leave ... On several occasions my brother forced me to kneel at his feet and lick his shoes ... I was sickly at school, and I remember the teacher calling me a smarmy little sod (MF-PR 136).

Childhood transvestism

Accounts by some transsexuals indicate how cross-dressing in their early years was linked to the experience of nervous timidity and victimisation described above:

My earliest memories at school were of being bullied by an older boy. He got his penis out and forced me to hold it. I was very nervous and scared and, whilst other boys used to like to play together, I was happiest by myself. Otherwise I could be happy if I was with girls. Some boys dressed me as a girl substitute and the first to catch me would kiss me. At first I thought this was odd, but later when one older boy forced me to the ground and lay on top of me, I remember liking it. I was considered sissy and soft. When I was seven, I put my sister's skirt on myself. I was envious of her, how attractive she was, and how nothing seemed to bother her. She would never scream or shout at anything (MF 31).

Early feelings accompanying cross-dressing are often of comfort or security:

When I was young, I was teased a lot by my brothers and sisters and schoolfriends. Then I used to cross-dress and I would always feel secure and I would find some nice cosy little room, such as my sister's room, when my relations came (MF-PR 181).

Otherwise, the 'discovery' of cross-dressing might be almost accidental:

Once when I was seven or eight, I was dressed for a school play as a flower girl. I liked it and kept those memories until the age of 15 ... Once I had a wrestling match with a girl who lay on top of me, and as a result I felt placid and did not struggle, and felt safe (MF 40).

When I was 12, my mother got a new dress and used me as a tailor's dummy, and my initial reaction to this was, 'yes', I wanted to have this, and to please her (MF 84).

Childhood sexual behaviour

Where, in a minority of cases, childhood sexual experiences are recollected, they usually had 'troublesome' connotations:

I was first 'aware' of my penis when I was at primary school, when I had to climb up a rope, and I had an ejaculation. I found it unpleasant, and I was ashamed, but later, I did try to experiment to see if I could get this effect deliberately on the rope. One time, I fell off in fright. I had done this from curiosity, but it was definitely unpleasant, and definitely a mess (MF-PR 136).

I had a lot of sexual approaches made to me by other boys at school. Later I had such approaches from men, and I never felt these immoral suggestions were right (MF-PR 30).

Disturbed behaviour

It has already been mentioned that a minority of cases involved clearly disturbed childhood behaviour, for which the boys were usually taken to see child psychiatrists. The behaviours so classified included violence, antisocial acts, extreme withdrawal, inability to communicate, eneuresis, encopresis, delinquency, *e.g.* petty stealing, running away from school, and a variety of phobias. Neither the clinical practitioners nor the children classified these disturbances as gender disorders at the time. The following is an articulate statement from an individual who attended many years of child guidance and was sent to a school for maladjusted children:

I was extremely shy when young and I made up games by myself with lots of 'pretend' people. I didn't like rough and tumble games, and there were days when I didn't speak to any other people at all. I was spurned by other children, I think, because of the physical appearance of my face, and children are very cruel. Even a teacher believed I must have had a grandfather or something who was Chinese. I was sometimes called 'Chink' or 'Chinney'. I would be bullied and give up in tears. My alternative fantasy world made me feel better and I used to belong to a secret society with me and robots, and I would try to follow children and not be seen. I was sent as a young child to the doctor because I wasn't eating enough. I used to feel physically sick if I had to undress for P.T. I used to stay in the school in the play time, and people would regard me as not being any good at being a person. I had no feelings of wanting to be a girl because I always felt so low. It came to me that I needed to be a girl when I was 19 (MF-PR 78).

Female to male transsexuals
Tomboy behaviour

Although there is some variation in females' experience of themselves in childhood, it is, as we have seen, more common and unproblematic than is the case for males. Preferred tomboy behaviour is virtually the rule for female transsexuals-to-be:

I was a tomboy as a child, although I went round with girls too. I didn't like dolls, and I was always out climbing trees, playing cowboys and Indians, and riding on motorcycles with the boys. Our family was very poor we were called 'flea bags' - and I was never picked as a good looking husband or wife in any school drama (FM 17).

I liked to explore the countryside and prove how strong I was. I did well at games. I remember feeling some resentment in my junior school when one changed for P.T. and I didn't like being made aware that I didn't have the same physique as other boys (FM 21).

I got punished at school for fighting with boys. I was quick tempered (FM-PR 4).

I asked my mother to let me have a boy's suit because I wanted to join in the rough games and climbing trees. I found girls dainty and discriminated against, for example, they were not allowed to play formal games like football and cricket and do woodwork. I was however a happy person as a school child and accepted my assigned (gender) identity (FM-PR 50).

Family Life

Male to female transsexuals
Family difficulties affecting childhood experience

From the statistical survey, it was estimated that 38 per cent of male to female transsexuals experienced significant family relationship difficulties in their childhood. That means of course that 62 per cent did not, so this factor has limited value as a strict explanatory 'variable' of transsexualism. Most transsexuals came from families with unremarkable histories of behaviour and interpersonal relationship. However, severe family conflict can undermine an individual's sense of self. In our sample, male transsexuals who did have such a severe history were over three times less likely to achieve reassignment surgery than those without such a history. Some examples of individuals who experienced severe family problems were the following:

> Paul's father was a labourer who spent years in prison for violent offences, and violence in the family was common. Paul was beaten for defecating in his pants and was later put in a children's home when his parents broke up. He had shared a bed with his sister and incest was vaguely admitted (Medical report on MF 140).

> I was beaten and sexually abused by my uncle (MF 106).

It was not always possible in retrospective accounts to

unconfound possible genetic and environmental effects:

> My parents used to argue and have violent rows, and in truth, their marriage was dead before I was born. My older brother was treated in hospital because he was 'into' drugs, and I recently discovered he had a homosexual phase. My father was a bit effeminate (MF 63).

Some children by their nature experience a relationship difficulty which may not objectively be the result of serious objective deviance or deficiencies in parents:

> My parents were loving, kind and loyal. Everything my brother ever did was interesting and important and everything I ever said was regarded patronisingly and with amused tolerance. Even now as an adult, I often see myself treated as a child (MF 145).

Extreme closeness to mother

Notwithstanding the importance of this topic to psychoanalytic theorising, such recollections were found quite rarely in only a few cases. One was the following:

> My mother treated me as a dear with many close cuddles and I love her dearly. I used to sleep with my mother until I was 11 years of age, from the time that I was a baby. Mother thought I was delicate. Father would be in the same bed, I would cuddle up to her body. We would both wear night clothes, but as a baby, I was actually on the breast until I was nearly five years of age. It was comfort suckling (MF 104).

Father figures

The lack of a good male model to encourage masculine behaviour is associated with marked childhood effeminacy. This may not always function simply as a 'lack'. In this subject's case, it does seem to have played a role in his closeness and 'identification' - at least in a loose sense - with his mother:

> My father had an accident and was killed when I was small. I

was shunted around many relations. When my mother touched and caressed me, it was very soft and she smelled different to my brother. I wanted to be like this mother and we were alike in many ways, in not being very demonstrative, for example. At the age of ten, I admired the fact that she had lost a leg in the accident which killed my father, but was still able to carry on. I noticed that as a woman, she received courtesy from men. Men deferred to her (MF-PR 136).

A father figure might well be present and functioning all too well. The simple functioning of a masculine model may disturb a boy child if he already has problems:

My father was strict, but he used to play with me. He wrestled with me but he was always too rough and I always ended up crying. I was close to both my mother and father (MF 14).

A minority of fathers were rejecting and abusive:

My father used to put a pillow over my head as a child from when I was six years old till 13. He also beat me a lot because I wouldn't do weekend work with him in an abattoir, but preferred to do household duties and I used to like animals (MF 189).

Female to male transsexuals
Family difficulties

The majority of female transsexuals in our study did not report serious family problems. Most had:

Parents who were pretty stable and happy people who cared for each other and me (FM-PR 50).

A minority of females have to deal with great antagonism:

My father and brother have been unbelievably antagonistic to me. My father has told me he believes I can do nothing right and I am evil. He takes the view that only God can make males and females. Ever since I was 11 we have had lots of the most terrible rows. My father has told that on my next visit home he will confine himself to his room, he finds me so repulsive. He has put his hand over his face in my presence to avoid seeing my existence (FM-PR 56).

A very few families are grossly disturbed:

Father, a nervous man, can be uncommunicative or impulsive. Mother subject to break-downs and threatens to kill herself or her husband. Older brother, with history of violent criminal behaviour, has spent time in borstals, and prisons. Older sister has not grown up properly and has paralysed arm from polio. Paternal grandfather very violent and has beaten his wife and son (Letter of referral of FM 153).

Childhood Gender Identity

Male to female transsexuals

A standard answer to a standard psychiatric interview question such as 'when did you first feel like this?' almost always locates this time in childhood. Typically, a presenting transsexual will state he has known he was really a member of the opposite sex since some childhood age. Typically, he will produce 'evidence' such as an account of cross-dressing, preference for girls' games and company and so on. If scholars of normal development have trouble being certain whether certain behaviours or statements by children reflect gender awareness, gender stability, gender constancy, gender role or 'core' gender identity, then it really shouldn't be so surprising to find that transsexuals-to-be also find the categorisation of experience and behaviour problematical. Where the account collected from a transsexual is progressive, *i.e.* moves forward in time from the earliest memories available, and when the examination of those memories follows the ethogenic method (described in Chapter 2) then the pre-transsexual problematic status of gender identity constructions of one kind or another becomes apparent. The following excerpted quotes illustrate the variety of constructions which almost always could be found.

Original gender assignment accepted

> In childhood I assumed myself to be a boy, because that is what I was told (MF 93).

An early imaginative hope corrected by an appropriate cognitive exercise of gender constancy:

> I realised one day I was not going to grow up like my mother, but like Dad. This was a disappointment but it didn't matter too much. My mother had strong fears about aggression and crude masculinity (MF 84).

The above quote is interesting in that an early gender desire is going to have massive future implications. To that extent only could natural history go along with psychoanalytic fixations. As it turns out, this 'disappointment' is not the end of the story, and mother's fears about 'crude masculinity' will affect this lad's evolving concept of himself as an adequate male, but not because his bedrock early 'core' gender identity is female.

A quality of femininity

> The feeling I had when I was dressed up as a flower girl at primary school, was a nice clean feeling. This was a feeling which I thought indicated I had found my identity, it was decent, unshackled, good (MF 40).

Being like a girl

> I recall being female in my behavioural patterns, mannerisms, emotions and feelings and I liked to be chased like the girls when I was at primary school. At grammar school, there were no other girls, so to a large part this seemed not to matter, just doing schoolwork. As a younger child I wanted to play the role of girls in games, but I didn't necessarily feel different from boys. I was taunted that I walked like a girl, and I became conscious of being someone feminine because of this (MF 34).

Desire to belong to the company of girls

I was envious of the girls, for they seemed to live a much fuller life, because of their gentler selves. You could see that one day they would grow up to be like their mothers and would stand outside the school just nattering. I used to like to stand there and listen to their conversations. If fathers came, they just collected the kids. It wasn't just the topics they spoke about, it was their mannerisms. It reflected the girls' company, that I wanted to join a group I felt I belonged with. It was friendly, wholly sane company. Even so, by the age of ten or 11, I had no specific ideas of actually becoming female (MF 14).

Feeling 'different'

At primary school I had one girl who was a very good friend of mine, and we did things together and I felt we were on the same level and we were different from other people. I felt different from other boys, but I didn't know why. I had three brothers who were all loud and noisy and doing naughty things. They all liked football which I never did, I never like changing rooms, I found that oppressive, I hated the clothes you put on for games and I thought I looked stupid in them (MF 83).

Cross-gender behaviour and interests without a crystallized cross-gender identity

Up to the age of ten, I think people thought me a bit sissy and soft, but I didn't feel any different myself. When I first met my foster mother, she was lovely and I became sensitised to the glamorous materials of her dresses. I used to get into her clothes when I could. I collected pictures of beautiful people and I fantasised being in a movie, singing and dancing with spectacular dresses. I would be the heroine to a leading man. My foster mother and I had the same weakness and refinements for art, dancing, the theatre and sewing. I began to realise my behaviour was a serious matter only when I was 16 or so. I was never 'one of the lads'. I had some crushes on some of the boys (MF-PR 37).

Female to male transsexuals

Among female to male transsexuals-to-be, it is even more common for gender to be taken for granted in a tomboy role. As and when gender derived expectations begin to make themselves felt in an unacceptable way, then certain psychological adaptations may begin. The following quote from a highly intelligent subject, illustrates this in a very typical way:

In my first primary school, I wasn't particularly aware in those days of the division between boys and girls, and it didn't cross my mind I was 'female'. My first fleeting experience of hating my identity went with my mother having a lot of make-up on. She put me in a skirt, made up my hair and I hated my appearance in the mirror. I wanted to be a postman and only men are postmen. I was told I couldn't tear around with the gang which my brother had joined. I enjoyed active games like football whereas most girls preferred pretend games like 'horses'. In my second school, there were quite a few girls who were tomboys, and that's what I imagined I was. I was convinced enough to have phases where I came out of my (real) body and imagined I was a boy. There would be a flash in my mind and I wondered if that was self- brainwashing. I had short hair, and was thrilled if someone called me 'son' in a sweetshop. I had a male nick-name. I began to feel out on my own when the other girls who had been tomboys began to wear bras. They became antagonistic to me because I didn't want to, and I tried to flatten myself with sellotape (FM-PR 56).

Sometimes even the above early foreglimpses may not have occurred to anticipate the forthcoming gender identity crisis:

Before the age of 14 I was a tomboy and did not have any distinctive idea of being the other gender, but I felt there was something different that had not come to the surface. As a young child I got on well with everyone ... and was very happy (FM 71).

Adolescent Nature
Male to female transsexuals
Cross-dressing and homosexual orientation

The minority of transsexuals-to-be, whose adolescence most clearly forecast such a fate, typically reported cross-dressing behaviour and homosexual desires:

> As a teenager I used to be called a sissy and was afraid of other lads who said I ought to have been a girl. I felt very bad and mixed up, and would go home and get crossed-dressed and would feel over the moon that it was me After my father died, there was a marked increase in cross dressing (MF 104).

> When I was 14 or 15 I used to cross-dress, and was sent to see a psychiatrist. I was afraid of most of the boys but was very attracted to some of them. I was interested in reading and drawing. I felt a second class citizen, but when I was in female clothing, I felt nice (MF 96).

Adolescent effeminacy

Signs of effeminacy, either behavioural, or through late or less strong pubescent virilisation creates anxiety.

> My voice didn't fully break until I was 17, and I was teased about my femininity at school. I tried to grow out of it by not cross-dressing for two years. I hated compulsory games because I always seemed to get hurt (MF 198).

> I was sent to boarding school but my body was not like the average young fellows. I had to get measured for a uniform ... and there was laughter that my hips were so large. Later this gave me satisfaction for it told me I must be in the right direction for becoming female. It was, however, a very

shameful thing at the time. My voice did not break till late (MF 26).

The behavioural link between 'nervous timidity' and 'effeminacy' is referred to by this subject:

When I was 16 or 17, I was such a nervous and very shy person. During puberty I became unacceptably pretty. I wore specs, looked odd, and I walked in a kind of wiggly fashion. This was due to extreme nervousness when I was out and I wanted to get back as quickly as possible. I didn't want to rush in a running kind of way, and that led to short little steps with the toes inwards, which is conventionally known as 'mincing'. I didn't know what I was doing until it was later pointed out to me at work. If I had moved faster in a kind of a run or stride, that would have been like an athlete. My short inward steps were enclosed like, which reflected my inability to step out confidently (MF 31).

Defective appearances and disabilities

It has already been mentioned that defective appearances and disabilities play an important role in the development of a spoiled identity in the pre-adolescent male child. Adolescence brings a new wave of sensitivity to these matters. Occasionally these deficits appear to be due to a real clinical biological syndrome. The following is from a medical report:

This boy has suffered from delayed puberty and an unhappy background. There is concern about his poor body build and his feminine voice. He has smallish testes for his age and plasma testosterone levels are on the low side. This may indicate an androgen target organ deficit (MF 2).

Whatever the causes, the social fact of deficits brought on very hard times for some boys:

I was very artistic and nervous, and timid as an adolescent, and my diabetes interfered with my ability to take my exams, and all I got was O-level Art. During that school year, I also had problems with my knees and I was teased about this (MF 63).

At school I was called 'Tubby' and I was embarrassed. I didn't want to be marked out, so I stayed home and withdrew completely, even from my friends. I put up with a lot of mockery on the school bus and I felt that boys and girls could be very malicious. I couldn't understand why this was happening. I developed a problem with my eye-sight, and the optician described this as being due to nervous strain. I was unable to read the blackboard, and so had to sit at the front of the class. I started faltering at school and got more and more abuse (MF 31).

I was ridiculed in my teenage years because of my epilepsy, and also because of my eczema. Sometimes I would be called scabby, or sometimes a leper (MF 124).

The losing struggle for masculinity

It is clear from many accounts that adolescence was a crucial time in gender construction. This was not simply a revealing of some cross-gender 'core', but it becomes easier to see how a future cross-gender construction can evolve from the adolescent experience of failing masculinity:

I had no girlfriends at school, although I constantly tried to get one, so I could be one of the lads. When I cross-dressed I may have provided myself with the desired girls, but I'm not sure. I had aversion therapy at hospital, and for a while I did manage to control my desires. A girlfriend would have been a solution to this (MF 150).

As an adolescent I didn't think I was as manly as the other boys. I had less hair on my chest and legs. My voice never really broke, and I had a sensitive body. I would have felt better if I had had strong male features. I wanted to be part of the herd. Later I was mistaken as a homosexual and I had to fight to defend my maleness. All my life I feel I have been acting. Deep down, I couldn't mix then as a teenager, or now because I was sensitive to people's hurtful comments even though I was really quite good looking (MF 143).

Undifferentiated anxieties of adolescence

For a considerable number of boys, relatively undifferentiated adolescent anxieties preceded the sexualisation of their feelings:

I went through a funny stage when I was 14 or 15, when I thought I was adopted. In a funny kind of way I wanted to be adopted because I was so different and this seemed to be the answer, it was no-one's fault. It would explain why I was different from my brothers and sisters and why I liked to climb into a big cardboard box which was warm and cosy (MF 48).

In my teens I didn't feel I enjoyed anything, I wasn't attracted to anyone or by anyone (MF 75).

I did less well at secondary school because of troubles at home. There was an awakening of an idea that I did not want to be successful, because then I would be identified with it. I realised my personality was not really emerging as an individual so much. My father was dominant, and I was expected to follow all his wishes. Although I had done well at school, I would deliberately fail examinations; somehow it didn't seem to matter, passing exams for someone else. Whatever my father turned to, he went to the top. I never knew how to reconcile my desire to please him and yet not identify with his success. My mother used to ridicule him in front of us children and I knew there was a danger in success, I wanted to express myself rather than my father's wishes. However my personality couldn't come out. I had no joy inside of me. I became introspective and thought other people, like my father, were simply superior. I felt little and insignificant and depressed (MF 40).

Female to male transsexuals

The limitations of female socialisation in adolescence

For female transsexuals-to-be, it is most often adolescence which is a watershed for their identity. Even where life has been relatively free and unproblematic up to this point, the experience of the role expectations and constraints of what it means to be female, now become 'problems'.

> Pressures were put on me by my parents and teachers, when I was about 12, to be more feminine. I knew if I dressed as a girl, I would be treated as one, and expected to behave as one. I began to be rejected from the boys fraternity around this age, when sexual differences began to appear. For example, I was not allowed to join the model aeroplane club at school. Other girls had started growing up, and I was clearly not like them, I didn't fit. I prayed to God to do a miracle. My periods came late and I was distressed. I was still into rougher games. I was friends with one girl who was plain and interested in books and we were a kind of exclusive duo. I found myself drifting onto the edge of things (FM-PR 274).

If a person doesn't fit into the real world, development can still take place in the world of fantasy:

> I used to enjoy reading boys' fantasy stories and adventures with real heroes, who would be men. I was bad at socialising in company, and felt different. I felt odd and eccentric and wanted to play my own imaginary games and read, rather than not relate well. I remember my female clothes as being uncomfortable, vulnerable, freezing and thin. I felt like a pre-pubescent boy (FM-121).

Appearance

Problems of appearance are much less common than for boys. When they did exist the reactions of others could add to the feelings of rejection:

> When I was a teenager I had hair on my face, and people called
> me a billy-goat, which hurt at the time (FM-PR 52).

The crisis of sexual feelings

In comparison with males, the experience of sexual feelings
towards the same biological sex, early in adolescence, is a more
consistent phenomenon, and plays a central part in the female
transsexual-to-be's labelling of herself, and her own behaviour.
Female homosexuality is still not as well 'defined' or recognised or socially organised into 'gay scenes' as is the case for
male homosexuality, and this is especially true as regards the
understanding of adolescent girls. Many experiences and ideas
expressed by female transsexuals-to-be are not much different
from full adult lesbians-to-be. This, of course, is not realised,
and the 'track' the individual eventually takes will be contin-
gent on a number of circumstances. The relationship between
sexual desire and identity is reflected in the following account:

> In my teenage years I had crushes on girls, and wanted to play
> doctors and nurses so I could touch them. I was jealous when
> the girls flirted with boys rather than me. I was eased out of
> serious games like football and slapped for calling my mother
> 'mom' rather than 'mummy darling'. If I could have just been
> allowed tomboy behaviour, that would have been O.K. even as
> a girl, until I began to have sexual feelings. Then my wishes
> crystallised to be male. I kissed girls, but my desire to be a boy
> increased with my desire for real sexual contact, which I
> eventually achieved at the age of 13, with a girl (FM-PR 35).

Female transhomosexuals

The development of transhomosexuality involves certain variations on the feeling and fantasy themes expressed by transsexuals. Indeed, the problem of classifying one's own gender
identity can be acute. The following subject, never reached a
full transsexual status, even when she knew much more about
these categories than she did at the time she refers to below:

My parents were happy with me being a teenage tomboy, and I quite liked my grammar school uniform, and wasn't bothered at the time about the skirt. It lost its significance because everyone was wearing one. I tended to pair off with one particular friend and that friendship was really like a Greek ideal. My friend and I took the part of boys and acted fantasies from films and the wireless. We always took the part of heroes, and I was never addressed by my proper name, but rather by a nick-name. I felt actually more like a boy during the time when my breasts were developing. I had had early sexual feelings when I saw a film poster of an attractive man. He was standing with his hands on hips in a rather decadent image kind of a way. In my early teens I had sexual feelings all over the place for males of the delicate type. I didn't like it when heterosexual blokes fancied me. I thought of myself inside as a man like, although I didn't think I was anything else but a woman in reality. I had not heard of the transsexual categories (F-THO 157).

This account shows just how complicated the relationship between gender identity and sexual desire is turning out. The anchor for gender identity can affect the way self is constructed and the sexual object choice, including the significance of special discriminative attributes (*e.g.* 'delicacy' in men, and the type of relationship aspired to). What's more, the 'anchor' can move!

Adolescent Behaviour
Male to female transsexuals
Transvestism

Many male transsexuals are cross-dressing at some time in their teenage years. This is more likely to lead to fuller gender dysphoria if it is not associated with sexual pleasure.

At 15 I became very tense if I could not have a period of cross-dressing. Only very occasionally did I get sexually aroused, and I found that to be like a burning experience (MF-PR 136).

Poor social relationships

Apart from the continuation of childhood nervous timidity and poor social effectiveness, some male transsexuals-to-be did not behave in a markedly gender deviant way at this time:

> A sissy image was imposed on me as a teenager because I wasn't good at football or gym and I was very thin and not strong. I had very few friends, but I don't remember behaving overtly unlike any other adolescent boy (MF 34).

Sexual behaviour

For those males who did manage some kind of experience at this age, this often created great difficulties and these could be of many different sorts. The following are simply a selection:

> At 13, I started to masturbate and I found this enjoyable. Sexual relationships with girlfriends later were O.K. for a month or two, then I would have difficulty in having erections. I thought I had a rather small penis. I was self-conscious about undressing. When I was 15 I dated a girl who everyone expected me to have sex with. I didn't have the personality or dominance to carry this off. I wondered if you got a certificate for seducing a girl for the first time (MF 40).

> I was attracted to females when I was 15 or 16, but I was often impotent. I had to identify with a female. I cross-dressed a lot anyhow without sexual feelings. Later I got sexual fantasies associated with being in the opposite sex. I wanted to be normal, and I wasn't interested in foreplay or petting. Usually a session would last 15 minutes from the first kiss. I had inflamed nipples as a teenager and I was frightened I was changing sex. I often had daydreams where I took a passive role and had a partner with no face, a male I suppose (MF 126).

> Identification with the opposite sex only occurred after sexual feelings had developed further in adolescence (MF 9).

When I was 12, my sister wanted to have intercourse with me. I was so shocked and repulsed I never wanted to have this kind of intimacy again with a female (MF 49).

For some males, sexual experiences were not a 'shock' as such. For these subjects, there was an 'experimental' or discovery aspect to their experiences:

I did have a girlfriend when I was ten and I was flattered that I must be attractive . I went out with girls in my teens because that was expected, but none of the sexual encounters did anything for me. After I got involved with boys, I had a fantasy of being a female film star in a love scene with one of those boys (MF 34).

I experimented with anal intercourse and enjoyed that. Before I wanted to be a woman, I would allow my penis to be put between a man's legs and for it to be wagged to a climax! By the time I was 16 I wanted to be a woman (MF-PR 11).

Disturbed behaviour

There exists a minority of male transsexuals-to-be who show clearly disturbed behaviour in their adolescence. The following is from a medical referral:

In Dublin he was in the homosexual scene and was beaten up at least once a week because of the obviousness of his orientation. He came to England at the age of 15 and obtained female hormone pills illegally on the scene. He has also used barbiturates and heroin and made a number of suicidal attempts. He has engaged in pickpocketing and has been arrested for importuning and male prostitution (MF 68).

Another mixed-up subject states:

I was a mixed-up adolescent, unsure if I was heterosexual or homosexual or if I desired really to be a woman. I felt uncomfortable and sick when I had sexual intercourse with a girl. I was badly treated on the gay scene by a couple of men, and that has made me nervous. I also contracted syphilis. I used to swear and fight and I used to get the ambulances out on hoax calls. I also made a couple of obscene telephone calls. I broke a court supervision order with the same offences and a care order was made sending me to an approved school (MF 133).

Female to male transsexuals
Antagonism

As females feel gender role expectations appropriate to their biological sex, increasingly imposed, then often strong antagonism develops between the subject and parents, teachers, peers or doctors who try to engineer conformity. This is a typical example:

> At the age of 15, I found out about transsexualism through reading and immediately it clicked. I began to really hate boys who tried to shut me up. I was in love with a girl and I was forced to tell my parents and a doctor. I was so unhappy I tried to throw myself off a railway bridge. My father got really angry and rigid and our arguments came to blows. I was sent to a psychiatrist because it was thought I had a delusion. I refused to go on a course to learn female skills (FM-PR2).

Disturbed behaviour

For a minority of subjects, their history of 'antagonism' shades over into more severe emotional reactions or even frank psychiatric disorder:

> When puberty occurred it was hell, and I smashed up a lot of furniture in a rage, and then I refused to eat any food. At another time I overate because I was so unhappy at having to wear a uniform. I got called 'fatty'. All the teachers hated me because I was a trouble-maker, and was verbally abusive and occasionally physically violent (FM 153).

A more severe case:

By the age of 15, I'd been out with nine girls. Because of the difficulties, I had a nervous breakdown and overdosed and slashed my wrists. No-one would listen or understand. I had met no-one like me, I was a freak, the odd one out. I became very aggressive and was put on drugs at the psychiatric hospital (FM 74).

Sexual behaviour

Sexual behaviour, and its rules of what was 'possible or permissible', begins to evolve in relationship to gender identity, and is not necessarily in its final form at the end of adolescence. Consider the following typical example:

I remember crying on my last day at school because I was becoming fond of girls. With one girlfriend we used to go home and practise things and take it in turn to be in the male role. I had some sexual activities with girls, who all had boyfriends, and it was terrific. Even then, they understood that I didn't want my breasts or genitals touched and I was a bit of a strange female. Getting into bed with a woman always made me feel I really wanted a penis. At the age of 18 I had no idea about the full adoption of the male role because I was content in a way. Looking back, I think I was testing myself to see if I was putting on a fake image, trying to be two people (FM 17).

Adolescent Gender Identity
Male to female transsexuals
Adolescent troubles

Adolescence, heralded by the physical changes of puberty, is a key time for gender socialisation and adoption. For most male transsexuals-to-be, gender role development is fraught with conflict and is highly problematic. However, the form and the stage of their transsexual 'resolution' is highly varied. For those with significant early failure or 'trouble' in boyhood, adolescence heightens these troubles:

I was considered effeminate at school, and in my teens I did try hard to get a girlfriend. I found myself trying to find something in common with girls, identifying with them. I got wrong feedback which said 'you are nice (boy) but I only want you as a friend'. It was a sexist stereotype of what women want you to be. After an intense period of this, I stopped feeling the need to have a girlfriend. I had a mixed gender presentation (MF 63).

I was very slender for a man and some people thought I was homosexual. It was ironic and a tragedy that when I had perfected this slim masculine image in practice, I then realised I wanted to be a woman. In my teenage years, I thought such desires had just been a 'way out' for my mad behaviour (MF 145).

Adolescent memories re-collected and revised

This latter quotation is the beginning of a retrospective revision of biographical attitude, which his ambivalence at the time made him open to. The same subject goes on:

Now I am certain I spent that time in my life in a pathetic attempt to cover up what I really was. When at 16 I had a strong relationship with a man, I knew I should be a woman with him making love to me. My desire got stronger and stronger after this (MF 145).

A Chinese subject re-interprets this time of life likewise:

I began to feel feminine in my teenage years because before then I had been passive and quiet. That made me feel I should think of myself more as a female. I thought I looked a bit like a woman and my Chinese name can be interpreted as female. I liked to be treated gently and early teenage homosexual experiences were enjoyable, although at that time I didn't feel so much feminine (MF 138).

For some males, the pain of feeling different pushes them towards feeling they should have been a girl:

At secondary school I hated changing rooms because I felt out of place and couldn't match the other boys for masculinity, and I didn't want to anyway. I didn't like any rough activities and I blossomed in the stamp club. My voice deepened and I had erections from an early age and this disturbed my concentration at school, and I didn't do so well as the other boys. I couldn't tell anyone and I was very jealous that others didn't have this problem. It was not enjoyable but it was a nuisance and very frustrating. Once I was forced to undress with a girl and I had never seen a female body before. When I did I thought that was the key to my problem. I should have been like her, and something had gone wrong. All the way through, my problem made me feel I should have been a girl (MF 147).

Sexual desire, self-image, and gender identity

Some individuals had more than their share of difficulties to resolve during adolescence. The following subject was intellectually gifted and physically disabled, notwithstanding which he was subject to strong sexual desires. In fantasy life he struggled to 'fit' these together. This is an atypical case and it was not until many years later that this subject embraced a full transsexual identity and achieved sex reassignment surgery. Then, the transgender components of adolescent fantasy were returned to and granted a fuller significance than was given during the teenage years when they first occurred:

When I was 14 I tried hard to go out with girls but they were wary of me getting emotionally hurt. Their instinct was right and I didn't get anything more than a kiss until I was 16. I did get erections and I realised I could manage intercourse even though I was paraplegic. This would need a lot of masturbation and after a while this tailed off. Ejaculations were not possible. My libido was strong, but I had no opportunities. I had a lot of fantasies about a strong competent woman who would take the dominant role with me. This was all mixed with the science fiction I had been reading in hospital. In my fantasies, we would be journeying around space in a space ship, and she would rescue me from scrapes. In the space ship there was zero gravity so my legs were not frightfully relevant. Sex would be partly conventional, partly oral. If it was oral, she would sit on my face. I remember having a passing thought that if one has got to be paraplegic it is better to be the woman from the point of view of my imagination. I didn't indulge this imagination too much (then) because I thought my face too poor. Then I read an article about April Ashley (a highly publicised transsexual case in U.K.) and I was fascinated. I hated my nose and teeth (MF-PR 66).

For another young man, a new social image solved a previous trouble:

At 12 I was hospitalised for an undescended testicle, and there was a certain amount of ridicule after that. I followed expectations to go out with girls, but I preferred boys. I had a crush on one girl, it wasn't sexual but it was important for her to like me, to be equal with me. I found my accomplished prettiness something which gave me the idea that I might have a real change of sex, because prior to that I felt I was ugly. Suddenly, being considered pretty became really exciting (MF 34).

Desire for normality

The transsexual development is highly abnormal of course, but for many individuals the full compulsion was preceded by a more normal adolescent urge to be normal:

I realised there was a difference between boys and girls in terms of voices, aggression and genitals. Girls wanted me to accept boyish standards, but I found I preferred their company, and to have long hair and nails and be treated in a genteel way. I failed at sports, but at puberty, my penis meant I could have a sexual relationship. I didn't want that, but it did mean I could be accepted as normal. I was beginning not to be accepted as normal, I have memories of that. I was out on a limb socially, people talked less and less to me, some days no-one at all. My private desire to be a female developed alongside my isolation (MF 47).

Female to male transsexuals
Menarche, a watershed

Whilst, in general, the childhood of female transsexuals-to-be is experienced as less problematic than that of males, puberty often comes as a shock for many females, who have often kept up a belief that it won't really happen to them:

> My periods started when I was 13, very suddenly and I never thought it would happen, I was absolutely miserable because it meant I was like the other girls (FM-PR 56).

Lesbianism and transsexuality

Female transsexuals seem to 'work out' their homosexual orientation, and the fact that there is a transsexual aspect to this, in a fairly methodical way through adolescence. The following two quotations are typical:

> When I was a younger teenager, 13 to 15, I had some sexual experiences with other girls, but I always wanted to be the dominant one and have them regard me as male. Some of these girls were mixed in their orientation but I didn't want them to treat me as a woman, and it took me two years to realise this. Although some exclusive lesbians are attractive, there is something unpleasant in their being attracted to me as a girl. I don't like them to be pushy and dominant (FM-PR 95).

> I felt I was a man in a female body around the age of 14, and I was really confused. I knew nothing about anyone else like this, and wondered what the hell was going on. I did not feel like my girlfriends felt, or my mother's image of me. When I was 16, I felt I was strong enough to make sure my feelings were right and that I wasn't a fool. Although I thought I was

going through a funny stage when I was 15, nonetheless, I reached a firmer conclusion when I was 16 that I wanted to be a guy (FM 71).

Usually teenage female transsexuals do not socialise with other gender dysphoric females, i.e. self-proclaimed masculine lesbians. Even if they have female sexual partners, they wouldn't want anyone who they would consider qualified for the masculine lesbian label. However, there are some who do socialise in the gay world in their later teens and early twenties. Their accounts indicate there is a lot in common between these two 'versions' of gender dysphoria.

I had worked out I was a lesbian when I was 12 or 13, and I didn't feel positive or negative about that. I was still mucking about and I was popular. Although I was horrified when my periods came at 13, I still had affairs, and was happy, no hang ups! I wasn't bothered by biological differences because it was all so accepted anyhow. I began to get frightened when I developed a bust, that I would no longer be accepted by the blokes. We used to sneak into cinemas, steal fags, chat up girls all together. I had relationships with straight and gay girls, and I had to be careful not to upset everyone with my wanting to be a bloke - or I would tear myself apart. I had to allow myself to be accepted as a masculine gay female. However, when the chances came for gender change, I couldn't turn that down because I knew I would be happier. Many butch lesbians dress as men and deny their girlfriends the right to touch them in the genital areas. Feminine homosexual girls enjoy being touched. It could be that these masculine dykes would like to be men, but haven't the guts to go through with it. One friend of mine told me that during sex there must be no mirrors around and she objects to her partner looking at her. Some of these girls just don't want to tamper with nature (FM-PR 197).

CHAPTER FOUR

TRANSSEXUAL ACCOUNTS: MANHOOD AND WOMANHOOD, DOUBTS AND DESTINIES

Adult Nature: Appearance

Awareness of abnormalities

Setting aside the obvious problem that a biological male may not look much like the woman he wants to be, and *vice versa* (a problem of passing, dealt with in a later section), abnormalities of appearance in the subject's own mind often predate a final adoption of a transsexual role. These matters, when significant issues, were so almost always for males:

> I developed a large inferiority complex that I was not as good as anyone else because I was so embarrassed having (epileptic) fits, and having a left eye which turned inwards (MF 20).

> My whole appearance has been more suited to a female, I have small hands and feet. I used to get odd comments from friends and 'looks'. When I joined my newspaper at 18, I was told I would make a good woman in fancy dress (MF 111).

For some individuals, this issue of appearance is so severe it becomes a central part of their desire for change, even though living as a member of the opposite sex would not remove the problem.

> In private I cross-dress as a young girl of 20 or so, in mini-dresses which make my ugly bodier tidier. I can't go out

dressed as a girl because of my appearance, I just want everything taken away. My body has always been untidy. Some of my toes overlap, and I have a crooked little finger. I have always thought I was ugly while my brothers were handsome. Ever since I had an army medical at age 17, I thought I was unattractive to the opposite sex. Male clothes were always ill fitting, and I used to cross-dress then periodically, for a girl only needs a piece of material and she is dressed. This made my ugly body tidier and I wanted colour. Later I found a penis spoils the (female) shape. I put make up on because I have an ugly face and I dream tremendously about being a beautiful girl at night in society, it is a different world in my day dreams. Apart from the penis, I don't think anything else can be done about me (MF 128).

A sense of spoiled appearance then may continue to be a problem in the projected cross-gender future. Another remark from the subject before last manifests this:

I have had a hang-up about my nose which was broken when I was eight or ten. If I change my gender it would bother me even more (MF 111).

Poor masculine appearance

The awareness of a poor standard of masculinity is a common precursor to a transformation of that standard to 'feminine':

I have small testes, have always been dreadfully small down below, and life has been hell. I have always been conscious of never having to shave and my neck being so small. I never had a proper Adam's apple. It was a woman's neck (MF 49).

I was extremely self-conscious about undressing, and worried about this and my (small) private parts. Even in my early days I was so self conscious about my private parts that I would go into the cubicle in the men's toilets. If I tried to use the urinal, I couldn't pass anything (MF-PR 78).

Whilst at later stages, remarks about a male transsexual's femininity are welcomed joyfully, an earlier conflicted stage can exist where reactions are not clear cut.

I was in a supermarket some months ago, and somebody said they didn't know if it was a man or a woman. They were definitely referring to me in my working clothes, and the effect on me was that this hurt so badly. I feel I must go to hell, and then I go and drink, and then go to my shed. My reaction is, why can't I be a woman and have done with it. At least they would not be able to make all those sarcastic remarks anymore. Then this leads to thoughts I am not feminine enough (MF 193).

Some subjects will have tried other remedies to deal with their image discrepancies before moving along towards a further transsexual commitment:

At 20, when I went back into insurance I thought my face was long and thin and not attractive. Because I wasn't very tall I sent away for a variety of exercises to make myself taller, and I wore things inside my shoes. (MF 30)

Adult Nature: Personality Problems

Setting aside once again, the conventional presentation of the transsexual's personality as 'fitting' the sex role of the opposite sex as such, a sizeable proportion of males particularly are acutely aware of personality 'deficits', some of which border on the neurotic:

I went to India as an engineer, and tried to be a man, suppressing everything. However, I was never able to mix on an equal footing with males (MF 80).

I have always had difficulties making relationships with either males or females. I am tongue tied and solitary, and my interests are model-making and walking, bird-watching and gardening (MF 148).

I have very few friends and tend to stick to people I know well. Until recently I was miserable at home and virtually a recluse. I made a mess of getting on with people and at times my acquaintances were terrible and I tottered on the brink of depression like being a prisoner. I got involved with a girl in the house I live in. She left me and it took me six months to recover. I worry about things and I ruminate in case I fail, and these ruminations can go on for hours. This sometimes prevents me from doing anything at all. I would like to have a proper relationship, with sex and true feelings for each other, but at the moment I am not on it (MF 75).

Whilst female transsexuals try to maintain their masculine personality, males, especially of the type mentioned above, discover a new comfort and competence in the cross-gender role, which unsurprisingly commits them:

Since I changed my role to female, my whole personality has changed and it is like being reborn. In this way, I have to cram five years of my short life into one of reality (actually in cross-gender role). I have many new friends and I have been socialising more than ever over the past year. I no longer have to take all the tranquillisers that I did and visit psychiatrists as I did before the change over (MF 38).

Adult Nature: Religious/Spiritual

Not a few transsexuals espouse a religious commitment. Some have very strong experiences, which can be considered together with dissociative experience in a later section. For some individuals, their religious beliefs provide a framework to understand and support them through their cross-gender career:

At 15, when I was having treatment at a clinic, I went through religious experiences. I passed from believing in a personal God to something that was not me and is outside of myself. I have this idea in between the waking and sleeping stages, rather like meditation (MF 63).

My philosophical attitude is that I have taken religion more seriously and am now a member of a theosophical society which is a kind of Christian sect which believes in divine revelation through one's self, and that one's spiritual self is God. One has to use meditation. There is also a belief in reincarnation. The link with transsexualism is that I am destined to change from a boy to a girl somewhere along the way in ten years time. Meditation causes a crystallisation of light on transgender problems and it's a gradual revelation from the simplest right versus wrong basis. I started a kind of religious reflection in my teens (MF 47).

However a religious belief can also be antagonistic to a cross-gender commitment. The following subject was a member of a fundamentalist Christian group:

There is a conflict between my wanting gender reassignment and the tenets of my evangelistic religion, which I joined 12 years ago. My mind is in constant conflict. I have to recognise that a sex change will mean eternal damnation. However, if the condition is something beyond my power, then it's not my fault. I did feel free after I went to a 'casting out' of the (evil) spirit. I broke down and cried, and felt free from this deception. I laid hands myself on a girl who was suicidal and I felt the power pushing back, and after that she was not suicidal (MF 126).

Adult Nature: Physical Disorders

A significant minority of transsexuals report somatic complaints, which in various ways precipitate, or are woven into a developing transsexual picture:

I used to have a variety of medical complaints, for example, I couldn't urinate and then I went deaf in one ear and my left arm seized up and became painful, and I had pains in my left knee. I am scared about deciding I am transsexual. It is similar in a way to MS and it's going to change my life, and not just control of things in private. All my physical symptoms have dropped away since I have taken this on full time (MF 198).

I was fine until I had a motor accident coming down a hill in my van when my brakes failed. I hit a brick wall and sustained a crack in the neck and was very shaken up. I lost a lot of weight and strength after that and felt awful. I had this bleeding from my penis into my pants and then I got pains in my chest and began to develop breast tissue. One day I got out of my bath and hairs fell out from my private region. Since that time, I have never felt masculine (MF 183).

Adult Nature: Psychiatric and Psychological Disorder

Male to female transsexuals

The statistical survey of all the subject samples (Table 6 refers) indicated that nearly two thirds of all male to female transsexuals consulted a doctor for some explicit psychiatric complaint, other than the gender problem *per se*. Some 17 per cent had suffered a disorder with sufficient severity at one time to warrant hospitalisation as in-patients. The relationships between these frank psychiatric symptoms and the transsexual picture seems varied. Most other psychiatric patients of course do not present with transsexual compulsions. Even on these figures (above), it is fair to say that most male transsexuals are not exhibiting psychiatric symptoms most of the time. However, the evidence does point to psychiatric vulnerability in many subjects, which may be part of an overall underlying psychological trouble, and/or reflect the stress of trying to cope as a transsexual, something which often calls for superior psychological resourcefulness and emotional robustness. In general, the statistical table shows that success in finally achieving sex reassignment surgery is more likely for subjects who do not have a significant psychiatric history.

Neurotic anxiety and depression

The majority of psychiatric problems fall into this category and the accounts given by subjects indicate the varied links these problems have with a sense of gender dysphoria:

> At times my depression gets worse, and I am on a variety of medicines. I get withdrawn and nervous, and have a craving for nicotine. I am hardly living at all and it is difficult to get over my physical debility and tenseness. I can't make plans for the future (MF 63).

> I became obsessional with respect to washing and this took up over an hour a day. I became paranoid that people would try to break my nails and so I developed a strong feeling that they must never be broken (MF 34).

Desperate, angry frustration can break through a depressive reaction:

> I have attempted suicide before and am considering it again. Then I left my bedroom windows open with no clothes on. It was -2 centigrade that night. I have some explosives at home, and a gun and a flick knife. I have been responsible for some sabotage. I don't want anyone released from jail. All I want is my rightful quota of female sex hormones, which I have been deprived of since the age of 11. If I don't get it, I might do something silly, I am becoming that desperate. I may come armed next time, I am a very sensitive person, usually very gentle, not violent, I may have to do this (MF 47).

Just as with some somatic complaints, some subjects claim gender role controls the experience of a complaint:

> I have to get headache tablets from the chemist because I get depressed from pressures in the head. I only get depressed as a man. As a female, I feel restless but not depressed. It's as if I had to get on and do something (MF 54).

Simply waiting for reassignment can be a great strain:

I get quite badly depressed from time to time and have to go on anti-depressant tablets. This is brought about by my knowledge of what is under my skirt and fears I will be confronted, especially in female toilets. Since I have been on the (surgical) waiting list for 21 months, I keep thinking that may be a mistake has been made and people are being admitted ahead of me. It will be dishonest of me to say I was not feeling more than a little suicidal (MF-PR 136).

The reticence in this subject's last remark reflected his knowledge that strong suicidal tendencies were taken as a contra-indication for the surgery he desperately wanted at the Gender Clinic of Charing Cross Hospital. Following his finally obtaining reassignment surgery, he continued to have serious problems, continued to be depressed, and eventually did commit suicide.

Psychopathic tendencies

A number of male transsexuals manifest psychopathic tendencies. Some psychiatric practitioners would extend that label to the majority of transsexuals, who are judged by these professionals to be 'manipulative' and 'superficial' in their relationships. However, for this report, this label is reserved for individuals who likely would have attributed such a diagnostic term whether or not they were transsexuals with the special problems that brings. The following is an example from a medical record, and indicates the very great difficulties in clinical 'management' which exist. Usually prospects are not good, and usually these subjects are not granted reassignment surgery. They often are very poor clinic attenders anyway:

Man polymorphous perverse. History of heavy drinking and wife battering and episodes of violence towards his own children. Strong feelings of shame about incestuous feelings towards mother. Beaten up as a child and eventually sent to a residential children's home. History of truanting from school and being forced by his father to tear up newspapers until his fingers were sore. History of violence and theft (from medical record of MF 204).

I was sent to a special hospital for psychopaths because of my violence, drug abuse and overdosing. I believe this was all due to my failure to resolve my sexual identity problem. I resorted to drug abuse because of this. I have become filled with loathing and disgust with myself and I did anything no matter how mad or bizarre rather than confront my problem. I tried to commit suicide because there was no hope for me. I always have at least five pints of beer or a bottle of vodka before going to bed. I do the same if I have to go out 'on the game' (prostitution) (MF 145).

Multiple problems

A small minority of male transsexuals manifest multiple problems together. Often these are associated with low intelligence or unequivocal mental handicap. The special problems of mentally handicapped transsexuals will be considered in a later section, but the following quotations reveal something of the dreadful life which these most unfortunate people suffer. In comparison with these records 'simple' transsexualism is almost a picnic!:

Patient with multiple pathologies, depression, alcoholism, homosexuality, inadequate personality, many overdoses, binge drinker, failed marriage. Six psychiatric hospitalisations (from medical record of MF 87).

Patient with cerebral palsy resulting in spastic paraplegia and low intelligence. Hospitalised as a result of regressive/catatonic state. Exhibits aggressive and regressive (infantile) manipulative behaviour. Difficulties in controlling urinary functions. Believes he has a witness from the Holy Spirit and has tried to take his own life on a number of occasions (from medical record of MF 180).

I suffer from depression a lot. I can read a newspaper but can't spell very well (subject borderline mentally handicapped). I don't like shaving and I have no friends. I can't understand being alive. Sometimes I am standing outside my body and looking at it. I have no interests, I don't know what people are. I would kill all people if I had a gun and myself. I like killing cats and birds. I have to go to hospital because I have disease in my hips and knee joints. I am registered disabled (MF 102).

Psychoses

Since most subjects attending Charing Cross Hospital's Gender Identity Clinic have been referred from medical agencies, it is unusual for anyone to be seen who is currently going through a frank psychotic episode. It is well known that some schizophrenics suffer from hallucinations and delusions concerning their bodily functions, and this includes sexual functions and gender aspects of body image. However, occasionally some individuals do arrive. They usually have a history of psychiatric treatment and, although they are currently maintaining themselves in the community and the most florid symptoms are not presented, the psychotic form of psychopathology is easily examined:

I don't go out with girls because I am more a person who stays in bed. One time I smashed a car up to relieve tedium. I wanted to be close to my sister, to put her in a cage and call her mine. I always feel awkward with girls and go out of my way to be different *e.g.* giving myself girlish finger nails. I used to look at my body and think it was a bit like a diver's suit, it didn't feel me inside. Sometimes I lie in bed with live electric wire around the door because I am afraid of other people. You could say I am afraid of nothing. I am finding it hard to keep myself together. It is a losing battle. I don't think my face is right, not ugly, it is a general feeling. When a car doesn't work, it's not a car. I haven't been accepted as a man, I don't suppose I'll be accepted as a woman. I carry this big elaborate radio tape recorder around so people will look at it, not my face. What I see in a mirror is not me. When my parents die, I will brick up the house and just have lights on so I don't see anyone (MF 178).

My anger knows no bounds because of the female intrusion into my field of electronics. Female society puts too many restrictions on me. I get black marks from all quarters. I had hoped to experience my wife's pregnancy and child birth and I was prepared to have hypno-therapy to instill labour in me. I was manipulated and told I could share and then I was expected to run around doing things. I used to have fantasies of having sex with girls. At the moment of ejaculation, I found myself, in fantasy making love to myself. I have this feeling of tauntness before ejaculation and when I sense threat from the male role. I used to imagine (during sex) that the male semen was running within me. As soon as I 'switched' back to the male role I would lose this. I see sex reassignment as the only way of keeping out of psychiatric hospital. My sexual desires (in the male role) are all tied up with my getting nasty and violent in the past. I have an overwhelming feeling of dominance and hostility and swearing and taking everyone on. I fear that power to fight. Anyone can be the target, even my own children (MF 106).

These gentlemen need continued conventional psychiatric treatment.

Female to male transsexuals

Females consult for explicit psychiatric or psychological problems (other than for the gender dysphoria itself) less frequently than males. Less than half of our sample did so, compared to two thirds of males. Furthermore, a mere three per cent were hospitalised for psychiatric problems and in general their problems, when they did occur, were less severe. Most problems reported are associated with coping difficulties and the strains of a cross-gender identity. There is a 'battling' flavour to female transsexuals' determination to be accepted as males, and that comes through even when there are psychological problems, often in terms of aggressive responses to frustration:

> I overdosed when I was 15 because no-one would understand or listen to me. I never met anyone like me. I felt alone and a freak and the odd one out. I got very aggressive and there was talking therapy at the hospital. I was also put on drugs because I was aggressive to other patients. At present I am on a mugging charge because a bloke approached me at midnight and put his arm around me. I took out a sheath knife and threatened him (FM 74).

> I am not happy being female and I am only just coping with the way I am now. I have no confidence and I get wound up and have started hitting my girlfriend. I have a history of nervous states, feeling I was dying and ill. That is all over now (FM 18).

> Eighteen year old girl who has found it difficult to express her sexual orientation to other people. She has found it difficult to go out to work and has hardly been out at all in the last eight months. She has developed secondary symptoms of depression and stays in bed until mid-day and has no patience or tolerance at home. She has smashed several glass panes and three doors (from medical referral letter concerning FM 58).

Dissociative experience

Transsexuals

It is arguable that all transsexuals exhibit some degree of dissociative phenomena simply in terms of their gender dysphoric conviction. Around half of our subjects gave accounts which included further revelations on the extent of dissociative experience in their lives. The most common of these related to the differences felt in one gender role as compared to the other.

Gender role dissociation

Sometimes a cross-gender role would herald new likes and dislikes. This includes shifts in what or who is sexually desirable, but this aspect is dealt more fully in a later section:

> The...gains for reassignment are that it would result in lower pressures being put on me. It is a notable thing, for example, as a man I find I don't like yoghurt, whereas as a female I do. As a man I tend to smoke heavily whereas as a girl, I don't. Men have more directive conversation, and women tend to leave loose threads. I am more conservative in my taste for food as a male, whereas as a female I tend to go for salads which are lighter and more suitable for diets. I am less decisive as a female driver and less fast. I believe my handwriting is better as a female. I think there are two roles in the brain. As a male I am capable of mending a car and as a female I don't relish it. I have only begun to find men sexually attractive (MF 150).

Some motor habits may be differentiated:

> My female voice is different to my male voice to an incredible degree. I was first aware of this in my early teens...I have been admitted to psychiatric hospital three times for complete loss of memory (MF 205).

Mood and temperament states were often genderised:

> I am two people in one body. My male personality is uninteresting and quick tempered. My female personality is quiet and tries to be neat and tidy (MF 90).

> My temperament is different when I am cross-dressed. I am shyer, but I talk more. 'She' holds the love of nature and gentle things and I can't get it clearer than that. 'She' is freer, not aggressive, more creative, and less inhibited to try things out. I am Margaret at home, and 'she' is more quick thinking than Bert. Bert has built himself a shell so he can do his job and be a provider (MF 84).

Some individuals' response to prescribed hormones, is so fast it is clear that it is a placebo type psychological reaction:

I have been prescribed hormones and...I think some of my feelings have changed. I don't feel so flat and all this has occurred within 18 hours. My male sex drive has disappeared completely, and I now recognise which males are sexy to me (MF 47).

For some individuals the changed gender role and life stages result in wholesale personality changes:

Paul my love has no idea why I have certain problems. He regards John - my former self - with reverential respect. Once we visited Paris and met up with a previous confidant of John, of some 20 years ago. Somehow we managed to get through that conversation and I indicated that I had worked for John and saw him as my boss. I had a completely altered ego and was entirely unrecognised. For some years I had lived two lives. My former self was a very successful professional who dealt with foreign diplomats and heads of companies. He was chairman of the disciplinary committee of my profession. It was politic at an appropriate time to have him 'emigrate' to Africa. Sometimes I have instructions to go and consult him. I refer to him as my boss because I lack the confidence to make the kind of designs he was able to do. I am not as experienced as he was. Often these days I cannot understand the mathematics he used in some of our old projects. People have commented on how good my handwriting is compared to John's. I am much more extravagant now as a female, and have never been happier (MF-PR 39).

Some individuals can exercise a degree of control over their dissociative or conflicted experiences. The following is a quotation from a young man, bisexual in his sexual desire, but these divergent desires did not co-exist easily:

When I am feeling very randy, I have different levels of masculine feelings and feminine randy feelings. This is...a kind of embarrassment. I can rapidly switch imagery...and my feelings switch by themselves. My facial expression will change within seconds, my eyebrows go up, my hair is back in place, and I have very different smiles. A male smile has a strong jaw, it's manly, cheerful, moderately aggressive, and a bit cocky, not so petite, delicate, and subtle....These reflect the personalities of males, who like my father and brothers are aggressive, use swear words and are all for sex and nothing else, and want as much of it as they can get. A feminine personality is so opposite, just like my mother and sisters, gentle and affectionate, considerate, houseproud, hardworking, virtuous, and in general having a lovely personality (MF 31).

This young man's family background has clearly given rise to very polarised gender stereotypes. His attempts to fit the masculine gender stereotype to his own sex role conception as a male would be clearly fraught with difficulties, given his perception of his own nature.

Imaginary companions and alternative personalities

The recovery of details of childhood 'imaginative involvements' from adult transsexuals is limited. A lot of time has passed and those original 'naive' fantasies are often represented, for reasons that become understandable, in a form supposedly typical for a transsexual history. However, some subjects do make a link with original fantasies of imaginary companions, alter egos, and the transformation of one to the other. One eloquent example is the following from a man of low intelligence and a very disturbed childhood:

I have another person inside me, and I want to let her loose....When I am not dressed I am moody. Dressing calms me down. I have conversations with this other person inside me, and that's why I don't need to go out with anyone. Tony and Sheila look after each other. She tells me how to help out, and for example, she has helped me with my reading, we just got our thinking caps on together. She wasn't like anyone I know. She was much better, long black hair, looking nice, a nice personality...I see her as a friend, a wife, a mother. I would like to be a wife, or mother to someone and I would be a lot different to what my mother did to me. Tony has been in a load of trouble all his life. His history is all trouble. I wish to have a good history but you can't change that. When you think of Sheila, she doesn't have any history of trouble because she is good...There is no struggle, she has taken over my body. I want to be on the right track with God, and talk to him by myself. I need the hormones to be a new person, to overcome my past history (MF 140).

Another subject, of above average intelligence, also speaks from his loneliness:

When I was cross-dressing before, I wondered if I was providing my own female company, and I was possibly splitting into two people. I have an active analytic mind about this....Through the change, I find I am not stuttering so much now (MF 82).

'Reality' came to exist on different planes for this atypical female transsexual:

I read a story about a boy who was hidden and kept in a big house by a wicked uncle until he was discovered. In this story, he was disguised so he wouldn't be recognised. He was just different, he wasn't a girl, but I thought of myself as a boy deep down and that my parents may have disguised this, and one day I would be discovered and it would be put right...I had a fantasy about the future that I would grow up to be a man like other normal men. I knew this was wishful thinking and it was clear that there was no way for me to change, but in fact I lived on two planes (FM-PR 27).

Intensively vivid 'imaginative involvements' and 'psychic' experiences

Although intensive imaginative involvements were not recounted among all our subjects, they were common. They were reported by around 40 per cent of subjects, mostly males. The following are typical examples:

I have always had a very good imagination. I could always vividly see things, even when I write things now. I have looked into investigations of UFOs and am interested in science fiction. I believe I have been in contact with a girl from Liverpool from the last century. I take a view about parapsychology that everything has a form of energy. I am a firm believer in reincarnation and I could have lived before...When I was 12, I saw five apparitions, one of whom was my dead grandfather, standing at the bottom of my bed...Recently...I would help my father with his car, and then I would have the odd experience that it wasn't really me doing the work. I felt more or less like a puppet, as if a string was pulling my left hand (MF 20).

I remember when I was ten years old, waking and finding a white shape standing at the foot of my bed. In my teenage years I would sense a poltergeist around...I have intuitive feelings that I have existed in a previous life as a female(MF-PR 136).

At the age of 25, I met a woman who liked me to cross-dress whilst she was dominant for a while. Towards the end of that year, I thought I was going insane and coming out of a dream state. Then I had a special experience. It was an instance of the sun coming out behind the clouds and I knew I was a woman, and that my body was wrong and that my whole life was a stream before my eyes. Events came back that I had forgotten. My whole life made sense for the first time, for until then I thought I was an odd transvestite...I joined a clairvoyant circle in the spring time and began to be aware of my capacity for physiognomy. I developed a friendship with a medium which was a bit sexual. I have always been psychic and a bit hypersensitive and I joined the Divine Light missions. I was aware of something impenetrable to investigation, and that was my transsexualism. Now that has all been dissolved and, since 1981, I have had no overt psychic experiences. I have had enough to do with my transsexualism (MF 117).

This is a rather dramatic 'rapturous conversion' experience. Other subjects have similar if less vivid moments of sudden enlightenment, as will be discussed in a later section. Some subjects' experiences are so vivid as to be on the borderline of, or beyond, the threshold of psychosis. The following is an account given by an elderly subject, a Klienfelter syndrome individual, who in spite of the extraordinariness of his experiences was not diagnosed as psychotic:

I had complete intercourse in fantasy and I never felt so happy and content. I couldn't see the face of my partner, but it was a marvellous feeling going tight inside. The feelings spread outwards. I felt alive. Then my stomach was going in and out and after this, the baby came. I felt it was the birth of a baby. I had some pains and my body was relieving something to come out. A voice of mine said 'push', just above the penis it came. Then I saw the head emerge. It was an adult head, in fact it was my own head on the body of a child. I saw in this vision of a child my own face. It was as I had been as a younger man. I realised the child was me. It was my head and I wanted to lift the baby up. It was terrifying trying to bring the boy to my breast. He would not move. It was connected to my body. It was connected by dark black sinews. The child was joined to me like a Siamese twin, and the child had female genitals. It went on for some time and then disappeared (MF 49).

Amnesic barriers to early history

It is not uncommon for subjects who have crossed over full time to the opposite gender role, to claim memory difficulties in accounting for actions and experiences belonging to their 'previous' self:

Whenever I am asked to talk about something that happened

before my full time proper change to female, I think that I am talking about someone else. I have de-personalised this part. Now I have switched. I could not go back, even if I were refused reassignment surgery (MF 12).

Identification with another person

It is rare to find genuine identification with or as another specified individual. However, it does seem this can happen, not as an absorption of an infant self by big mummy, but in response to intensive experiences of loss. The following is the clearest case in our sample:

After my mother's death I grieved for her very much. People told me I looked like her when I cross-dressed. I developed more like her, and I used to kiss her photograph every morning. When I was with the coffin at home, the coffin lid opened and my mother said, 'Please don't leave me on my own'. I was a daughter to her, and she was disappointed she did not have a real one. I have had conversations with her, lying on my pillow kissing her, side by side. When I looked into the mirror, I saw my mother there. Sometimes I felt inside she was controlling me through her mouth. This had developed all the way through. I see me in my mother, and I am my mother now. Mother had a daughter called Irene, which she lost when Irene was 9 months old. This was before I was born. You are really talking to Frances, my mother, the same body. My mother has not really died, nor has Irene. I am Irene in name but I have been taken over from Irene. It's not the real me that got lost. I never had a real me. My mother's burial was just a show (MF 104).

Hypnosis and sense of gender

A few transsexuals dabble in hypnosis. One of our subjects learned a basic technique and used this to treat other people he considered were not 'real' transsexuals. What happened was a surprise!:

After I treated this transvestite to remove his transsexual feelings, I found my own transsexualism was 'unwinding'. I was beginning to have the same feelings as he was. It was a big emotional drain...I was drained and after I had played him the loud confidence tape, I found my feminine feelings had gone. I couldn't have cared less if I was male or female at that time. I didn't need to be transsexual. Therefore I made myself a special hypnotic tape to keep my transsexual feelings. I was aware of the (female) identity I had built up and the environmental pressures not to give it up already (MF 40).

Transhomosexuals

Transhomosexuality is a descriptive classification. No-one claims to be born this way, and as a reasonable generalisation it can be stated that among our comparatively small sample, there is more readily reproduced, more extraordinary accounts of fantasy and imaginative involvement, than is the case in transsexuals generally. These imaginative involvements with their strong dissociative aspects are more varied and extraordinary and the 'development' to a transhomosexual 'stage' is more eccentric and time-consuming. For these individuals, there are no simple classifications of their experience such as a transgender conviction, although these might have existed in the past. These subjects are so individualistic, it is not possible to use accounts of some as typical examples. The following subject produced disturbing and indeed menacing accounts. Of below average intelligence, he had suffered a dreadful childhood of family losses and violence. His own propensity for violence put him in prison many times. The use of his imagination to creatively cope with his pain and deprivation, and the unexpected direction they took are very striking. Apart from using fantasy to restore what he had lost, he discovers that a cross-gender identification helps him control his passion to brutally murder. As with some transsexuals, the step-by-step development of his use of part of his own body image to substitute for his unfulfilled yearnings for another, may imply to psychoanalysts a 'narcissistic' orientation, but it would seem to be a travesty of the ordinary meaning of that word. For once in his life this subject had found a woman who seemed to love him, and whom he adored. However, he again went to prison, and his Betty left him for a black man:

Learned my wife had gone off with a nigger and she was now a prostitute and a drug addict. I was determined to kill them both. I would cut off his genitals and stuff them in her mouth. I tried to plan it all, I ate, slept and drank murder, and searched for them throughout England. I began dressing in the mini-knickers Betty used to wear. I wanted to look like that of which I had been deprived, that's my Betty. I played with myself and had a relationship with Betty, with Betty's bottom. I was seeking for all things Bettyish. I wanted high heels and knickers, no higher than my chest. I wanted a female bottom, the top half of me was ugly...I would lie at an angle in front of a mirror and see only the bottom half. Just before my climax I would think of that as Betty. I would often cry and fantasise I was a full time girl and not the sort of homosexual who hangs around toilets....I began to fantasise more about the fellow who had seduced Betty, and I reacted with less disgust. When cross-dressed I was Betty and I fantasised about the coloured guy doing things to me. I spent all that time wondering what she got out of a nigger...As Betty I was insatiable and this guy was making love to me in my vagina. I got all mixed up because I was not a separate person. Betty was a connection but then I became a female who could be loved, that is, 'Kate'...When I stayed with a friend of my sister, I didn't cross-dress or feel effeminate. My murderous and violent feelings returned and I had to leave the house. I decided to live as Kate, because then I could tolerate being rejected, agree with those I hated, and my desires to kill Betty and her lover went down completely...I need to have breasts now. I want a breast emotionally given to me. If a woman's breast is not there, I want a substitute. If it's a matter of choice between someone else's breasts and my own, well no one can steal (my own) from Kate (M-THO 200).

Bryan Tully

This next subject, a highly successful practitioner in his own profession in his middle years, has had a lifetime progressing in his submissive/masochistic rituals to the point of compulsiveness. Not only are his feelings 'as' a male and 'as' a female split off, but orgasm is experienced as a shock and let down, since normal post orgasmic satiation has been replaced as the goal of sexual activity by something else:

I fluctuate from being an excited and over-fawning 'maid' female, in which I am completely overpowering in my desires to please my wife, and accept her will, to being a 'scholar-male'! In my conventional male phase, I get no enjoyment from being considerate... Ejaculations are the ultimate disappointment because it means the end of all pleasure, rituals and foreplay. My unconventional female phase is ended, and I feel empty and ridiculous. I am mechanical in my professional life, as a male...I believe I have developed a dual personality, where I sense gratification at the outward display of the humiliated 'class' female, and couple that with enjoying the castigation and degradation of the body of the male. I must totally give pleasure, cunnilingus is the height of delight. Not getting pleasure back satisfies the female in me. To ejaculate is to fail and I feel cold and deprived of my driving force. If I am punished before ejaculation, pleasure occurs in my mind. Afterwards it simply produces pain as my mind is no longer receptive...My summary of myself is that I am a male transhomosexual dual personality. I have a compelling desire to experience life as a submissive male lesbian, that is, to be dealt with by a lesbian mistress, as a degraded female(M-THO 166).

If that case seems complicated, then the imaginative involvements of the following female transhomosexual subject defy simple classification. This young woman who admits to a 'confused gender identity', and is primarily interested in male effeminate homosexuals and transvestite 'queens', is turned 'on' or 'off' by unusual fantasies, depending on her level of consciousness and other contextual triggers:

I have peculiar sado-masochistic mechanical fantasies. These tend to happen when I am semi-conscious and half asleep. If I am fully awake they turn me off. If I am half asleep, then my wide awake notions tend to turn me off. It's like being in a different world. In my semi-conscious fantasies I am assaulted by machines in a violent way. People in laboratories are being raped by machines. White coats are all around. At first I am an onlooker, then naked, I fit into place as a victim. Awake, I tend to be the one who is a bit sadistic, a controller, an aggressor. In dreams I am a victim, raped by jets of water. In reality I hate pain and am a pacifist. At some level, horror stories and sadistic literature appeal to me, there has to be some glamour involved. I am then a proper young girl experiencing the injurious breaking of skin, instead of my wide-awake confused gender image. The machines coerce the boys and girls to do things to each other so conventional heterosexual (fantasy) acts occur only in dreams. Sometimes, however, I enter a boy's skin in the story (F-THO 164).

Finally, one female transhomosexual subject exhibited such a range of 'dissociative', 'psychic', 'imaginative' and floating gender conceptions, that in a sense it was impossible to find any primary category for her at all. At different times in her life she manifested *dèja vu* experiences. psychic healing, precognition, telepathy, clairvoyance, fugue memory loss, split personality, transsexualism, transhomosexuality, family history of psychic powers, bi-sexuality, shadow body image, and adopted spiritual twin brother. The following small quotation provides just a glimpse of some of these phenomena on her sexual orientation *etc*.:

I used to have fantasies that I am making love to women and I was the male...Then I found I liked passive men. I have since modified that, and I can be passive part of the time. I was always aware without anything being said that I behaved in a way women ordinarily do not. I had fantasies whilst with a male, that I was a male, we were two homosexual men. I realised that although I had a real body (female), I also had a shadow body which was male...In that shadow body I have dreams of places I have never been to...Earlier this year I met a gay man who matched my fantasy of having a twin brother by one of his own of having a female twin. Although it was not sexual, we loved and trusted and devoured each other like two snakes. I don't see myself as neuter but one who has and lives two genders - plural (F-THO 154).

Marriage

Male to female transsexuals

According to the statistical survey, 66 males out of a total sample of 143 had been married before attending the gender identity clinic. Nine of those individuals had in fact been married twice. This was not a bar to achieving reassignment surgery, but males who had been married - in the male role - were less likely to achieve reassignment surgery than those who had not. Although these married males freely entered husbandhood, believing at the time it was a viable role for them, they tended to see this retrospectively as a mistake, out of order with the new (female) order, their present convictions proclaimed them to belong to. With careful questioning it was possible for many subjects to at least partially re-collect their entry into the marital role with the perspective operating at that time.

Compatible marital relationships

Some males have had quite long term relationships with their wives. Usually there has been strong personality and emotional compatibility in these cases:

I met my wife when I was 22 and a friendship developed firstly. She fell in love with me, but I just wanted to be friends. Eventually we got engaged. I never told her of my 'problem'. She was my kind of girl, not flashy, rather literary, 'blue stockings'. We decided to get married and things turned out reasonably well. I saw marriage as a continuation of our relationship, and my desire to be female was not constant. I wanted to be a good father to our children, and also fulfill my professional work as a civil servant (MF 147).

I have very few close friends, perhaps one or two. However I am very close to my wife, as we are both emotionally and financially dependent on each other (MF 96).

For a good number of males who get married, these compatibilities are not so easily slipped into. Rather they are 'experimental' and purposeful commitments to overcome a defective sense of manhood:

I was extremely fond of my wife and I married in order to conform. I would feel I had a sense of belonging. When I was in the role of male parent, I tried to meet expectations. When things got on top of me, however, my transvestite desires came back. I would certainly have traded these in if I could have been a proper family man (MF 12).

At the age of 18, I met my wife-to-be who was very shy like me. I had a few girlfriends and had never gone beyond kissing. I wanted to be good friends with them. I convinced myself I was a transvestite, and then an effeminate homosexual, after I tried and failed to consummate my marriage during 18 months. I had a lot of unlearning to do (MF 198).

Incompatible marital relationships

As might be expected incompatibilities in marriage frequently emerged. These appear to have caused great distress and both to have reflected a failure to fulfill a conventional male/husband role, and to have moved the individual along the reconstructed sense of his gendered self. Sometimes this happened quite quickly:

My wedding night made me ill and I don't know why. I wanted to marry because my male part thought I was not good enough without a wife. When she left me I cried a lot because I am very sensitive (MF 49).

I got married when I was about 20, and I was in love. Marriage deteriorated after five or six months, and this was my fault because I had made a mistake. I could not take the responsibility of being married, and I still wanted to cross-dress. Although I still wanted straightforward sexual intercourse at the time, my wife didn't want me near her sexually. I found myself full of self pity and remorse at my failings (MF 124).

Other marriages continued for much longer until an irretrievable breakdown:

I fell in love with the woman who was to be my wife and she was the masterful type. For five years we were very close, interested in music, painting, and flowers and so on. My wife wanted me to be a man but I wasn't very good at decision-making. My wife was a career woman and more intellectual than I. I was able to play the male role sexually, initially. In 1939, I caught a chill and I felt she knew I didn't measure up as a man and she began to despise me. I wasn't as successful as her in the political field. We were both active communists and, in 1936, I was charged in the Central Criminal Court for spying and was acquitted only with the help of wife (MF 80).

Sex was generally OK in my marriage....However, my wife divorced me because she wanted me to be more aggressive and more masculine, to take an interest in the household repairs and to take a fatherly interest in the children, and be fully responsible for the finances (MF 84).

Sexual problems in marriage

The great majority of males who were married reported sexual difficulties with their wives at some stage of their marriage. Some individuals reported problems right from the start and the following subject 'accounted' for his child in an extraordinary way:

In his marriage as with all other girlfriends he has had inadequate capabilities to have erections and has never had intercourse. Although his marriage was not consummated, he masturbated on occasions, and on one of those times, semen ran into the vagina of his wife and consequently his daughter was conceived (medical report on MF 46).

Sometimes other aspects of the marital relationships would sustain the marriage *per se*, but this would not necessarily prevent reconstructive changes happening to the males sense of self:

I felt I had been under pressure all my married life, hiding my cross-gender feelings. We only had sex four or five times a year and so my wife suspected something. I got married and I wondered if it was possible to be happy in a simple way because I felt something was missing and I had become introspective. I thought my wife Vera was perfect and I was so happy to be with her, we didn't need much sex. I wasn't much of a success on the work side, or in finding accommodation. Vera then became ill with colitis. All these feelings meant that I could identify by the end of my twenties that something was not right (MF 40).

The impact on a spouse can be very serious:

After the marriage, Sally, the wife became depressed and would take small overdoses, and lock herself in her room and pretend to take overdoses. She started drinking heavily and sex was practically non-existent, all because of Bill's cross-gender problems (medical report on MF 189).

A final crystallisation of a cross-gender identity may occur at some crucial crisis point:

Things came to a head when my wife tried to break out of the role of wife and mother, and slept with another man after she had been away for a week-end. We tried to make love when she returned, but I couldn't and I realised that I didn't need to be a man anymore. I don't want to be part time because I don't want to spend my life going from one role to another (MF 196).

Some individuals try again and again to 'make it' in a

conventional role, in spite of the trauma that, for example, their homosexual orientation causes to their relationships:

> I got married and it was disastrous and the parting shot of my wife was 'You don't want a woman, you want a bloody man'. I was shattered, but later I got married to a woman who was a bit butch. I still wasn't very good at intercourse, but she didn't want it much either. I just wanted cuddles really and then later she told me she wanted other men. We had adopted a little boy, but she stopped me having access to him by telling the Court that I was homosexual and I might molest him (MF 26).

Female to male transsexuals

Marriage is extremely uncommon among presenting female to male transsexuals. Marriage was entered into by five of our 61 subjects, usually as a result of social pressures and a genuine liking for the husband-to-be. In general these marriages occurred when the individual was young and had not experienced a homosexual relationship. The following quotation summarises the typical situation:

> I married because it was expected by my parents and he was my first and only boyfriend. I suppose I was out to prove I was as normal as the rest. I suppose I used him, which was a shame, he was a nice bloke. Every time he came near me I felt queer, it was like two men going to bed, and he was more of a 'mate' to me. We never had intercourse before or after marriage. We separated after a few months (FM-PR 4).

Children

Male to female transsexuals

The fate of children of male to female transsexuals seems to depend on so many factors that generalisations cannot be made with confidence. Relevant factors include the age of the children, the degree and management of their exposure to their parent's gender change, and how this affects other aspects of their relationship. The attitude of the transsexual's spouse is very important as is the presence of any other problems in the family and the availability of good social support and professional help where needed. A good number of children do seem to come through this extraordinary change in family circumstances without significant emotional trauma. Honesty and openness is clearly very important.

Adjusted children

> My two teenage children have accepted what's happened after being fully briefed by a third party. This was suggested by a child psychiatrist (MF 19).

> Although my children were initially curious and worried for me, and then one was disturbed enough not to want to talk to me, we have had long discussions about the operation. They have asked all kinds of questions, and seen a television programme about a sex change too. Now, none of them express reservations when they see me (MF 38).

In order to confirm what we were being told, the research team at Charing Cross Hospital followed up and assessed 20 children of male transsexuals where access was made available. Of these, 60 per cent showed no significant emotional disturbance at that time.

The underestimation of the impact of parental transsexualism on children

Notwithstanding the above remarks, transsexuals gloss over more than a few areas of uncomfortable realities, and this is certainly the case when some reflect on the impact of their behaviour on their children. Their judgements can be based on trivial criteria, and the lack of proper thought on this matter can extend into the future, placing the transsexual in an unforeseen dilemma. The following quotes are illustrative:

> We have two children, a boy aged five and a girl aged two.

Dennis (my husband) asked the boy how he would feel if Dennis was to become a mother. He simply pointed out that mother couldn't drive the car, and he wanted his father to do that (wife of MF 184).

Until I crossed over the female role I hadn't thought what to tell my two younger children. I don't think I could revert to an intermittent (male) role when I have access to them. These younger children have not been told of my plans and I miss them especially. I can speak to them on the telephone and have indicated I will not see them for some years as I have some kind of disease which means I can't be with them physically. Once I had a friend take them to a hamburger bar where I sat in a corner, (cross-dressed) and could see them. That tore my heart out, not being able to say anything. What can be done? (MF 40).

Disturbed children

The following subject didn't see any link between his trans-sexualism and his children's behavioural problems:

My 6 year old didn't query anything when I switched to a full time gender change role. She called me 'Daddy' for a while, but that faded and she calls me 'Mummy' now. I told the children that their (real) mother was gone for good, and then they tore up all the photographs of her. We didn't need them anymore. I have two girls and a boy. The girls are very tomboyish and very antagonistic. All the children have got into stealing. The boy is backward at school also (MF 192).

Attitudes of the transsexuals' family members to each other complicate the picture:

I have a son Peter, aged eight, and seven year old triplets. If I get any pastel coloured clothes for the boys, or any toy that is doll like or anything like that, my wife leaps in and removes it, shouting abuse. Peter never got on with the triplets and has been very violent to them, once trying to suffocate them. Peter is actually of small build and backward, and has a mark on his head, which I believe came from when I hit my wife during her pregnancy (MF 115).

Sometimes a family seems so full of disturbances and problems, it is difficult to disentangle what may have influenced what:

My gender change has caused no real problem with my children. One child is in fact in his 20s and I hardly ever see him. A 14 year old boy is at a special school because of his aggressiveness. He doesn't know of my present situation. Another boy aged 11 is slightly built and has a speech impediment, and has been seen by a child psychiatrist after a series of thefts. He has been aggressive at school, and once set fire to his bedding at home. Another younger boy rejects his older brother, is aggressive and has a low IQ. We have a daughter who is backward and tends to stumble. Up till two years ago, two of the children wet their beds and their clothes, you could smell the urine. One would soil himself and had a fear of going to the toilet. My ex-wife is of low intelligence, is epileptic and tends to drink a lot. She has suffered from depression (MF 12).

It seems a wonder this family could even notice the father's latter day gender eccentricity!

Transsexuals' problems in relating to their children

Even in those circumstances where children of a transsexual seem to be living a stable life, *e.g.* with an ex-spouse, the problems of managing these relationships can create genuine distress for the transsexual:

I have a son, Jack, now 18, and a daughter, Joanna, aged 13. They live with their mother. They know all about me, and regularly come and stay with me. My wife has offered me a divorce (needed for reassignment surgery) if I agree to never seeing the children again. Sometimes I think this could be for the best, and then I get depressed. I have to guard against getting close to anyone. Both my children call me by my stage name 'Lena'. I don't ask for a formal right of access because there is no way my wife can stop the kids coming to see me. However, looking back I think it might be better to commit suicide, as the price for all this has been too high, in terms of distress and conflict for the whole family. I didn't foresee my wife would be so stubborn. I daren't love the kids too much as I'm not their Daddy anymore. I daren't love them because I have to be on guard, and so do they when they go back to their mother. There can always be a row (MF 122).

Clearly, family members should be included in the help made available by gender clinics.

Female to male transsexuals

Female transsexuals' own children

Only three of our sample of 61 female transsexuals had children of their own. One other gave birth, but the child was taken away for adoption. Just how these unusual pregnancies came about in the first place is a matter dealt with in a future section on sexual behaviour. The circumstances reported are unusual including rape, and brief liaisons with homosexual males. Since female transsexuals are committed to their cross-gender role earlier than many males, their children have a more uniform experience of them as males and fathers. However, these relationships also have their worries and problems:

My child has called me father from the age of four or so. He has no recollection of me as a mother. I tell him his mother is dead. I do have an anxiety he would be taken away if I go through with the operation (FM-PR 25).

I am bringing up my own child as the father. I had intercourse unwillingly with a man on one occasion and this resulted in the birth of my son when I was 38. My son knows my history, I never lied. I 'married' Laura and I never hide in the bathroom.

I told my son he was a little boy and I loved him and wanted to be like him. He has shown emotional difficulties in his childhood because I was in hospital and prison. I think he was insecure. He has turned out to be a con merchant and is under threat of expulsion from school. He has exhibited disruptive behaviour in every school. He has been surly and complained of headaches. He tells the school I give him a lot of hidings and he runs away from schools. He had to be put in care at the age of nine, after he tried to poison the tea of my mother. She was very evil mouthed and suffered from cancer. We've had a lot of problems with Patrick. He will go off somewhere far away, then phone and demand I go and pick him up. I get desperate because I was brought up in a children's home and I don't want him to. He had an operation last year for an undescended testicle. A prosthetic testicle was inserted. He used to deny it bothered him, but now he is much less embarrassed at going around in his underpants. He feels overjoyed at being a normal human being, rather than caged up (FM-PR 13).

Female transsexuals' partners' children

Many female transsexuals seek female partners who have children and thus take on an adopted family. Again there are problems to be managed:

The woman I live with has three children. Jackie knew her mum was a lesbian and stuck by her and wouldn't let anyone degrade her. Colin, aged 18, was a problem child and didn't want to learn, and truanted from school all the time. He does express some jealously and doesn't know about his mother's sexual relationship with me. John who is 14 asked embarrassing questions, for example, asking what I have got and what his mum has got sexually. I asked him what he thought and he said he didn't know. I will let him know at a suitable age (FM-PR 50).

Consort Relationships: Pre-Reassignment

Male to female transsexuals

Once a male transsexual has 'crossed-over' full time, but before he has achieved sex reassignment surgery, he has a special problem in procuring 'suitable' intimate consorts. As his body is, the men who are most likely to express an interest will be homosexual. Yet it is this classification of sexual orientation, experience and identity the transsexual is seeking to escape. His ability to gloss over incongruities in orientation, experience and identity permits some 'slippage' in giving an account. Still if he does indulge with a homosexually orientated partner some mind-work effort will be needed.

Glossing homosexual incongruities

> I let my boyfriend have anal intercourse because it is a way of expressing deep feelings. It is not sheer lust. When he caresses me I feel feminine and it is an expression of closeness. Recently he asked to see my micropenis to see if it had developed at all, and when he saw it hadn't, he understood and now takes no interest. As a result of this I am now less self-conscious. It was necessary for him to see I was not just playing as a woman (MF-PR 152).

Most transsexuals of both sexes try their best usually to hide their pre-operative genitalia from their sexual partners. The significance is made even more clear by this next subject who, forced to acknowledge the sexual orientation of his boyfriend, glosses the incongruity in a very precarious fashion:

> I am with this guy Paul now. He is gay so we don't really have a sexual relationship. It's like a sort of stagnant marriage, and there is a bit of affection, and we sleep together. He doesn't really want a woman, and at first this was a threat to my gender identity. Not now. Peter can treat me as a woman up to a point, and when he touches my penis, I can tell he is 'going gay' (MF 12).

Fairy tale dreams about consorts

In the presence of so many practical obstacles to a fully intimate consort partnership, many males indulge in extensive wish fulfilment. The following quote is from a rather inadequate low intelligence male whose naivety and desperation is made clear. Even so, his own final sentence shows he does have some awareness of the status of his hopes:

> I have been approached by men on several occasions with a view to sex. I don't expect much until after the operation. I have never had an affair with anyone, because morally I don't believe it is right until everything is OK. Once when I was out walking with a group of people I realised that Bert was taking Joan into the sand hills. I hoped Gerald would ask me to go, but I felt guilty, a poser, making a 'promise' I could not live up to. After the operation I shall not be worried about dancing with a guy and saying to myself 'What will happen if he asks me to go upstairs and have sex?' I have met a young man, Barry on the train and we have got to know each other a bit, and had a bit of kissing and cuddling. He knows about my condition and is happy to wait until after the operation for sex. I only know his first name, but we are considering setting up house together. Instinctively I feel he will be interested in me physically. I am having correspondence with him, but I do feel that I will like his kissing too much and will become dependent on him and then be cruelly disappointed (MF-PR 136).

However major difficulties with consorts during the pre-operational period are not confined to naive and inadequate subjects. The following extracts are from a University graduate whose wish fulfilment fantasies were apparently shored up by open and informed assessment and planning.

The best laid plans

November

Recently I have met someone who was suitable for me in every way. He is my walking fantasy - physically, mentally, spiritually. The relationship got to a point of permanence without any explaining. Apart from genital contact there is 'plenty' of everything else. He is a senior lecturer at the University and an honourable man. I have told him I have had some kind of sex change and am waiting for an operation for removal of penis and testes. Biologically I've told him I am not a female, but in every other way I am. I gave him a book to read by Money and Green. I don't want to pretend, or have a relationship based on lies. Initially he was floored, but not disgusted. We've been away for a pretend marriage, and everyone knows we are 'married'. We have developed an inter-crural position with my penis tucked away between my legs.

The following May

Our marriage of six months is not going as well as we thought. Sex is not satisfying for him at all. We hadn't slept together before marriage and I tried to kid myself it would be alright. He is now experiencing what he calls 'cunt hunger'. I call it a violent insult. I am panicking. I enjoy love making more than the final climax. If my relationship breaks down it will kill me. I am trying to be a heterosexual wife, but apart from my physical limitations there are other difficulties *e.g.* I am a striving female and a committed feminist. We have many arguments over housework. I am really shattered after work and all the meetings (MF 171).

In consideration of these kinds of problems, it is perhaps not surprising that most pre-operative male transsexuals who have committed themselves full time to a female gender role, do not have stable intimate consorts most of the time.

Female to male transsexuals

Even before reassignment surgery, many female transsexuals do have stable consort partners. The moves towards further masculinisation do not always suit consorts' desires but often they are happy to see their transsexual partner achieve a status which means so much to them. Female transsexuals seek out consorts whose prior heterosexual experience is highly valued, and who are in any case willing to submit to the transsexual's dominant demands as to how the sexual and social aspects of the relationship will be conducted. Courtship is vigorous on the transsexual's part and often the consort has formed a strong affectionate or loving bond before being completely enlightened as to the transsexual's problem. Problems which arise are either practical - arising out of the pre-operational status, or emotional if the transsexual feels insecure about her masculinity. The following two quotations reflect these concerns:

> I am living with Maureen and that has lasted five years.Her three children know my history and are not sure whether to call me 'Daddy' or not. Little things show me I'm not fulfilling my male role completely. I would like to go swimming with the lads, or just walk around with an open shirt. Social life can be screwed up if I can't take my coat off at a party (FM-PR 4).

> My girlfriend likes men and she treats me like a man and I get very upset if she doesn't reject other men quickly. I get bad tempered when people make comments and remarks about me and I can explode at the slightest thing. Sex is more or less OK, but there are limitations and that makes me irritated, although my girlfriend gives me good feedback and tries to reassure me over and above what she really feels. Then I confront her with it, especially when we are at our closest, and I will say that is not enough, and she will say that it is and it doesn't matter that I cannot do things to her that a real man can (FM-PR 194).

Crime

The statistical survey (Table 13 appendix refers) showed that about half of males and a third of females get involved in some type of illegal activity sometime. This is usually petty crime, but such activity is usually associated with marginal life styles.

Marginal life styles

The following excerpts from medical reports refer to individuals whose criminality was above average. They illustrate how this activity is part of a wider picture of social and psychological difficulties:

> In Dublin he was on the homosexual scene and was beaten up at least once a week because of the obviousness of his orientation. He came to England at the age of 15 and obtained his female hormone pills illegally on the scene. He also used barbiturates and heroin and made a number of suicidal attempts. He engaged in pickpocketing and was arrested for importuning and he has also resorted to male prostitution at times (medical report on MF 68).

> Convicted of theft and involved in the soft drugs scene. Sentenced to detention centre and borstal, where he became somewhat agoraphobic. Developed transvestite tendencies and thinks the operation will fix everything. Subject to depression (medical referral of MF 118)

Legal problems

A few transsexuals get around their legal problems by illegal deception.

> I had a problem with my birth certificate when I was applying for jobs, and so I forged it. For superannuation (pension) purposes, so far I have only had to provide a photocopy of this forgery (MF 171).

> Me and Angie got married at a registry office. I don't accept it is illegal really because I think and act as a male. I have been in trouble with the police for forging documents, and messing with drugs (FM-PR 4).

Victims of crime

The statistical survey (Table 12 appendix refers) indicated that around half of all transsexuals had been the victims of criminal violence at some time or other:

> When I was 15 I was beaten up and kicked very badly, including in the testicles (MF 33).

Some victims have been victims of very brutal assaults including sexual violence.

> Last month I was waiting for a bus, late at night having been to bingo, when six or seven young fellows came by. They thought I was a fellow and 'queer'. They began to rip my clothes and then they found out with their torches that I was female. They thought they might as well make use of this. I thought I was in danger of death. They spreadeagled me on the common and raped me. I didn't report this to the police because I didn't want the publicity of being someone who was attending hospital for a sex change. Since that time I have been hitting the bottle pretty hard. I have been booked myself a couple of times for driving under the influence of drink (FM-PR 35).

> At the age of 19 I was bludgeoned in an assault and sustained seventh nerve paralysis (which renders part of the face immobile). The nerve was sutured and cosmetic surgery was necessary. Later I went for a job as a home-help and a man wanted sex with me. I couldn't stop him from stripping me because my injuries were fresh in my mind (FM-21).

Although there are special aspects to the victimisation of transsexuals, they share a common experience with other victims of violent crime, that is the 'effects' of the assault carry on into the future, way past the moment of the original trauma.

Drug Abuse

As has been made clear in the above section on crime, drug abuse is often associated with the marginal social worlds which some transsexuals inhabit. It is impossible to classify fixed categories of abuse for statistical purposes because trans-

sexuals obtain drugs in so many different ways and the significance between neat definitions of 'use' and 'abuse' is not easy to
draw. Most transsexuals obtain various psychotropic and
hormonal preparations from their doctors. They do not always
tell the full truth and are often aware of the 'story' the doctor
expected to hear which will bring him to make the appropriate
prescription. Some transsexuals 'shop around' going from one
medical practitioner to another. Public service medical practitioners generally prescribe according to honest clinical judgement, but a small number of private practitioners will provide
a prescription in return for a high 'consultation' fee. For this
reason, in the UK the prescription of narcotics has been restricted to specially authorised doctors. However, these are not
the drugs transsexuals ordinarily seek. The 'scene' and the
transsexual network is another source of supply and 'information' and may or may not involve an exchange of money. Some
drugs can be bought legally and used excessively or even quite
improperly, *e.g.* some desperate transsexuals will buy hormonal preparations which are sold for animal husbandry purposes. For many transsexuals, the use and abuse of these
drugs follows a similar pattern as with non-transsexuals, it is
a chemical means to escape suffering. For others, the experience is an important part of getting through a crisis, and a
contributor to their future genderised personality development towards a transsexual commitment. The following excerpts are examples of each of these patterns:

> Between '76 and '77 I did a lot of drug taking with motor-
> bikers in Brighton. I always felt a bit of an outsider, and to
> some extent when I was high I felt less unacceptable. This
> group was made up of outsiders anyhow. I felt I could wear
> what I wanted without any anxieties (MF 63).

> After my wife left me, I went to Canada for a year. I had plenty
> of money with my new job, and I began smoking dope and
> living in mountains. I did a lot of fishing and went to dinner
> parties. Whole new areas of feelings and emotions were

opened up to me, and the paranoia I used to feel was reduced. They were not even repeated during acid trips and I was now eating vast quantities. I discovered the beauty of the mountains, colours, tactile sensations, fabrics, music, and I became something of a gourmet. At the beginning I felt emotionally inadequate. Under the influence of dope I decided to get out or rather to change the record of my physical circumstances (MF-PR 66).

Beliefs Concerning the 'Cause' of Transgender Feeling

For most transsexuals the believed cause of their feelings plays a strong part in the justification of their transgender commitment. Sex shares with, for example, ethnic identity, or membership of hereditary royalty, the feature that it is an 'ascribed' status, something an individual is endowed with, he or she cannot earn, or achieve. Achieved statuses include being a doctor, a married person, or a 'nationality' that is granted by a state. When transsexuals seek reassignment in effect they seek to be granted a new 'achieved' sex status on a matter normally treated as 'ascribed', not subject to personal choice. There are a number of ploys that can be presented as 'cause' for reassignment. An ideal one is that the original status was an error, a mistake, and so the granting of reassignment becomes simply a restoration of the proper order. Many transsexuals realise that biology is the ascribed substrate that most doctors work on, and they may feel that some kind of undetected biological force must be at work. Many researchers claim the same thing so this carries some weight.

Some transsexuals share with other investigators a view that the phenomenon of transsexualism compels a conclusion that physical sex and psychological sexual identity are two different entities, which usually go together, but in transsexual cases, by definition, they do not. The requirements for a happy life require a harmony between these two. If psychological identity seems intractable to medical therapy, then a mutation, (or as some would say a mutilation) of the body is called for. Thus in the UK genitals may be altered as a therapeutic intervention to accomplish 'adjustment', but a birth certificate's legal statement of genetic sex cannot.

Apart from the 'ascribed' *vs* 'achieved' status issue, there is also the dimension of the seriousness of the cross gender desire. It cannot be presented as simply one type of unattainable fantasy of which most people have one or two. It must be enduring and seriously disabling,classifiable as a 'disorder' thus warranting medical intervention. In telling their stories, transsexuals not only report past 'facts', but proclaim or 'avow' that what they are telling is beyond their control. Once the individual has committed himself or herself to this fateful view he or she has a powerful call on medicine and also thereby undermines future changes which might have been brought about by the self as a directing agent.

In surveying transsexuals' proclaimed beliefs, it becomes clear that they are quite varied, and their role in the transgender career varies depending on the stage reached, and the orientation of the medical and psychological practitioners through whose hands they have passed.

Biological state causes

Many transsexuals proclaim their beliefs in the biological basis of their experience, *e.g.* this may be because of genes:

> I think the cause of my condition is that there is a natural division in the human race between those who are going to be dominant and those who have to bring up children. It probably comes down to some kind of genetic code (MF 12).

> It's chromosomes you know, a small mistake can make a lot of difference (MF-PR 11).

Some transsexuals look to the sexual differentiation of the brain:

> Although I have been told it is a delusion to think I am a woman, I have also been told my brain has feminised in some way (MF 176).

The cause of my condition is definitely some difference in the brain, although I could have been influenced as to what kind of female I could become (MF 33).

Hormones of course are known to have an effect on sexual expression:

It has been considered that I have brain washed myself into thinking that I was unattractive to girls and therefore to think I look like a girl. You cannot explain away physiologically the development of breasts. You cannot explain this by anything other than high oestrogen levels (MF 47).

I think it was a hormonal imbalance during the foetal stage (MF 127).

Programmes or forces

These are closely linked to biological ideas, but without the specificity of the above belief statements:

Transsexualism is when man's innermost feminine feelings are forced outward to the surface where they become concrete. This is part of witchcraft theory (MF 14).

There are subconscious programmes which blur things and make you solve problems unconventionally. I am solving my problems by continuing in the feminine role (MF 40).

Strange happenings in the womb

The womb is where a person is made. A variety of events can affect development:

It is possible there was a release of hormones into the womb before I was born (MF 186).

My mother wanted a girl, and that was in me when I was born because she carried me (MF 61).

When I was in my mother's womb, she was told my father was

dead, and on that day she told me she felt me go all funny inside of her. The shock she went through may have prevented a proper issue of male hormones. Other transsexuals may have been psyched into their gender and talked themselves into it (MF-PR 134).

Psychological influences

Some transsexuals cite childhood as the watershed for them:

I have implanted in my mind that all this started in my childhood (MF 115).

Now these 'psychological' aetiologies can be quite complex:

When I first came to hospital I felt I was female in my mind. My real identity is that I am a male person. Because my father was old and often not at home, I was dominated by females, and have grown up a copy of my sister and mother. My adopted female identity has pushed the real male identity to the back of my mind so it has not had a chance. It has not been apparent, but I have had the odd heterosexual contact (MF 31).

This next one combines a biological disposition with psychological consequences:

My model of causation is, first of all, that there was a biological predisposition due to sexual differentiation of the brain prior to birth. This gives rise to an inability to develop emotionally along masculine lines. In early childhood, consequently you are treated as a girl, though not necessarily in obvious ways. Even after 30 years as a male, the female hormones and the way people treat you mean you react completely differently (MF-PR 131).

Another linked congenital and learning paradigms:

I think the cause of my condition is something to do with my mother when I was in the womb. She had four boys before me. I was dressed in their 'hand-me-downs' and I had no dolls to play with. She got my brother to take me to the toilet. He stood up, so I stood up. I did everything my brothers did, climbed trees, played football and squash (FM-PR 4).

Apart from biological, ethological and social learning, theoretical viewpoints, there is also to be found a psychoanalytic representative!:

As a child I reacted to the lack of awareness and wholeness to my mother, while identifying more closely with the longed for object, therefore filling the gap, and thereby reducing tension. A child may use this identity bit to play through roles. The child uses the fantasised mother to fill the real gaps. In school, the obvious role in identification will result in being put under pressure to become homosexual (MF-PR 30).

The creation and dispensing with 'causes'

Some individuals, at least at certain stages, recognise their own agency, in creating a 'cause' to deal with certain uncomfortable 'facts':

I think one of the causes of my condition was that physically I looked feminine, and I did not want to accept (myself) being homosexual (MF 142).

My feelings of being male crystalised and now I can attribute my earlier feelings to this, it makes sense (FM 184).

These two later statements refer to relatively early stages in cross-gender commitment but sometimes a long standing transsexual can dispense with it:

I never discount options. It has taken me a long time to come to this point. I have stopped trying to find a cause for my condition (MF 116).

Conversion, Conviction and Compulsion: The Transvestaholic Road to Sex Reassignment

Historical, cross cultural, and clinical reviews (*cf* Chapter One), all indicate that there are diverse meanings to cross-dressing, especially for males, in the clothes of the opposite sex. Many contemporary male transvestites have discovered a fetishistic sexual arousal which is associated with their inhabiting the female costume. These men tend to be heterosexual. The strong fetishistic arousal to female clothes *per se* often fades over time, and may be replaced or elaborated by an increasingly discriminative sexual response to theatrical or scripted scenarios or stories (as often found in transvestite pornography) where fetishistic elements, exaggerated parts of female anatomy, dominance and submission themes including bondage and sado-masochistic features are all developed in a highly fanciful way. For others, the sexual aspect simply fades in overall importance, and a more complete, sexually less exaggerated, cross-dressing develops, often involving the individual carrying out traditional domestic female roles, *e.g.* housekeeping and shopping. Such individuals claim they feel more relaxed in these roles and are expressing a side of the personality which is not possible in the male role. Many such men, often married, continue quiet lives with their unpublicised 'hobby' and will only come to doctors' or psychologists' attention if a significant conflict arises, *e.g.* objections by a spouse, or if the man is unhappy about reducing sexual powers. These transvestites, the great majority, are the most reliably distinguished group from transsexuals who come to wish to live fully as a member of the opposite sex. Transsexuals are generally not sexually excited by wearing female clothes (and if they had a history of this, it was weak), and are much more likely to have a homosexual or bi-sexual orientation.

The variety of early transvestite experience

Those transvestites who do become transsexuals will have had a stronger cross-genderised sense of themselves which cross-dressing reinforces. Even among this group will be found a diversity of early experience associated with cross-dressing. The following individual became turned on at the new image he had created:

All through my childhood when I cross-dressed, I sat in front of mirrors a lot. In my teens I did this for hours, I wonder if this was really 'narcissistic', but I did like to see the beauty I didn't ordinarily see. At 17, I did in fact have an orgasm, fully clothed, just by looking in the mirror, I was rather shocked. At that time I was attracted exclusively to girls. Now it seems I am bisexual but then I could not be what I wanted, to have other girls, so I chased the girls in myself, in this other person (MF 117).

The divided sense of self in two gender roles is often found:

This experience of cross-dressing in the early stage of my marriage provided me with a sense of elation and relaxation which I never had as my ordinary self. I would go shopping, and I would delight in being accepted as female. I could be wined and dined and express a part of me I never usually could. However, I did have some good times in male clothes (MF 175).

It is unusual in this group to find early transvestism associated with comfort of sexual arousal. If it occurs, it is weak:

I had cross-dressed out of curiosity: occasionally I got sexual excitement, but I really did it for personal comfort (MF 116).

If sexual arousal did occur at all, then sexual dysphoria was a far more likely result in these transsexuals-to-be even before full cross-genderisation had developed:

I first cross-dressed when I was 15 and this brought about some sexual arousal, which was not welcome at all! I did not want to have erections, and I did not have any distinct feelings of identification with the opposite sex. That identification only occurred after further sexual feelings, later in my adolescence (MF 9).

For comparison purposes, the following excerpt is presented from a psychological report on a young transvestite who did not make a transsexual commitment. Other dimensions of the transvestite experience, than have been mentioned hitherto, are manifest and a weak cross-genderisation of self is also present:

> Began cross-dressing at age 12, two years ago. This led to sexual excitement, not so much so later. Had strong feelings of being different and dare-devil and wanting to get involved in hazardous activities, such as being on a speedway bike. He found it difficult to stop the habit of cross-dressing as he derived great pleasure from deceiving people. In his mind's eye he would have liked to get to know people in that feminine role as it would have meant he could be a different personality. When out of doors, he enjoyed knowing he was really stronger than he looked (psychological report on 14 year old transvestite).

The following individual took a transhomosexual rather than a transsexual path. His quotation reveals the specific genderisation of sexual responsivity, rather than the more general genderisation of personality expression exhibited in transvestite transsexuals-to-be:

> My cross-dressing developed in my teens and I enjoyed the arousing feelings of stockings and suspender belts and so on. I was only interested in what it was like to be a woman from a sexual point of view. I was fascinated by the vaginal area, which was not then normally shown in magazines. One could see breasts readily, but there was a mystique about vaginas. After I went out with a number of girlfriends, where heavy petting took place, this sort of fantasy abated (M-THO 160).

'Transvestaholicism'

Some individuals with long histories of periodic cross-dressing, find that this activity begins to assume a greater and greater role in their lives. This may well create problems as the need for increased frequency of cross-dressing takes on an addictive dimension.Alternatively, a new future with bad feelings and troubles shed, which this more central activity is seen to herald, may be a matter for rejoicing:

> For years I think my transvestism was partially repressed. Now it has come out fully and there has been a move. I don't see my new need to do this as a compulsion, it's something about me. I feel brighter and lighter as if I was having a dialogue with myself. I don't want to throw it away, and I may find it represents the larger part(of me), and will give joy and delight (MF 84).

> I first came to Charing Cross Hospital in 1959, about a year after my marriage. I used to have these phases, for two or three weeks a year when I would have an impulse to obsessively cross-dress. This would happen several times a year. Then, I wanted to adapt to normality. Now, over 20 years later, I do not have the same urgency, I am cross-dressing more often and taking hormones, and having joined the Beaumont Society (a British transvestite organisation), I have a new social life. I have found my direction and can see the idea of a full time change in three or four years time (MF 111).

The addictive model and 'craving'

In conformity with an addictive model of behaviour acquisition, it is found that individuals who have reached the 'transvestaholic' stage of cross-dressing dependency, suffer from withdrawal symptoms or 'craving' if timely opportunity to cross-dress is not available. There is developed an anxiety reduction function, not dissimilar to other ritualistic compulsive behaviours:

I would become very tense if I could not have a period of cross-dressing. I would look at myself in the mirror and have fantasies of doing housework and being feminine in social situations. When I lived in a migrant hostel I used to cross-dress every night in order to reduce the disgust and difficulty I felt when in close proximity to other men (MF-PR 136).

It got to be an addiction and I would do it (cross-dress) more and more in order to relax, however, it also led to feelings of guilt (MF 116).

The subject above also found that once a major commitment to his fantasy to make a full time change had been made, and acted upon, by becoming a customer of a gender identity clinic, then:

Since I have come to the commitment of going full time to be a female, it has been less necessary for me to cross-dress. Since I am treated as a woman (by attending the gender clinic) I do not need to make such a strong announcement. When I do get treated as a male I need more explicit cross-dressing (MF 116).

Again, as with other addictive behaviours, a highly involving event can lead to a temporary recession of the compulsive activity:

It can be overridden if there is a strong interest in my life. For example, when I was a driver and I had a chance to buy a new lorry. However, this doesn't last (MF 70).

Some events are more 'involving' than others of course:

I was in the Air Force during the war and during that time, and some years afterwards, I cut back on my cross-dressing a lot, as I was preoccupied with my career, work, and new family (MF 77).

Sexual dysphoria on the other hand can strengthen the compulsion. The same subject goes on:

The discomfort I have over my sexual feelings often leads to a desire to cross-dress. This discomfort reminds me that it is not me to be like that. If I am in a role pushing me to behave like a male, or I felt sexual arousal, or I felt anxiety, this would lead to an urgency to cross-dress. My urgency could be due to anxiety. I used to get hooked on valium (MF 70).

Renunciations

As a problem behaviour causes more conflict and social disapproval, there may be dramatic renunciations. Transvestites may throw away their entire female wardrobe, and then buy new ones in the future when they 'relapse'. Motives for the renunciation, and the factors which make therapeutic 'rituals' such as aversion therapy work for a while are likely to be mixed:

Throughout my marriage I have cross-dressed and had various aversion therapies. Somehow things were just controlled enough to keep the marriage together for the sake of the children (MF 19).

He was forced to stop cross-dressing when his parents discovered him. He felt that the confrontation and the subsequent admission to hospital for aversion therapy brought him closer to his parents, especially his father who had separated from his mother recently. He believed aversion therapy worked because he felt humiliated and felt sick and tired of coming back to Charing Cross Hospital. He didn't like the unpleasant treatment, and the prospect of going through it again. He dreaded coming to London, which he despised. He did not like all the strange and crowded groups of people in London (medical report on MF 8).

A new tool for British behaviour therapists, the capital city as one aversive stimulus! There are shades of the play 'Equus' in the following subject's appraisal of the prospect of aversion therapy:

My mother found some (female) clothing, and referred me to a psychiatrist. It was thought I should have aversion therapy. I never went back though, for I was scared he would destroy me. If there had been a quick way to restore my masculine part, that would have been OK, but I thought that all I was experiencing was all there was to me and I was terrified I would be emotionally destroyed, from which there would be no replacement (MF 96).

A plea, if there ever was one for unknowledgeable practitioners not to 'prescribe' instant therapies because a text book says this is an indicated treatment for a diagnosed condition.

Re-labelling transvestite behaviour

Just as narcotics addicts and alcoholics re-label drug taking and drinking depending on whether they are in a period of renunciation or relapse, so the transvestaholic on the final stages towards transsexual commitment relabels the instrumental purposes of his (and others') cross-dressing and reconstrues it in terms of having a deeper and more authentic significance for his personality. This often coincides with his coming out of the closet and finding affirmation by various organisations which exist for people like him, a sympathetic family and of course, his 'acceptance' at a gender identity clinic. Previously satisfying activities including work, family, and leisure interests become increasingly unsatisfying and grey. They compete with cross-dressing for time and energy. Other people are inveigled into the organisation of time for the cross-gender role, and there is even a division of talk in the two roles. Eventually, even extended time cross-dressed is not enough to satisfy the individual. An increased 'tolerance' to the power of costume to present a cross-gender role develops. Already existing antagonistic attitudes to the bodily insignia of gender continue to grow until the cliche is uttered of having a woman's mind trapped in a man's body. Now, in response to the above tolerance, tailoring must be extended to the body. The terminal transvestaholic may be prepared to completely forsake his family and presents at a gender identity clinic as a full candidate for sex reassignment surgery. The following excerpt from a successful British scientist touches on many of these issues:

When I first got married my primary occupation was my career. I had to do a lot of travelling and I always took (female) clothes to change into in hotel rooms. At home we were very happy. Both my wife and I are very interested in opera and concerts and we went out a lot. That did tend to reduce after my little daughters were born. I found myself not looking forward to coming home, where I was the only man in a female household. After my wife discovered my problem, she would accuse me of sitting and fantasising about my next dressing session rather than thinking about what we could do as a family. I'm afraid she was often correct but the more she attacked me, the more I withdrew into these revelries. I met a couple of other professional men who 'dressed' up and sometimes we would meet up. In the female role, our talk was completely different than as males, we never talked about our jobs for example. I managed to persuade my wife to attend one or two Beaumont Society functions but after that she refused. She thought we encouraged each other. That was true in a way, but some years ago I ceased going myself because I could see that for many of them it was a dressing up 'game'. For me it has become too important, really the most important thing. These days if I am not dressed I am always depressed. My wife understands more now and we will separate amicably soon. That will solve a lot of problems. Now I have seen the doctors, she realises this is something I can't control. She has stopped trying and is quite supportive really. I have agreed not to dress in front of our daughters, now 13 and 14, but everything has been explained to them. I am planning to go full time (into the female role) after I leave home, and I have to sort some things out with my company. They too have been very kind. I feel everyone understands now. I am now able to spend all my time organising social events with those friends who accept me in my female role. It's always a come down when I change back. I feel I have found myself and this is what I was heading towards all along (MF 161).

Sexual Fantasy and Behaviour Related to Gender Identity

Male to female transsexuals

Gender roles in sexual intercourse

A common theme of male transsexuals is the strong response they find in being the recipient or passive partner to the active role of usually a male partner:

> I like to feel someone else's hands run over my body and stocking tops. In my mind, it doesn't matter if they are male or female. I feel female. A female body is that which is done to....and the male body is that which does it. I have never connected or thought of a situation of a woman caressing male legs (MF 124).

It was not uncommon that in early stages, the transsexual's desire for recipient status was independent of the sex of the partner:

> If I have to take the initiative in sex I get bored. It is all a feeling of wanting to yield and have her (my wife) make love to me (MF 126).

> I had intercourse with a girl in 1970, and it became a chore. I had a strange feeling that one didn't know who was fucking who. It unnerved me....and I had to maintain the mental imagery that it was me being fucked. If I was on my back, my partner would cease to have an identity in my fantasy. It was not necessary for a penis to be in me, so long as I was experiencing passively, somebody doing something to me....it was purely a tactile sensation (MF-PR 131).

For some transsexuals, at this stage, anal intercourse is practised with varying degrees of acceptance, so long as other conditions exist which genderise the 'copulation'. This can be the vigour of the male partner, for example:

> Psychologically I get satisfaction from anal intercourse. I lie on my back and Peter is very aggressive in his physical actions. I am the woman because I am not used as a male body. Being attracted to Peter is this way, is a characteristic of women (MF 31).

The taking of female hormones may accomplish the same acceptance:

> I was only able to enjoy even anal intercourse, after I had hormones, for they made me relax because they made me think of what I want and what I am (MF-PR 181).

Alternatively, the face-to-face position, as opposed to the rear entry position may function as a heterosexual construction of intercourse, with the transsexual as female:

> A homosexual male will expect me to bend down whereas a heterosexual male will take me from the front, and not pretend I am homosexual. He is screwing a female, as he has other females. I would not find it natural if he has only screwed boys (MF-PR 152).

Once a homosexual construction is put on anal intercourse, it becomes genderised unacceptably, because a male transsexual does not accept an act or role which exists between two men. This construction can then be extended to initial courtship activities such as kisses:

> There are a lot of fanciable lads. One I like a lot is gay, and this affects the pleasure I would anticipate from a kiss. He would see me as a target for his gay sexual outlets....I get impressions that his follow-up I couldn't agree with....I don't know why anal intercourse is unacceptable whilst vaginal intercourse with the same man would be, I think people are just born with an instinct (MF 40).

Homosexuality

Homosexuality is a construction of sexual experience and behaviour with implications for an individual's notion of himself. For some subjects early experiences were categorised and accepted as homosexual:

> When I was a teenage boy we engaged in (sexual) acts with other boys, *i.e.* other homosexual boys. I was like them then (MF 33).

However, as is well known, transsexuals generally reject homosexuality, and that can have a comprehensive and unyielding implication for the subject's own behaviour:

> Before five years ago, I did see men who were attractive to me. I knew if I had made a move, that meant I was homosexual, and that switched me off (MF 43).

Generally, homosexuals were seen as being in a different and rejected stereotyped category of persons:

> I've come across homosexuals, and they want just one thing. They are all lust (MF 26).

This is contrasted with the desire of male transsexuals to be 'loved', in a romantic sense:

> Whenever I sense homosexual interest I cut it short. I visualise the homosexual as buying favours. I don't want to be taken in by a homosexual. I would feel I was being used....I find it hard to visualise a loving encounter (with a homosexual) (MF-PR 66).

One way to manage 'homosexual' signs in partner behaviour is not to look or think much about it:

> I was very cautious about letting this man see and treat me as a male. Actually we just 'accept' each other, and don't ask questions. I don't put too much on what we do, I accept things from day to day (MF 142).

Others' imagination allows them to tolerate or gloss certain signs of homosexuality, but only up to a certain threshold. The following subject's need for complete passivity as a 'sign' of femaleness is also less established:

I was distressed sometimes to be approached by homosexuals, but it didn't strongly repel me. I knew that it was not 'right' that someone should find my maleness exciting....If a gay male kissed me, my own imagination would say I was a female being kissed by a man. This wouldn't work if he said things which reminded me of my maleness, or touched my penis. Anal intercourse is difficult but I'm not a passive female, and don't mind doing in return what is done to me (MF-PR 97).

The need for love can be sought in homosexual experiences, and this is sometimes reported from transsexuals' youth. As the following subject found himself making substantial changes in life, so the more superficial 'signs' of maleness ceased to carry the same weight of meaning:

As a boy I was very willing to go to bed with male people because I was looking for love. I got very little out of it. Now I am looking for genuine fondness. I don't mind so much now having a male partner who has had homosexual experiences....or using swearing words, which are masculine....or remembering childhood (male) experiences. I am changing so much as it is, and it is OK so long as it is not required of me to dress and behave in a very masculine way (MF-PR 37).

It needs to be remembered that 'attraction' has strong dimensions that go beyond or may not be associated at all with a physiological sexual response:

There is a feeling of arousal by men which is difficult to describe. It's like going into a stare and a mesmerisation and I have to wake up out of it (MF 76).

Aggression and vulgarity associated with masculinity

Very many male transsexuals express nervousness or repulsion of normal males' loud crude and 'aggressive' behaviour. For some, even going into a pub or bar where such behaviour is likely to be found *en masse* is likely to create anxiety to a level that is virtually a phobic state:

> The main difference between men and women is that men are rough as opposed to gentle. I find men's behaviour sometimes makes me sick. Their drunkenness, their boastfulness. A few men are nice (MF 44).

> I don't talk in the way they (men) do, about women, swearing and making rival sexual jokes....They leave things lying around and are slovenly....I can talk to women about sexual things, humorously or seriously, but not vulgar, that does not suit me....Men are shirkers (MF 31)

Sexual attraction to females

A significant number of male transsexuals have a history of some degree of sexual attraction to females. Some 46 per cent of our sample were married at one time. The following subject was married twice, in fact, and had a long history of heterosexual fantasy, without any homosexual elements. Once movement along the transsexual career commitment had gone far enough, things began to change.

> My attraction to females has been changing *i.e.* reducing. I know many other transsexuals who were heterosexual before the change of role, and following the change would never think of that....My relationship with Jean was very important in this. Jean had a lover, Marion, and I began to fantasise being in Marion's role. Jean became like a husband. My soft clothes and increasing desire to be enfolded passively gave me a freedom to express what I never could before. She began to make all the decisions, as a man would....During the past 18 months, I have looked through women's eyes at men. Most

I couldn't go for, so I was worried. Now I've met one or two who might be possible. My attraction for the Jean type woman has gone down (MF-PR 66).

For some other male transsexuals, a minority, their attraction to women continues through their change of gender role. The following subject comes close to the transsexual transhomosexual category. However, since he was not interested in, or specially empathic to, lesbianism *per se*, he is not so classified:

I have sexual feelings towards Vy, but not to males. I don't like to be touched in the genital area, and Vy doesn't want to know about this anyway. We call this relationship homosexual. I think two girls are closer than a man and a girl because one understands the other to a greater depth. A man cannot really know how a female mind works and does not know really how to touch, or how a woman feels and he will go to sleep after ten minutes love play. There is a mutual understanding between two women in terms of touch and passion and knowing when to do what and where. It is a kind of harmony, like a dance (MF 137).

Bisexuality and the social function of the female role

Many male transsexuals, at different times and to different degrees, experience sexual arousal associated with men and women. For some, this is linked to their gender identity. Like transvestites whose transgender commitment develops in social directions, so for some transsexuals, their identity reflects more the social role of women, rather than the sexual one:

Feels aroused by sexy television programmes. Has fantasies of being both male and female, but does not know which to be. Attracted to the greater repertoire of clothes, ease of making friends, finding suitable gentle work, and because social life is very poor at present (medical report on MF 2).

There was a dominant period, and then when I was married

and female things were close to hand, things started up again, and I began to resent masculine things....Over the last few years, I have wanted to take this further although I enjoy sex with my wife, and being a father to my children. I fantasise doing all the social and domestic things a woman does, and being accepted in female company in a non-sexual way (MF 190).

Non-sexual relationships with females

For some transsexuals the desire for relationships with 'other' females is a major component of their feelings. Usually this centres on the nurturing qualities of such relationships:

At the moment I can't explain my real emotions, my concern, my love. My daughter-in-law had trouble with a roving husband and I wanted to cry with her, and have her tell me and not just my wife. I wanted to take her in my arms and be closer to her. I feel closer to women, happy sharing their problems. I want to show my wife love, not as a husband. As a woman I feel domesticated, tidy, and happier (MF 115).

For some subjects this identification seems to offer an escape from oppressive masculine expectations:

I can't meet anyone else's expectations. I can't do a narrow job, or go out with blokes or run meetings, and pass exams. I am expected to be sexual with women and I want to like them in another way. My own expectations don't suit anyone (MF 75).

This subject, a good looking male, had desperate feelings, when he was respected and found attractive by females. This seemed to force him to fulfil expectations he couldn't:

It's hard to say why I want to be treated as a female, and maybe it's just because I don't want to be treated as a male and no-one believes me....There is an etiquette where men treat women with superficial respect, but women have much stronger respect for men. It's wrong for me to be getting this respect. I should be the one respecting and serving others. I did think once of being a monk or priest. This respect involves finding security and a dominating figure to play on. It means pretending to be helpless. When women fancy me, I am angry because they expect me to make a move (MF 83).

Androgynous roles

Rarely, an individual will attempt a synthesis of male and female gender roles. This is not easy! The subject below, freed from conventional male expectations, could then be more assertive in a female role. In fantasy, having it both ways may not be uncommon, when it extends to real life, then, in the vernacular of the times, comes a real 'gender bender':

> Everyone knows me at college, and I am generally treated as a feminised man. My personal identity is that I am a woman with a penis....If I was just a female, I would want such male structures removed....I was fascinated by David Bowie. I developed an *alter ego* as a hermaphrodite pop star, that is to say a woman with boobs and a penis. This fantastical person became the ultimate ruler in a fantastical domain. I wanted more and more to become very powerful. In my fantasies most satisfaction would come by performing as David Bowie, with hundreds of thousands of people worshipping one. This was very fulfilling and the appeal was that this creature would have no one gender. The kick was getting noticed. I was ambitious with both masculine and feminine characteristics. This androgynous person was female with male genitals and capacity....People have realised that I am an assertive female and have a strong character which they quite admire. When you see me as a man, I am weak, effeminate and wet, but as a woman I am respected (MF 34).

Other sexual deviations

It may or may not seem surprising but transsexuals rarely report other sexual deviations outside their own gender dysphoric syndrome. Many transvestites do have overlapping interests in sado-masochistic and fetishistic activities. These transvestites who enjoy such sexually arousing activities tend not to be the ones who move on to become transsexuals. However, this is not an absolute rule, and the following individuals did have long transvestite histories before subsequent transsexual commitment in later adulthood:

> From the age of 15 I was a rubber fetishist....I had been interested in (female) clothing from the age of 11....As an adult I discovered male activity to be quite enjoyable, and I became a happily married man. In later life my desire to be a woman has decreased my interest in all activities except those associated with being a female, *i.e.* housework (MF 44).

> Stimulation between the urethra and anus easily brought me off. The whole thing was complicated right up to my 50s because I was a masochist and liked being bound and beaten. Normal sex life was impossible for me if my penis was touched it killed all feelings dead. Now, (after reassignment surgery), I find it repulsive and sickening (MF-PR 39).

Sexual conflict

Transsexuals who describe major sexual conflict in their histories before the resolution of a transsexual commitment indicate major incongruities in fantasy, behaviour and identity. There is no set pattern to these, and they can be very distressing:

> My fluctuations have made me wonder if I am really two people....I might bring a girl to my place and attempt lovemaking. Foreplay can be pleasurable and although I have trouble obtaining an erection, I feel inside there was a heterosexual man trying to get out....My masturbation fantasies always have me as a woman. Sometimes I try to use this fantasy when I am with a woman. After orgasm I feel sick. My active role with females is completely contrary to my fantasies where I am completely passive and gentle (MF 89).

Although sexual problems and post-orgasmic reactions will be discussed more fully in a later section, the following subject is here noted as citing these as part of his conflict:

All my feelings were for girls. Now I find it difficult to get used to men. I suppose all women feel like that initially. I enjoy conventional sex, but I like to cross-dress and then have sex as a male. Immediately afterwards, I feel absolutely horrible as if I have done something wrong. I have to fantasise the female as a male. We both end up crying after intercourse (MF 122).

This subject's sexual arousal was full of conflict:

During my courtships my reactions to touching and kissing were not normal. The sensuous sensations helped me imagine myself in a more truly female role. My problem with erections (priapism) was getting me into a jam as I longed to be one thing or another, and my male and female sexual dimensions co-existed in discomfort....My erotic fantasies, when my breasts are stimulated, are marred by the half male/female response (MF 147).

Imagination and the body

Fantasy about the functions of the body extends beyond the purely sexual (dealt with in a later section). The range of these genderised fantasies' intensity is broad, from mild wishfulness to reports which are virtually hallucinatory or dissociative. The following subject reports a typical mild form of fancifulness:

I try not to be clumsy and oafish. My behaviour fits in with who I'm with, *e.g.* when I sit down. The way my voice changes when I am with women has been noticed (MF-PR 181).

This next subject, having read about hormones, is sure he is:

Producing lots of female hormones and the effects are dependant only on the sensitivity of the target organs. The brain is most sensitive and has feminised and is rejecting everything masculine (MF 47).

This next Afghan subject's subjective and rather narcissistic 'experience' of his own body prompts him to highly dubious and indeed dangerous behaviour:

I want to be admired, loved and fondled....I indulge in self-play as my whole body is extra sensitive....I have a sensitive belly and I press my testicles very hard until I get a deep pain in my belly. I made them slip under my fingers with the pressure and this gives me a twitch of pain and I tremble like a bird whose throat has suddenly been chopped off. The pain reminds me of a lovely long penis very deep inside my belly inserted from the front just like a woman getting it....I take an eye dropper which I put into the hole of my penis, repeatedly pushing it deep in and out until it bleeds. It is torture but I get satisfaction that I can have intercourse like a woman and even bleed like menstruation (MF 139).

Some people worry about prospective problems:

If my penis is removed in the operation and a small amount of tissue is left to be engorged on sexual excitement, then if I have an orgasm, would it be right to consider it a female one or male one? (MF-PR 181).

Finally, an example of a virtual hallucinatory fantasy from an older transsexual:

I went to bed a so-called man, and then woke up and felt like a woman down below, and everything. I had an awful feeling I was different here in my genitals and hips. I never had a proper Adam's apple and I have a woman's neck. I was washing one day when I was 62, and my penis went back inside my stomach. Even when I masturbated it felt like a skin over my penis. I even thought I had given birth to a baby (MF 49).

Lack of sexual desire

A complete lack of sexual desire is rare, and when it does occur it raises the question of an atypical gender dysphoria. Some individuals who have been depressed genderise their self-as-depressed and seek reassignment as a transformation of that self:

> Although I have not looked at any woman with a sexual intent for ten years, I do not have any tendencies to transfer my attention to men. This lack makes me wonder in all honesty if I am truly transsexual (MF 50).

> Man who has never been sexually or emotionally involved with anyone. During the last few years he has been increasingly withdrawn and claims he could not make it out. He wants the appearance of being a woman after hearing casually about this. He has no desire to behave sexually as a man or a woman and thinks of sex as a weakness (medical report on MF-PR 69).

This young man was granted reassignment and spent the rest of his life in and out of psychiatric hospitals as his mental state deteriorated and he developed an obsession about his birth certificate not being changed. This was a very unfortunate case where the lack of specific sexual or alternative social plans or desires should have been a warning.

Female to male transsexuals

The need to take the active and controlling role in sexual activity

Almost all female transsexuals emphasise the importance of taking active, leading control in lovemaking. It is an issue which is intimately tied up with their sense of gender identity and role, and capacity to enjoy sexual experience with an acceptable partner. The following subject provides the archetypal account:

> I always felt disgusted at a female wanting to touch me and wanting me to enjoy it, it was noxious to me to lie there and let them satisfy me. Even if they left my nipples and genitals alone, their styles would be wrong....I think it would be different if I were a man and had sexual organs, I wouldn't

mind lying back at all. If I am passive (now) and a woman does something to my body, it is uncomfortable and not nice and sends burning pains down my legs. This is just by stroking. I don't like to be touched down there (on the genitals) by men. I have tried to touch myself there, but I avoid it now. Probably I have an image of penetration and that makes it worse (FM 23).

This quote illustrates several important things. First, the common strict rule that nipples, breasts and genitals shall not be touched. Secondly, the physically noxious reaction to being a recipient of another's stroking behaviour even when that other is a regular sex partner. Thirdly, there is an admission that if the subject were a real man with male sex organs, then this reaction might not occur. This is a first indication that the role of these noxious reactions depend on the meaning of the situation which prompts them and they are associated with other anxieties such as being treated like a woman, *i.e.* someone meant to be vaginally penetrated. The insistence that the transsexual's role as male is to provide satisfaction can be a very absolute definition of gender role:

It was enough for me to give satisfaction. She didn't see that I did not want satisfaction from her anymore than I wanted it from a man. If I had wanted it I would have gone with a man! I was satisfied by her being satisfied (FM 21).

Being on top during the sex act also carried the male connotation of an active initiating function. However, when two partners have become very secure in their roles, then the dominating feeling, which is so important, may not need to be shored up constantly by the specific role of the transsexual being on top. The following subject explains the significance of this:

I express a lot of love with lots of active touching. I want to hug and hold. Being on top all the time I found leads to the same intensity of feeling. As time has gone by I have been able to have sex with Jean on top and I can feel dominant even when I am not on top or not doing anything....You see a woman on the bottom normally pulls a man down on her differently to the man pulling her to him. There is a difference, more strength and impulsiveness more noises. I can swear but, I like Jean to be more ladylike in bed. I am less restrained (FM 17).

There are moveable thresholds of acceptance of dominant or passive behaviour. However, the 'right' threshold can be very precarious:

Sometimes my girlfriend takes a leading role in sex, and sometimes it is enjoyable. If it goes on past a certain point or is too active, it ceases to be enjoyable. I liked to be stroked, but I can be agitated at the slightest annoyance. If I lie on my back, then I cannot respond.... The same strokes on the same part of me would be enjoyable if I was in the dominant and preferred position (FM-PR 81).

Lesbianism

The needs of female transsexuals to take a dominant 'male' role with their female partners often precludes them from wishing to have a relationship with grown lesbians. Lesbians are interested in their partners female sexual parts, and many do not wish to be entirely passive. Many transsexuals seek out females with a heterosexual history, which confirms therefore their own masculinity. The following subject explains her thinking. Her first sentence is an interesting gloss. Her girl-friend is subject to a rule, but her following it is attributed to her 'unquestionable' heterosexual motivation:

My girlfriend treats me completely as I want and I have never let her touch me sexually, and I don't think she really wants to because she is not attracted to a female. If my girlfriend liked my female parts it would be terrible and the end of our love. Lesbians you see, touch each other all over, even if one is in charge in the masculine role. They are more understanding and gentle. In a male/female relationship, each wants to experience the other as different. She is under him, there for him. If my girlfriend took the lead, it would be worse if I was on my back, for fear something would be touched (FM 71).

So lying on one's back is both generally vulnerable and likewise undermines the active dominant role. As with male transsexuals, some female transsexuals have experimented with lesbianism, some in their early teens. The following subject notes that this did not accomplish the social expectations she could be comfortable with:

I've made various attempts to form relationships on the lesbian scene. I found that scene less acceptable than heterosexual society....I find that you get dismissed in conversation if you are a female, and it's not thought you can follow through your ideas. I want the respect men get from both genders (FM 32).

Some transsexuals can accommodate a lesbian partner so long as dominance rules are maintained:

It's OK with a lesbian if I am dominant, overpowering, and she submits. As soon as the table started to turn, I would be out. I would have to be on my guard against being taken for a ride both in bed, and socially. I am my own boss and not to be humiliated. If a woman did not conform to a submissive role, I would feel secondary. She would be getting the better of me and I would be vulnerable and anything might happen. I'm not sure I could stop it. If I were to enjoy it, it would be the 'woman' coming out (FM-PR 125).

Such a desperate sense of having to guard against certain reactions, again reflects the precariousness of the current constructions of experience. The power and submission demanded over a partner can be surmised by another remark by the same subject:

Catherine did not know I was using a prosthesis rather than a real penis for a couple of years. She was very embarrassed and rather hurt when she found out, not angry (FM-PR 125).

A subject who had had both lesbian and heterosexual partners gives a reminder that many females who classify themselves as lesbians rather than transsexuals do share certain gender and sexual dysphoric experiences with transsexuals:

> Some gay women I have known are not happy about being entered vaginally. On occasion it's OK for me. It was a heterosexual girlfriend who really turned me on, by wearing something sexy and seductive. She reacted to my male side. Lesbians want sex without foreplay, they are more demanding (FM PR 86).

For some of these masculine lesbians, a rejection of the female role may develop as they seek to gratify their strong lesbian desires, whilst seeking stability and social acceptability:

> I want to be accepted and be able to go down the street holding hands. The women I know are very dominant and stable and outgoing, whilst the men I have as friends tend to be submissive and uncontrolled. I don't want to be like 'men' or 'women', but accepted as the me I am (FM-PR 79).

Experiments with men

Only a minority of female transsexuals get involved in sexual experiments with men, usually in the early parts of their lives. What is interesting from the accounts given is not so much how men are unattractive sexual objects as such, but how the 'female role' in sexual activity is noxious:

> Five years ago I met a fella who was very nice. I wanted to prove to myself that my feelings were not just fear. I asked him to help me and he stayed a couple of weeks. There was a lot of sex play and he taught me how to make love to a woman. I however felt like a living person in a corpse, especially when he tried penetration. We parted as good friends (FM 21).

The following subject had an untypically weak cross-gender

identity in comparison with most female transsexuals attending a gender clinic, and a somewhat untypical history. Nevertheless she reports the dissociation between sexual attraction to males and sexual desires for their ministrations:

> I missed William a lot. I didn't really enjoy sex, but I liked kissing on the lips. I have a reservation about intercourse (which is) that I do not ultimately want to be aware as a woman. I liked being physically naked with him, but I didn't enjoy intercourse. In fact I was more aroused and thinking of him when he wasn't actually there. This man was special in allowing me to be myself, whilst others didn't understand and assumed things....I can't be treated as a woman because that is a put down. Intimate intercourse is the ultimate in being treated as a woman (FM 121).

Now the first part of this subject's account is not far removed from that which would be expected from a heterosexual woman reporting general sexual dysfunction or frigidity. However, the classification of the experience is different and the noxious conditioned response to the implicative associations 'treated as a female'... 'putdown'... as the overriding noxious reaction would not be such an acknowledged factor. As it is, the experience is seen not as a rejection of sex (frigidity), but rather a rejection of gender role. Some subjects try to operate occasionally in a conventional situation *e.g.* marriage and then try to impose their role unconventionally. It's difficult and in the few cases where a real effort is made, it doesn't last long. However, it provides another example of how sex role rejection can be dissociated from the rejection of an opposite sex partner *per se*:

> At age 21 she married in accordance with her parents' expectations. She found within her (marital) relationship, she was adopting the male initiative and in sexual aspects thought of her husband as 'female'. After 11 months she left him to join the army (medical report on FM-PR 35)

Although the noxious rejection of the sex role can be focused on sexual activity, it is not inseparable from wider social aspects of gender role:

> I had sex with Tim and I did get orgasms, but it wasn't 'me'. The dominant male was not for me....After two weeks of marriage, I thought of myself growing old and fat as a mother and I couldn't accept it. I could accept it as a man. Men get stronger as they get older, and I have always seen myself as stronger and fit and free from being interrogated if I arrange something (FM-PR 50).

Other sexual experiments with men include sexual intercourse with homosexual men. Although at first sight this seems unlikely, a couple of female transsexuals have claimed this is how they became pregnant! The following is one such extraordinary story:

> I have been on male hormones for years and had my mastectomy years ago. I look like a male (subject had a beard). Now I have this very close gay male friend who works for the same theatre company as I do. He's exclusive and has one stable boyfriend. He was leaving the company and we all had loads to drink. I didn't really find him sexually attractive, but somehow we ended up in bed. It was a kind of desperate affection. It never would have happened if he had not been a homosexual. Even then it was a momentary thing. Penetration was uncomfortable for me but it wasn't like what I imagine a heterosexual male would be like with a girl. He wasn't lustful, treating me as a sex object. We understood afterwards that it could never happen again....After 20 weeks I discovered I was pregnant! The doctors were really unpleasant with me, but I gave birth by caesarian section and the child was given up for adoption. I tried to put a brave face on things and consider this all part of life's rich tapestry (FM-PR 95).

'Abandonment' vs control

Although most female transsexuals refer to their own

inclinations to be active, and initiative taking in sex in comparison with women's supposed natural receptive passiveness, occasionally there is a glimpse of a fear of the 'abandonment' of female orgasm which requires the 'letting go' of control. It is rarely stated explicitly, but it is of interest since it is often just this that transsexuals see as the catharsis of their transformation to the female identity:

> Louise always makes noise and is more abandoned than I during sex. I like to be doing all the things that affect her like this, but I am relatively calm. I would feel much less comfortable if I was in her state. I don't think I ever want to be in this abandoned state (FM 153).

Residual fears of male rejection

Most female transsexuals reject out of hand any idea that they want to be desired by males. However, it is worth remembering that their early painful experiences involved male rejection of them as peers. Occasionally then a painful residual memory survives in a sense of spoiled identity that is linked with male rejection of the female transsexual as a conventional (sexual) object of attraction. No more can be concluded from this beyond noting that it can enhance a young female transsexual's sense of abnormality which in turn can make a transformed gender a more real identity dimension than a reformed heterosexual to homosexual status would:

> When males were on the look out for girls, they would think of me and say 'arrh! I don't want to know'. I would feel humiliated, small, embarrassed, not natural, a freak of some kind (FM 17).

Fear of rape and sexual aggression

In a few cases, female transsexuals expressed general anxieties about rape and physical aggression by men. These fears were highlighted in two subjects, who both happened to be of low intelligence. The first was classified as borderline mentally handicapped:

I don't want to be treated as a girl, and I hate perfume and high heels and people looking at me especially coloured men who say 'nice girl, I take you out. I go to bed with you'. I don't want to be a prostitute and thought of as easy....When I go up the West End I am afraid of being attacked and I am so frightened I run. It's of the violence and sex. There were two girls at school and boys tried to take their knickers off. I heard about it and didn't like the boys or the girls. I get warnings about going up to North London where there are funny men. There was a five year old girl there raped by men. I don't want to be a lesbian because you get named and disliked (FM 195).

The following rather naive Chinese subject did not know what her womb was, but eventually achieved sex reassignment:

Men can go out swimming and do kung fu, and face people and not have names called behind their back. If one is a girl, it is possible to get raped whereas a kung fu male can defend himself and others....No one has ever assaulted me, but I am afraid I may get raped in England (FM-PR 92).

Questionable feelings

As with males, but to a far lesser extent, some female transsexuals report conflicted or mixed feelings. The following subject had a weak cross-gender identification:

I realised I was not attracted to men when I was 15 or 16. I don't know if I am attracted to a woman, though if I was male I should wish to live with one. I have thought of kissing a woman....but I am not sure it is morally right....I have never met any homosexual people. It is not so shameful to be unmarried in Malaysia these days, but people do ask if there is something wrong with you (FM 182).

This next subject was highly intelligent and well informed and indeed a mental health professional herself. Her cross gender classification of her feelings remained questionable:

I think I am transsexual, and it is messing up my life and I would like to do something about it. I would like to be a man, and in a way I would like to be talked out of it, but I don't think I can be. I am out of place in my sex. If I was a male, I would be neuter in some sense....I have had intercourse with a man and it was mildly pleasant but a bit uncomfortable. My erotic thoughts are about men, but not involving intercourse. In these fantasies I usually have a male body. I don't generally get aroused by females, but I did once (FM 121).

This subject's account takes a weak and intermediate place between gender dysphoria *per se*, and those cross-gendered identified females whose sexual 'penchant' is for males and would like to be erotically part of an all male partnership, *i.e.* transsexual transhomosexuals.

Lack of sexual desire

As with males, a few females seem to have little or no sexual desire, as a component to their transsexualism. The following subject presented late in life, after retiring from public service:

I lived my life as a female as I thought I had no alternative. I was unable to cross-dress fully until 18 months ago when I was 56. I would very much like to be able to use a male urinal. My breasts are not a problem because they are flat, and my uterus doesn't matter as I am post-menopausal. I'm not aggressive and I don't want a sexual relationship with a female. I am not keen to be kissed. I would like to hold hands with someone (female) though. My need for phalloplasty is to overcome the constant reminder that something is missing (FM-PR 114).

Male transhomosexuals

The chief feature which emerges from examining transhomosexuals' accounts is the extraordinary plasticity of fantasy and behaviour, and in the case of such people who are usually actively experimental in their sex lives, these fantastical acts have a very variable relationship with gender identity. Many of their accounts overlap those given by transsexuals, and the range of underlying motivations is somewhat clarified. The following subject exhibits a number of important possibilities. Firstly two sex roles are claimed to co-exist and to a degree are divided from each other. High levels of sexual arousal seem to enact the male role, whilst at lower levels of sexual arousal, sex roles, experience and genderised fantasies become all mixed up:

> When I am highly sexually aroused I will escape entirely from my fantasies of the female role. After ejaculation everything goes back to normal and the two roles co-exist ....Everything the 'he part' wants to do is different to the 'she part'. If 'he' does the washing up, this challenges the 'she part'....When I am less aroused and my current girlfriend comes on top of me I think of her penetrating me. Penis and vagina are indistinguishable sensually. That kindles a desire in me to acquire female organs and have a penetrating organ in me. I want to know how lesbians relate to females and also how female-to-male transsexuals do (M-THO 161).

In the next subject, we have a familiar theme of a man who has failed and is repelled by a strong earthy masculine image. The beautiful and cool women who 'go with' such men are remote and god-like, not the type he has real sexual relations with. This leads to fantasy of transposition in Dorothy Clare's nomenclature, in which the subject 'becomes' the female underneath. This didn't happen when a particular female came on strongly in a sexy female role, whilst the subject was a teenager. From then, the above identity trend from not being a certain type of man, to a transsexual identity, where problematical sexual activity is given less emphasis, winds a highly complicated path:

> With girls I used to feel rather sexless. I was not attractive that way, and I would feel that attractive women were *grande dames*. They were clever, cool and beautiful and my feelings were not really sexual....I am repelled by the muddy rugby

player male image. Apart from the sexual side, if I wanted to be a great man, it would be as a scientist. I did not want to be like the boys in school who showed off their penises which were bigger than mine, and who were all at the bottom of the class, messing about....I find the idea of straight male to female sex unreal because I am not attractive. I would need a body I don't have, and therefore there has to be some reconciliation. I rationalise stunning girls out, so my girlfriends are only average....When I am having sex I have fantasies of being female underneath. Sometimes we are two women, sometimes she is the man....Attractive women I see and desire not to possess but to be....Once when I was 13 or 14 I ejaculated quickly when a very sexy girl touched me. Her sexiness and coming on that way meant I didn't have to make an effort, and I didn't imagine myself as a woman doing the shopping or cooking at home, and this is connected with my not being interested in sex to start with, and not seeking genital contact....I cannot envisage being attracted to a male who will treat me as a woman (M-THO 168).

The following subject retains his assigned gender identity, but his problem/desire concerning style in sexual activity has moved him towards a stronger transhomosexual status. In this case, the mutuality of lesbianism is more important than which sex the sex partners are:

My basic gender identity is male and I don't desire to change it. There is a female side to me which comes out....I am attracted to young gay lesbians, and a few older heterosexual women. I fantasise making love in a gentle, passive way rather than all that grabbing....The focus is the clitoris and the fascination that holds for me. If I am in the male role there is not any mutuality and that is of the greatest importance. Such female mutuality is not exclusively focusing on a penis but rather includes other sensations of warmth, gentleness, total openness....There seems something demonic about A doing something to B sexually, and something angelic where there is mutuality (M-THO 169).

Female transhomosexuals

The rejection of heterosexual males

The pattern of female transhomosexuals' fantasies are less chaotic in a way than males. Many have achieved this 'status' after passing through heterosexual relationships, usually marriage and such women react against all that is worst in the heterosexual chauvinistic male:

> Heterosexual men turn me off. My marriage was awful and disastrous. I see nothing in those men but dirty underwear and having to cook meals. I feel I have been used as a receptacle and that is debasing to me....I prefer homosexual men as human beings and I have had some nice cuddling relationships with them. They are more likely to talk to you in bed than just have intercourse and fall asleep, and they talk about things heteros don't, such as books, music, art, life and how one feels inside (F-THO 163).

That subject may have been rather unfortunate in her heterosexual relationships, but desires and perceptions of self have their own dynamic and, in the following case, middle age occasions a number of changes:

> I find male homosexual love scenes in films very arousing whilst heterosexuals ones not at all. There is something brutal, without gentleness ....Homosexual men are the best friends I have. I fantasise about an intimate relationship and it need not be very sexual ....Only a homosexual would accept the fantasising of a middle aged lady. I am seeking an emotional union, with or without sex. I'm not male, but I've tried to imagine myself inside a gay man's skin....I enjoy anal intercourse, and whilst I have been passive I have had fantasies to be active....A straight male would see me as a poor sexual figure now I am old. I need a dependent submissive man with whom I can play the male role. I want the social identity as a gay man so I can be in their company. I don't like the term 'fag hag' as I see it as a connotation of

women who just like to pick up young guys willy nilly (F-THO 162).

A female heterosexual transsexual, or transsexual transhomosexual?

The following subject represents a very rare type indeed. A biological female, she has a male identity, and is oriented to men - that's unusual for a transsexual - and then only homosexual men. A university student, she was very articulate and her account reveals exquisitely the precariousness of meanings attributed to sexual feelings and acts. She is quoted at length:

> I feel I should have a male body, because everything else seems to be male. So much of personality has to do with gender. When I knew I was attracted to males, it made it difficult for me to be male myself. I thought it was impossible for me to be transsexual, because transsexuals were attracted to their own biological sex, and that was not me. I am attracted to effeminate homosexuals and I have had fantasies of having a partner or brother, almost incestuously close. They would be close and particularly loyal to each other....I like the sonnets of Michelangelo which have homosexual themes and I would feed my own cerebral homosexuality going to western and space films where it was all comradeship...I used to become ill if anyone tried to touch my breasts. I dislike being touched up as a woman. Generally my males are passive in every way and I get excitement doing things to them, including using a prosthesis for intercourse. I used to resist being used myself for anal intercourse because that was too close to heterosexual sex for my liking. Then I was pressurised to try it with one man, and to my surprise I felt more intensely masculine - homosexual wise - than I had before! Now I am not bothered by fingers in my vagina. I only used to have a fear of being undermined *e.g.* I couldn't stand to have people behind me when I was in the middle of the room (F-THO 157).

This is really a very special and rare account illustrating

well the place of idealised male relationships in the transhomosexual schema, and the need to control so common in female to male transsexualism. Under particular circumstances however, which mediate the symbolic meanings of being attracted to men, and through discovering the feelings of anal intercourse, this subject is able to sustain a cross gender identity when two key elements of sexual life are entirely contrary to the typical female transsexual case. Similarly, male transhomosexuals seem to be able to sustain a more plastic schema in regard to who is doing what to whom, than typical male transsexuals, and consequently do not end up as clinic patients and escape psychiatric classification.

Dissociative Aspects of Sexual Experience

Male to female transsexuals

In earlier sections, transsexuals' propensity for dissociative experience in general, and the role of fantasy in sexual behaviour and gender identity, have been reviewed. Unsurprisingly, a fair minority of subjects experience dissociative levels of experience in respect to their sexual imaginings. The following subject illustrates what might be classified as intensive fantasy:

> If I lie on my back the identity of my female partner would cease. My fantasy of a consciousness of a penis inside me begins to develop. It becomes more realistic and the day dream develops into my being made pregnant, by the ejaculate and semen inside. This has all the connotations of a climax. This is not just an elaboration of an ejaculation (MF-PR 131).

This next subject would seem to be the object of high level suggestive 'placebo' effects, wishful thinking and selective recall, perhaps to a level which psychiatrists often call 'hysterical':

> Since attending the clinic and getting hormones, within three days there has been a marked increase in my breast size and

there has been morning sickness and a heavy feeling like runs. I have had pain around the midriff and my GP said that the slightly darkened perineum was not unusual, and likened it to a pregnant woman....I feel sore there as though there was a cut or something. When my children were born something moved inside me and strongly convinced me that it would be possible for that to happen to me. I believe I am capable of biologically carrying a child, it may need open surgery to correct the female organs (MF 106).

Orgasms

Male to female transsexuals

Male orgasmic dysfunction

Male penile ejaculatory orgasms normally lead to a highly satisfying and pleasing resolution phase. For many of those male transsexuals who engage in sexual behaviour to this point of climax, this post-orgasmic reaction is highly noxious. This may be reported as a simple physical feeling:

I feel pain in my sexual organs when I masturbate or make love. This pain is normally something which follows ejaculation (MF 67).

More usually there is a strong emotional feeling attached to a variety of unpleasant physical sensations:

Later in marriage I liked the excitement of regular sexual intercourse, but I felt very bad about the feeling following the climax. What I felt in my penis was alright first, but I had a general feeling of depression afterwards. I think this may have been associated with my ideas of sex being a drain on my physical resources. This feeling crept all over my body and was something akin to a panic or rawness or an irritability or a gnawing or loss of control. This feeling would start in my stomach and creep up inside me and around the back of my chest (MF 40).

Others would be disturbed by the sudden change in sexual 'tension' which could have an acute re-engagement effect on their cross-gender feelings:

> After ejaculation I hope to God that never happens again. When I come, I suddenly change from being very masculine and worked up in a sexual state, to feeling this is all a 'put on' and then I think of a sex change and want to talk in a high pitched voice, put my hair nice and so on (MF 31).

Others have mixed feelings:

> When I have an ejaculation I have mixed feelings, that is to say some enjoyment because of tension relief and some negative feelings which are hard to describe (MF 43).

It is only very recently indeed in the West that the issue of non-ejaculatory 'orgasmic' experiences for males has been addressed. In the East, prolongation and intensification of the pre-ejaculatory phase has long been regarded as highly beneficial. The benefits include heightened pleasure for the man and the woman, and a control over the ejaculatory climax for long believed to be an energy drain for men. The following subject's experience could have been understood in those terms but he classified them as 'like a woman':

> I can have orgasms just like a woman without ejaculations, I can come up and down half a dozen times, and this is the case if I am in bed with a man or a woman....I cannot say I didn't enjoy ejaculations, but I didn't really want them (MF 12).

Cross genderisation of orgasmic experience

Highly intensive and pleasurable 'female' orgasms are reported by quite a number of male transsexuals. The following account is from a post-reassignment individual:

> I have this kind of orgasm. A power comes over me and it lasts from three to five minutes, up to half an hour and it goes right up into my breasts, it is fantastic. It is a kind of all over feeling of arousal (MF-PR 11).

However it is not necessary to have an artificial vagina to experience this. Strong 'imaginative involvement' can take someone a long way. The following male had not yet had any reassignment surgery:

> If I touch myself where the vagina and clitoris ought to be, I get a prolonged experience of orgasm. This goes on until it aches. Years ago I had a medical examination of my rectum. Fingers were inserted and I had an enormous sense of orgasm, but it was short lived....when I touch myself now I am enveloped emotionally. It is difficult to distinguish emotions from sensations (MF 26).

Some of the actions and experiences accounted for by this subject may be partly due to stimulation of anatomic structures in the genital region, *e.g.* prostrate gland. Again it is worth remembering that a few transsexuals are quite accepting of male orgasm and do not see the mutilation of reassignment surgery as right for them. They may have genderised their personality style, and that may be dissociated from genital sexual pleasure *per se*. The following Malay-Chinese subject illustrates this:

> I want to keep my genitals to have orgasms. I want them for myself, and I see reassignment surgery as just creating an open wound which would be difficult to dilate....My inner self talks and expresses itself as a female. As a male my whole body language indicates I am hiding something, my desires to have nice decorated styles of antiques and pictures at home. Female personalities are interested in these things, and architecture and history and freedom for emotional expression (MF 149).

Female to male transsexuals

Most female transsexuals enjoy sexual arousal. It seems fair to say that, in a majority of cases, the style of love-making and the satisfaction of their partner is more important than a 'climax' to them. Anxieties associated with genital touching may interfere with the achievement of full orgasmic experience, though many subjects do masturbate to a point of satisfaction. 'Imaginative involvement', as with males, can carry an individual a long way. The following subject is a typical example. In general though, the intensity and specificity cited is not as widespread among other female transsexuals, as is the case for males:

> We are both orgasmic and we achieve this with our hands ....At times I have been so lustful in my emotions that I have felt I have had a penis and have gone on to carry out what a man would do, although I have got nothing there. Sometimes, I feel I have. I have the feeling of an approaching ejaculation and I have had actually the feeling of ejaculation, though not frequently....Eventually I feel exhausted, sweated, satisfied, and I don't feel like going on. When this happens, this is how I imagine ejaculation is. It is like something in your stomach, and I am hitting something with a hammer, it is like a big bell....Something comes away from me then. It is a kind of white watery substance, whiter than would normally be noticed (FM-PR 197).

Male transhomosexuals

One male transhomosexual in the submissive/masochistic category reported an orgasmic dysfunction with some features in common with male transsexuals. This subject, a highly respected professional, would escape from his cold, mechanical, efficient male-self by dressing as a servile girl and carrying out obsequious and intense acts of service and affection preferably for a strict domatrix, but otherwise for his wife. When and if this led to sexual activity and he achieved orgasm, this heralded a sudden loss of his en-roled arousal and it was experienced as highly unpleasant. The preorgasmic period of scripted ritual and service could be extended over hours and even days. Since orgasm did not serve a consumptive function of sexual arousal, this man felt compulsively driven to an unquenchable furthering of his desires through more specified role play. Real dangers and unhappiness can attend this compulsion:

> In cunnilingus I reach the heights of erotic delight. The desire to give pleasure without getting any back is the need to satisfy the female in me. The male has to be deprived, and I surrender even my right to masturbate to the woman. To ejaculate is to fail. The effect is dramatic. My body feels cold and my mind is deprived of its driving force...Ejaculation is the ultimate disappointment, it means an end to all pleasure, rituals and foreplay (M-THO 166).

Sexual Problems

Male to female transsexuals

Impotence

Over half of male to female transsexuals report some form of impotence or sexual inadequacy in sexual relations. These are obviously those who have tried to function as a male. This is not an unexpected finding, and to some extent it is difficult to unconfound cause and effect between sexual 'inadequacy' and gender dysphoria. However, for some individuals, it would seem that an early experience of sexual failure as a man was part of a genuine developmental history of transgender identity:

> In my teenage years, I tried very hard to make it with girls and I went out with one girl called Elizabeth. I had some spontaneous erections and one weekend I did manage to do it with her almost by accident. Then I felt depressed in every way because this was not stars and whizz bang....I started to get depressed and felt people were staring at me (MF 96).

> When I was 13, I used to masturbate OK. My sexual relationships with girls were OK too, but after a couple of months I would have difficulties. I was always self conscious of my small penis...One girl was nymphomaniac and she

really made me feel inadequate. So did a prostitute I went to abroad (MF 40).

For some males this problem has dogged them over a long period:

In both my marriages I had problems of sexual potency. After a few months of my second marriage, we couldn't have proper intercourse. If we couldn't do the proper thing we didn't want to do anything else. I would have done anything to save this marriage (MF 94).

Perhaps this man's fantasies would have been different if his attitude to not doing anything other than the 'proper thing' had been modified in sex therapy. For yet others a problem may occur at a certain time and for some it seems to have been at least contributory towards the transgender drift:

Although I have wanted to express the female side all my life, this became pronounced when at 30 I became impotent. There was a suggestion I had ovaries and was part and part female. Thereafter my (cross-gender) tension increased over the years in a fairly steady manner (MF 77).

Hypersexuality

This condition was found in only a few males, but it is a most distressing condition and not of course to be equated with super virility or potency. It is little wonder that these experiences contributed towards a growing antagonism towards genital maleness:

I have kept a graphical record of my erections, and half the time they are there and there is nothing I could do about it. Usually ejaculation is retarded or impossible. This increases the revulsion I feel towards my sex organs. I feel this especially when I sense the root of the penis, extremely large between the legs and uncomfortable....There is nothing about erections which is pleasurable....I get them especially when I am prone, lying down, and my (cross) gender desires are understood...Some nights in blind desperation I pace the

151

house. One night my wife found me in the kitchen with a knife, I was intending to cut it off...Age has not weakened the trouble (MF 147).

I used to have to get it (ejaculation) over every night or else I couldn't sleep. This brought about feelings of hatred because I had to do it....The whole thing was like going to the toilet and I had to work hard. Sometimes I got backache or hurt my penis where I rubbed the foreskin (MF 120)

Progressive Transgender Identity Developments

Male to female transsexuals

Throughout varying periods of life, male to female transsexuals struggle with feelings of being 'wrong', and a variety of attempts to 'make it' as a normal human being. The transgenderisation of experience and identity can develop slowly or take a sudden leap forward, depending on the circumstances. There are a great variety of circumstances too in which progress or retardation of transgender identity development can occur. Often, an individual will have experienced more than one set of crucial turning points until a 'final' adoption of the transgender identity results. This is more usual of course for individuals who finally present for sex reassignment later in life. Bearing in mind this fact, the following verbatim accounts illustrate the various possible turning points which arise most frequently:

Surrender of attempts to meet expectations to function as a member of the male sex role

For some individuals, a clear desire not to be required to act as a male emerges quite early *e.g.* in teenage years and it precedes a full transsexual identity. The following young man, doesn't 'deserve' to be treated as a male:

My father tells me women are never successful in business. I am not successful in anything....It's hard to say why I want to be treated as a female, maybe it's just because I don't want to be treated as a male and no-one believes me ....Women have a very strong respect for men and it is quite wrong for me to receive this....I should be serving others, not being a dominating figure who can be played on....I once thought of being a priest and going into a monastery (MF 83).

A priest of course is an alternate form of 'non-sexual' male. For other males the surrender comes later:

I was extremely fond of my family and I married to have a sense of belonging....I tried to meet expectations in the role of a male parent but they all got on top of me. My transvestite desires came back, but I would have traded these in had I been a proper family father (MF 12).

The surrender gives a new meaning to past experience, *e.g.* what this subject calls 'insight':

I have been unhappy trying to be a man and living up to my sex. Before my period of insight, I had feelings of strain but my malehood was there and had to be accepted. I couldn't relate to people....A year ago, this realisation that I need to be a woman came to me in a rush of emotions, and now I know where my emotions come from (MF 63).

For some individuals, a good surrender becomes a transformation of a message of male deficiency:

I married my wife to prove I was not gay. It turns out I am not the real father of our twin daughters. My wife has been out with 30 to 40 other men. Two years ago, I decided to change my life, and my style and my body (MF 100).

Occasionally this 'surrender' may be the result of a traumatic event, but there will be some predisposing history. The following man had a mild history of teenage cross-dressing, but not of nervous timidity or gross effeminacy. Married, with grown up sons, his family life had been dogged by various illness. Then:

I was fine until 1973 when I had a motor accident when my brakes failed. I hit a brick wall and was very shaken up. I lost a lot of weight - all muscle and I couldn't do anything. I felt awful and then I got pains in my breast, and hairs fell out from my private region. Since that time, although my feminine feelings have fluctuated I have never gone back to being masculine. I have felt a non-entity at times...I read a book about these people in South Africa who spontaneously changed sex. I began to cross dress again and asked myself what was the point of not co-operating when I couldn't maintain my masculine image anymore (MF 183).

The resolution of conflict and confusion

The experience of conflict and confusion in an individual's sense of self can be extremely distressing and damaging to their conduct of social relationships, and the satisfactions normally found therein. For many male transsexuals the discovery of the transsexual status offers a heroic challenge, an extraordinary hope, an achievable goal and a 'resolution' of intractable and incompatible desires and demands. A number of individuals report coexisting male and female (labelled) feelings and the way these are managed to a point where the transgender sense is granted priority or legitimacy is usually complex. The following verbatim excerpts are more lengthy than usual to illustrate this:

At the age of 17 I considered myself to be male and female contained in one body by the cross-dressing. If I masturbated whilst (cross) dressed I would think I was raping the woman within....I chased girls then and enjoyed intercourse. I saw myself 'in-between' and did not like to look at myself in the mirror. When highly aroused I was very masculine, but then with one girl I could only get an orgasm by fantasising myself as the female....I thought I was an odd transvestite, and I knew that in the eyes of transvestites, transsexuals are only transvestites with big ideas. Then in April 1981, I had a dream like experience, and the instant the sun came up behind the clouds I knew I was a woman, and my whole body was wrong and my whole life was a stream before my eyes, including things I had forgotten from four years old. My life now made sense I was a woman with problems rather than that odd TV (MF 117).

In my early twenties, I was on the gay scene - fine I was young. Eventually these relationships were unsatisfactory and I knew I had to subdue my baby-boyish ways and be left with my best side, *i.e.* an adult female...My female side is serene, cultured and dignified, mature. My male side is indiscriminatively sexy, and like my father and brother who are horribly vulgar and randy...I found my attempts to be more male revolting...When I was quite young I went to a hair salon and had my hair done by a 'change' (a transsexual). We all met up afterwards and experimented with make up and going to drag balls and so on...I need love and loyalty, and over the past few months I have felt my mind pulled around so much with uncertainty and depressing bewilderment. In the last few weeks I decided to make my mind up. Once made, my life has been revolving around it and I don't have any reservations anymore. It is such a relief to have decided (MF 31).

Another form of staged resolution is through androgyny, especially where genital pleasure has not yet become completely dysphoric:

Around 1972 I used to cross-dress once or twice a month just for a bit of fun...Women often saw me as a sexual threat wanting to go to bed with them just because I was a man. I am desperate to relate to women as persons. They are not arrogant and pompous and dominating. I was involved in feminism for some time. Lasting relationships are unusual unless there is something sexual...My cross-gender feelings increased around 1979 after I became impotent with several females in bed. I saw it as a sexual problem then ...Later I joined the Gay Liberation Movement, but I couldn't achieve any deep relationships. I wanted to define myself and what it amounted to was a desire not to be what I was...The need to become a woman became stronger and I changed from being uncertain to knowing that what I feel is torment as a man. I do want a sex change operation (MF 109).

Another subject, mildly mentally handicapped with a vast array of problems in life claimed;

I will feel happier because I will have achieved something in my life (MF 187).

For some individuals, the transsexual option offers the potential to simply break the amount of tension which is experienced, even though other thoughts may not be congruent:

I want to be cured of this obsession or converted. I must become an unremarkable person one way or another. My transsexualism is a vast energy, threatening to overflow the dam, which is my intellect. Before now I thought I could marry someone and use all my insights into feminine feelings as sympathy for the female and I could have been then a good husband, a normal male (MF-PR 131).

Following the previous subject's stated desire to be 'unremarkable', it is clear that for many male transsexuals the desire to be conventional, accepted and so on becomes overriding at some point:

I have reservations about (reassignment) surgery because I don't know how I'll feel afterwards, sexually. I want it because I need to be settled and conventional and not a freak of nature. My present partner penetrates me anally. It is painful and it is not right (MF 48).

A major class of 'turning points' or resolutions of problems are the discoveries of the existence of transsexualism as a medically recognised phenomenon with sex reassignment as the gateway to deliverance from despair. Such discoveries may be through books, television or other people. The impact of these discoveries goes beyond a simple recognition of what it is a person may be suffering from, it can crystallise the transgender identity, then petrify it so that the clinical criteria and the personal characteristics of the candidate meet.

The idea of a sex change occurred when I was a teenager and discovered this had been carried out. Before that I hadn't considered the matter as I didn't think it was possible. I had felt different but then I thought everyone felt different from anyone else (MF 22).

It was only when I was 25 years of age after my own marriage that I heard about the cross gender clinic and then thought about the possibility of sex reassignment. Up till then, I thought I was living the best I could have (MF 122).

I had had transsexual reveries in my teenage years. Once I read about the Christine Jorgensen story, I was on fire for months afterwards. I tore libraries apart trying to find materials on this (MF 135).

The impact of psychiatric assessment can contribute to transgender commitment:

I was given a lot of encouragement and help during an intensive in-patient assessment at Guy's Hospital. Although I'd had second thoughts I changed over full time after that. Everyone had accepted me in the hospital. I couldn't turn back (MF 14).

A crisis of another sort can act synergistically with gender dysphoria to precipitate progress in transgender commitment. The following professional man, with a 20 year marriage and intermittent history of cross dressing presented following his being removed from a pet project of his.

Over the past year my obsession has grown. I asked myself where life was going and it was like a flash of light, searching for a new direction in my life and career. This was triggered by a crisis at work when my special project was taken away from me. It wasn't the sack, but it was like it and I haven't got over the emotional shock yet. That rejection made me realise I had been shy for years and that whenever I got anxious, really that was a need for an outlet of feminine feelings...Perhaps because of the uncertainties about sex in my marriage, I turned inwardly to find the woman I sought, within. Even if this is not quite right, I suspect it is somewhere near it. The shock of rejection five years ago now turned me finally towards transsexualism (MF 111).

Again just to emphasise how limited information can affect a vulnerable mind, consider the following man of limited intelligence, voicing his anxiety about the operation:

I am concerned I might not find it all that sexually satisfying if I do have the operation. Last June was the first time I cross-dressed as a female. I wondered if I was transsexual because people I know, they know this other person who has been recognised as similar to me, and she is transsexual (MF 24).

Failure of alternative modes of gender functioning

A significant number of transsexuals have made serious attempts to live a viable gender role other than that of a transsexual. Over a period of time these fail, and this is seen to make sense retrospectively, (*i.e.* the subject sees himself as having been a transsexual all along, but it was not recognised until these 'failures' occurred, or even later). Notwithstanding this perspective, it is possible to discover some other types of reasons in mind from the time of the failing gender role enterprise. The following individual who has classified himself as an effeminate homosexual at one time tells how social changes on the 'scene' affected him:

In the 1960s, there were camp boys and ordinary men on the gay scene. Now all this has changed and feminine gay guys have polarised either to be more feminine or to become more masculine. One of the reasons I have changed over was I was a feminine boy and there was no future in this. Gay guys wanted me more masculine and then I realised I should go the whole way to being female (MF-PR 37).

Although transvestite histories usually move more gradually towards deepening transgender expressions, progressive shifts or developments can happen suddenly especially if a trigger, such as an important life loss, or a discovery of other people's transsexualism occurs. Both these were present for the following subject after 20 years of periodic transvestism:

I would be accepted as a woman when I was cross-dressed, and I was delighted to be taken out by men and wined and dined. I wouldn't want to go to bed with them. I knew then that only dates were practical. This is beginning to change lately. I have had good times in male clothes but I feel it is unnatural to be attractive to both men and women...I have to come to understand that homosexuality is not so bad. All of a sudden I met transsexuals and surgery could be there! (MF 175).

For other subjects, a set of progressive stages may be necessary through a number of role experiments:

I was discharged from the army and thought to be naive and immature. I didn't feel attractive to the opposite sex, but I wanted to be so then...At age 27 or 28 I had no transsexual feelings but I was aware something was not right. I had had various sexual problems in my marriage and I didn't feel I looked right...When I cross-dressed it was to escape from the world like into an insect chrysalis from which I might emerge transformed. I used to go away (from home) and do this in the dark. It wasn't enough... Only after the age of 35 did I give my imagination full rein to indulge in dreams of being of the opposite sex (MF 40).

The following individual illustrates a complex set of progressive periods towards full transsexual commitment in his thirties. A whole variety of experiences have moved him through a gender career pathway to sex reassignment:

> I suffered paraplegia at age 10, and was only able to have minor sexual sensations...I wanted to be with girls but they tended to be protective of me, I enjoyed kissing though...I struggled to overcome my 'role' as a paraplegic cripple and I didn't want to be seen as someone who couldn't do what other men could do...I got to University and got married to a girl who was very supportive of me. Later I went to an American university and used a lot of drugs and my appreciation of the sensual world expanded. Under the influence of dope and LSD I identified unconstructive and depressive patterns in myself. I became softer, less pushy and less mathematical! My wife went off, but anyway I found a woman who allowed me to express my passive, non masterful feelings...This woman also had another girl lover and I began to imagine being like her. My soft clothes reinforced my desire to be enfolded passively and gave me a freedom to express what I had not been able to express before. As this woman became more dominant, so I increased my feminine role and realised that I should have been born that way...Now I think that way, can I ever imagine liking being sexually kissed by a man ...I have now seen a fanciable male (MF-PR 66).

Finally a 'commitment' itself can fulfill its own promise. Returning to the subject before last, this individual took up practice as a hypnotherapist and tried to cure a transvestite of feminine feelings. He did this by use of a taped set of suggestions that his subject was more masterful and masculine than he realised. Our subject 'knew' that his transsexual feelings were real whilst his transvestite subject's were not. However he found his own commitment wavering. This is how he dealt with that:

> After I used the tape on F. I found my own transsexual feelings unwinding. I had to make another tape for myself, to re-wind my feminine identity....I was aware that I had built up a new identity, left my family and found a whole new social

and work life. There were these environmental pressures not to give it up after I had made the 'change' with my friends, my bank and my hypnotherapy institute   (MF 40)

Gradual transgender personality developments

A significant number of male transsexuals simply report their transgender desires getting stronger over the years. The most usual gradualist transition occurs in the habitual transvestite:

I have cross-dressed for many years and my girlfriend has been very supportive and helped me buy things. Then I had a shock. This wasn't just transvestism, it was going beyond. It was a gradual awareness from March last year, and it wasn't just that my cross dressing had been increasing, it was a mental change rather than a practical one (MF 84).

However, for some individuals, transvestism is an outcome of mental changes:

I was never a transvestite, I never cross-dressed. I knew I was more than a homosexual, but since I wanted men, it was convenient to be 'homosexual'. I would not give up my Andrea-ness though. Over time, through living my homosexual lifestyle, and getting counselled, I increasingly wanted to become a woman. I began cross-dressing and in the New Year I went out of doors as 'Andrea' (MF 33).

Sometimes a particular dimension of personality deepens and is transgenderised. The following quote is from a Chinese subject:

In my teenage years, I liked to be treated gently and I began to feel feminine at that time. I felt different but not a female as such. I enjoyed early homosexual experiences. The difference I felt increasingly was my being passive and quiet. I therefore began to think of myself as a female over some four or five years (MF 138).

A psychological limitation in these subjects is often that the female 'side' cannot easily co-exist with or form a synthesis with masculine propensities:

> I fought against these (transgender) inclinations for they would completely undermine my image of my masculine role. It didn't prove possible for that part of my feminine side to develop unless the masculine side deteriorated at the same time. There couldn't be a proportionate share (MF 90).

Few individuals foresee yet further imaginative developments:

> I expect to have a sex life after surgery presumably with a bloke. At this moment that leap of the imagination is yet to be accomplished (MF 84).

Gradual success feeds progress:

> I think the more successful you are in this cross gender business the more the desire seems to go on, whereas if you experience a lack of success - like when children chase you and jeer - well that tended to slow my progress. The desire grows to fill a space where restrictions are overcome (MF 150)

Transgenderisation of the longing for love

Many transsexuals claim that what they are looking for even in physical relations is 'love' rather than 'sex'. The following individual links this with his having been deprived of affection by his father, in favour of his sister:

> I wanted the affection my father was giving to my sister. By the time I was ten it was virtually non-existent because he wanted a proper little boy...I thought in school, life would be miserable if I couldn't be like a little girl. I was jealous of my sister who grew better looking from puberty onwards, whilst I got uglier and uglier. I still feel hurt that my father would not kiss me goodnight and my desire to be a girl increased when my good friend Jack turned to girls (MF 96).

The following is a typical romantic version of physical love:

My feelings come in waves at the moment. It is all a feeling of wanting to yield and have her make love to me. My fantasy role is elaborated into being loved, cherished, protected, being made pregnant and women's clothes (MF 126).

A untypical dimension is occasionally found:

I wanted this very close emotional relationship with Mark, but not sexual...I was part of an Anglo-Catholic group and I had an image of male perfection in a Christ-like figure. If I had stayed a man, then I would have perhaps been a priest, mystical and gentle. The Catholic theology holds that physical attributes are not necessarily the essential nature of a body or bodily love. That allowed me to fulfill my real nature through sex reassignment, although I started with the outward body of a male - and could only then have been a male lover (MF-PR 97).

Transgender feelings and despair

There are a few gender dysphoric males whose initial presentation is highly depressive. They are, however, sometimes considered psychopathic because of the chronic and desperate flavour of their words. Extremely hostile and manipulative, they become very unpopular with everyone. The demand for sex reassignment seems but one step in the progress towards personality deterioration as much as true transgender experience:

The stakes have always been against me. I have had so many dead end jobs. What's the bloody point in acting normally? I'll never own a home. I'll never get married, I've felt like committing suicide. When I got to 30, I thought I'd have another push for transsexualism. Friends just dropped away from me, but I'm not an idiot about the operation. It would have been an opportunity for a new person, a real me to come out. I've linked all this to a hangover from past lives I have discovered through regression hypnosis (MF 143).

The following man had the experience of a girlfriend leaving him after procuring an abortion. As a result;

> I was very angry and hated women. They leave you in the
> lurch, so I went back to my cross-dressing ways. I went
> drinking and abused females...I began to hate my genitals,
> they should drop off or else might breed something bad, evil
> and monstrous. It would be a bitter twisted ugly thing like
> me...If I'd been a woman, I would have been respected, as a
> nurse. I've got an obsessional respect for nurses (MF 128).

Expected gains from sex reassignment

Transsexuals go to considerable trouble to achieve sex reassignment surgery. The compulsiveness and desperation they
present plays no small part in persuading doctors to grant
them their desire when no other medical indication exists for
such surgery. It would be expected then that the expected
gains would play a part in transgender motivation and experience. It has already been shown that the availability of the
transsexual diagnosis and reassignment programmes often
crystalises the final transsexual status presented by a gender
dysphoric individual. Having travelled so far down the
transgender career road, it is a surprise to find that the value
of the gain to life of reassignment surgery is often quite small
and almost superficial. It may be that it is better to travel
hopefully than to arrive, and the function of the 'arrival' is to
provide the justification and direction of travel. Of course it
should be borne in mind that comments made to a familiar
and trusted researcher may be different from those given at a
psychiatric interview which is judging individuals' eligibility
for surgery. The following quotes are not untypical concerning
the advantages surgery *per se* will endow:

> When I have the operation I won't be as shy as I am, as I will
> have more confidence in the female role. It is shyness which
> prevents me from making friends easily. The major gain I see
> from surgery is the private satisfaction of not thinking about
> it all the time, and not having to stand to go to the toilet...It
> wouldn't be a disaster if I didn't have the operation, I am more

concerned about losing the breaks in my future career (MF 101).

After the operation I shall be more relaxed about being involved with men....They treat me differently now, they used to laugh at my effeminacy (MF 144).

The sexual possibilities do have new meanings of course:

Post-reassignment relations will define a oneness with my partner. Homosexual love play has been not so much distasteful as pointless (MF-PR 65).

Once on the road of the sex reassignment programme, not a few individuals admit feelings like the following:

If I don't get surgery it will be just one of those things. If I had a traffic accident and my female clothes revealed male organs underneath, that would be embarrassing. If I were treated completely as a female *e.g.* by the pension office, I would consider living without the operation...I have such a small penis, it wouldn't make a lot of difference (MF 46).

It makes a difference to the pension office however, and many public/legal institutions require sex reassignment as a medical 'imprimatur' of the transsexual's seriousness of desire. This then feeds the original motivation. For some other subjects too, making a final application for sex reassignment means they have identified their ultimate goal.

I do not know what I require to live my life fully, because the picture is not complete...I don't want to be a sexual cabbage...I see the gain in reassignment as meaning I will have adopted the life style to fit my inclinations of an ultimate goal. However at present I am not sure what is in me...Of course I would like a vagina to please my boyfriend, but I know many transsexuals who dropped out of the reassignment clinic once they found acceptable and accepting partners (MF 150).

None of the above should gainsay the transsexual predictable affirmation that reassignment surgery is very very important, and they would be distressed to be denied it. The benefits and value are as much in what it means however as the practical benefits it provides.

Clinical intervention

In several cases clinical intervention itself had the unintended effect of contributing to the progress of a transgender identity development. This usually arises when clinics or treatments are set up 'for' conditions X,Y,Z, but the meaning to the patient includes something more:

> Seen at age 16, because of compulsive masturbatory behaviour. Put on Androcur and referred for aversion therapy to overcome masturbatory stigma and castration wish. Discharged himself from hospital stating that treatment was successful and had had the opposite effect of that intended, in that he felt more feminine (medical notes on MF 120)

> I had read about sex changes, but I tried to live as a fellow doing hard physical jobs. I was a failure. I hadn't thought of losing my penis until I came to the clinic and realised it was not just for gay people...After the operation, initially I looked pretty awful, and had the feeling my penis should be there, as I had always had it and hadn't thought of losing it, until I came to the clinic (MF-PR 112).

Atypical childhoods and late transgender identity developments

There are a small number of males who present late in life and who have had atypical childhoods and adolescences in that the many features usually found are not present to any marked degree. Indeed such persons do not appear obvious transsexuals in young adulthood, though there may be other problems. These 'late developers' are difficult to examine retrospectively because the preceding life span may stretch over half a century or more. What are found are certain propensities for dissociative type experience coupled with either a schizoid sense of not being right, or an intense emotional reaction to a loss *e.g.* bereavement. The following man presented in his sixties. A professional engineer he was abnormally bothered by the way his name could sound if said in a certain way - an auditory form of dysmorphophobia perhaps. The death of his wife precipitated several psychological reactions:

> I have always hated my name, which could be shortened - and then mispronounced to sound like 'cheat'. I have a lot in common with my wife, and now she is dead, I am developing like her in appearance. I have this strong feeling she is always in my presence. I still talk to her, there is a terrific bond. I use her clothes - we were the same size. Then I feel I am much closer to her...I don't mix us up, but I could become her for there is something fulfilling in her that I prefer (MF 77).

The following two individuals experienced sudden transgender feelings without any obvious early history to understand it. However, even the short quotes convey a sense of psychological abnormality in personality or emotional makeup. Both these individuals discovered the low probability of being granted reassignment and dropped out of the clinic and research programme before a full assessment could be arranged:

> My desire for sex change was at least three years ago when I was 52. I want a pseudo-vagina as I don't want any other kind of involvement. I have religious reservations in that I am old fashioned and I believe intercourse should occur in marriage and with emotional involvement....I have never fallen in love, and I have never been to bed with anyone and have never wanted to (MF 41).

> When I was 65, I experienced various changes such as breasts beginning to grow and my penis seemingly going back into my stomach. I felt different even when I masturbated - like a skin over my penis. I never had such feelings until then. It was a nice feeling and it led me to thoughts about men for the first time (MF 49).

Female to male transsexuals

The failure of socialisation to prepare for functioning as a member of the female sex

Unlike male-to-female transsexuals who often struggle with a spoiled identity and become very distressed following the awareness that their masculine 'failure' creates, female transsexuals tend to find that new standards of their (female) personal worth are erected at or around adolescence. Their characteristic reaction is one of rejection of these new expectations. Pre-adolescent socialisation has not prepared them for this transition, and the pressures of puberty instead of easing the transition into young womanhood, become a psychic battleground. This sense of rejection can be recovered from some transsexuals' accounts as a preceding stage to full cross-gender commitment:

> I was an...adventurous little girl...Me and my brother were the same you see and did everything little boys did ...Then they separated boys and girls in the playground and I felt alone. I felt left out when the boys were showing their penises to each other - I had nothing to show. I used to masturbate in a very strong way to make something. This all led to me wanting a penis and a male identity (FM-PR 194).

Heterosexuality is part of the socialisation of young females and that may create a sense of rejection when a female discovers her own orientation:

> When I was ten I read stories about adolescent boys and I really identified with them and their activities...Then later I read a book *The Well of Loneliness* (a book about lesbians) and I was surprised how I identified with that character. At that time, I didn't feel all that much different from other girls. However as they got into dating, boys, cosmetics and all that, I found I couldn't move into the adult identity. I felt I was in limbo. I had thought I would make it in my original (gender) role. However, all the expectations on me made me feel tied

down. The male is dominant. Others want to clutch you and possess you and I felt this was a return to the control my father had over me when I was a child (FM 121).

Unlike the first subject, and indeed most female transsexuals, this individual had had long battles with a restrictive father to be permitted the freedom to follow her 'adventurous' inclinations. Although she had not been able to actually do so as much as she wanted, her desires, and book-reading and the battles had all sharpened her sense of needing to be unfettered, free, dominant, 'boy-like'.

The failure of alternate modes of gender functioning

The most usual alternate gender option that female transsexuals may pass through (remembering again that unlike males, very few admit such serious alternate 'experiments') is that of a lesbian, *a female* (if somewhat masculine) homosexual. This may not work out because of problems on the 'gay scene':

In 1977, I lived in London and mixed in the gay world...I was attracted to a female-female partnership then, rather than me being male...Later I found the gay female scene not pleasant. Women were treated as cattle, and were very bitchy, so I decided to continue as 'Mike' and get out of the sappho-scene. Now I have a straight girlfriend, and a future (FM-PR 86).

Sometimes it is a specific relationship which doesn't work out. In the following case, our subject sees the remedy as becoming a male, but provides a rare admission that this is something to be learned, not all already there, 'trapped in a female body':

I tried living with a woman, Theresa, once. It didn't work out. I need the support to know how to think like a man. I need to know how they think towards women, and the purpose and the stimulants that work, and how to make a woman happy, and this definitely requires me to be masculine (FM 21).

The full heterosexual female role is very rarely presented in the histories of presenting female transsexuals. Remembering that transsexuals report their orientations less in terms of what sex of body turns them on and off, and more in terms of who is doing what to whom, then we can understand this following subject's failure to be satisfied with her heterosexual relationship:

> I used to love a man, and had a four and a half year relationship. The first few years were terrific. I used to take the dominant part, and I even fantasised him as the female. This worked great for a while, then less so. I did enjoy penetration initially but my desires were never fully satisfied. Still he was loving and had a future. Then I found sleeping with other women much more enjoyable. Nicola now behaves completely as a woman in bed, and I am always on top, the active one. I could be more active if I had a penis though (FM 17).

Gradual transgender personality developments

In comparison with males, female transsexuals present earlier with strong transsexual commitments. In general their histories are less gradual, drawn out or elaborate. However, occasionally subjects have followed a longer path to the point of asking for sex reassignment. This subject, below, presented in her mid thirties:

> When I was in my teens I had crushes on girls. Then I had a relationship with an older teacher (female) and this was terrific. I felt easy in mind...I accepted my physical changes as part of growing up - I forgot about them really. As time went by I felt I wasn't doing enough during sexual activity. Then I didn't mind what was done to me...I wanted to be the aggressor and rough - not violent - and I haven't let other lesbian partners touch me so much...Over the years on the gay scene, my desire to change increased. People are very bitchy, and people have accepted sex changes over recent years more than female homosexuality. However I didn't want to be a freak...I have been with my present partner two years and

now I feel strong and confident and ready for reassignment (FM-PR 81).

Resolution of conflict

As is the case with males, a 'heroic' commitment to a transsexual identity can seem a way through distressing mixed or conflictful desires. There is usually a strong sense of social acceptability involved. For the following subject, alternate gender roles compatible with her desires were not a developmental option. Usually she had tried to be what her body said she was. Psychologically, it didn't work:

> I never dressed as a man before, because I never wanted a butch, lesbian, tom-boy image. I tried to be what my body says. To be a butch woman is not acceptable. I have to be one thing or the other, otherwise it doesn't seem right (FM-PR 173).

The desire to resolve the problem of 'deviancy', and become socially conventional or unremarkable, is a motivation shared with some male transsexuals:

> I see the future and the main gain from the operation as being that I can hold hands with my girlfriend in public. I'd like to lead an ordinary life as a couple - with me as the man. I hope to have a married life if the law will change, and buy a home and maybe own a printing firm (FM 23).

The escape from fears and foolishness often comes across in accounts from subjects with low intelligence. The following Chinese girl expresses this:

> I want to be able to face people and not have names called....touching yourself sexually is dirty, you should be married. A girl is very likely to get raped, but if you are a kung-fu male you can defend yourself and others (FM-PR 92).

Fearful feelings about rape, and jealousy at being endowed with a weak and vulnerable female body can lead to hostile demands for reassignment. The following female had a history of violence and initially refused any physical medical examination:

> G has had a history of feeling physically discredited from infancy when strangers would make errors about her gender. She was labelled as 'fatty' in preadolescent years, and was intensely jealous of the male physique following sexual maturity. She has felt particularly violated by being forcibly held down for medical examinations as a child. She sees such male examiners as the powerful and self-respecting kind of person she longs to be, so submission to them is particularly humiliating. The only time G presents as less than highly aggressive is when she feels completely flattered (psychological report on FM 153).

Some individuals have their desire crystalised as a result of unusual circumstances:

> I have lived with my girlfriend for five years, without knowing what I really wanted. I didn't want to live a lie, and I was tired of having decisions made for me...I went to various doctors who told me to go away and think about it a bit more. Then I heard that my own family doctor had the change. That really helped me decide, to be sure of it (FM-PR 4).

Male transhomosexuals

Transgender fantasy elaboration

In contrast to male transsexuals, male transhomosexuals' transgender desires and activities are far more restricted to the domain of recreational sex. Other aspects of their life are usually unremarkable. There is a tendency for them to be well educated and this may contribute to the creative and fanciful fantasy elaboration they are capable of. Free from the major implications of their created sexual gender identities, these forms of 'identity' appear to be highly fluid, free floating so to speak. Anything goes. The following is a detailed example and it would be difficult to dissect out particular circumstances which progressively develop the fantastic gender identities or set a limit to them:

> As a child I had an accident and had to stay in bed. My female cousins introduced me then to fellatio. That led to ideas of intercourse and fertilisation, *i.e.* seed dropping and giving birth. Later Rachel gave me enemas and used to say 'Come on, you will have a baby'....Later I knew a nurse who used to tie me up and use a dildo on me, in my anus. I could easily imagine discharging a baby. I imagined these women in the male role, treating me as a female....With my male friend sometimes we both cross-dress and imagine we are lesbians...When I was married I got turned on by the idea of a very posh girl being humiliated by a tart type of woman. Then I thought of myself as that posh girl. I sought out all kinds of pornography (M-THO 165).

Female transhomosexuals

Female transhomosexual transgender 'progressions' are not as 'free floating' and exclusively associated with sexual activity as are male transhomosexuals. There are important implications for the kind of relationships they seek. Furthermore, and perhaps partly because of this previous point, there is more structure to their gender/sexual career. Having said that, it is clear that the 'possibilities' for development seem to be a lot more open than is the case for female transsexuals. It is far more difficult to discover commonalities in the life stories of female transhomosexuals. For this reason, several staggered and edited progressive transitional life stories are presented in order to convey these points. It will be apparent that there are interesting overlaps in the content of experience reported. For this first subject, sexual experience *per se* does seem to play a critical role in development at particular times:

> As a teenager I didn't like (heterosexual) boys taking the initiative in courtship...I thought of myself as a real woman, but privately as a kind of male...This older bisexual man

recently asked to penetrate me anally, as I refuse anything vaginally. That was too close to vaginal intercourse which is associated with being a woman...However under pressure I agreed and then I began to see it in terms of homosexual intercourse, and I began to enjoy it...In the past I didn't think homosexual men would like me because I am a woman. Now I'm told some do find me attractive. I have to identify as one male, so the other must not be too different, *i.e.* must be a real homosexual male...I have always been active because I had hang ups about passiveness being feminine (F-THO 157).

What is interesting about the next case is that this subject's feelings vary depending on the sort of sexual partnership she was engaged in:

At 17, I had a lesbian relationship with a youth leader. I 'took on' the male role...Later I was involved with a bisexual bloke and I couldn't bear to think he would go with ordinary women. He used to treat me rough and ready, like an equal, so I didn't have to fantasise the male role. Then I met Richard who was effeminate and treated me delicately. I then had to fantasise I was another fellow. We got married but then Richard discovered he was really gay and we split up...Now I'm with an effeminate man, with a strong personality. I am dominant and masculine however, but sometimes I play the role of a submissive male and this brings back my sado-masochistic fantasies of being in chains and humiliated...I haven't gone with straight men or women since my teenage years...I did get pregnant by Richard and I felt tremendously womanly during my pregnancy. Afterwards it all went away. I felt left as a bystander when he went off with males - who had male bodies. I don't like being with straight people with all the talk of husbands, housework and kids. I'm expected to be what I'm not (F-THO 167).

Finally, this next articulate university student moved from a heterosexual female to the identity of a gay male over a period of years. Sexual experience, sexual politics and a dissociated style in relationships, all seem to have played a part in an unusual development:

> At age 18, I had a straight conservative boyfriend, and I liked sex with him. Then, intercourse became more and more painful. I felt the conflict of being female, subordinate...I didn't like girls discussing boys with me, in the way they do. I thought I should be discussing boys with boys. Later I came to London and fell for a gay man. He was concerned for what I was feeling...and I asked him for anal intercourse. His friends were gay and used to like touching my female body but now I restrict my partner to those who concentrate on me, rather than my female parts...I stopped intercourse three years ago and any touch down there puts me off...As a teenager the 'me' called Elizabeth was not really there, just responding to expectations. She was quiet, nice, and flirtatious with men. The other person in me was ignored, a lively expressive spirit who talks seriously with men. Elizabeth was careful, my 'B' personality was not...My personal identity was shaky (F-THO 158).

In spite of this development and other discrepant features with female transsexuals, *e.g.* having basically a neutral attitude to her breasts rather than a strong attitude of rejection, this subject was finally accepted on the transsexual/ reassignment programme at Charing Cross.

Transgender Identity Fluctuations

The other side of the coin so to speak of progressive transgender identity developments are the fluctuations in those developments, weakenings of desire, reversals, and changes, in direction. The transgender career path is not all 'progressive', and this is much more the case with many males than with female transsexuals.

Successes of the original gender role

For males who have usually not reached a final and 'complete' transsexual commitment, there seem to be times when successes in the male role turn the tide of cross-gender feelings at least momentarily. Where this is a sexual matter, it reflects a stage of development where efforts are still being made in a conventional mode:

> I met a girl at 17 and I was turned on completely. After that for a while there was a complete role reversal for my transvestite activities and I tried to be as masculine as possible (MF 117).

This didn't last however, and neither did a more specific fluctuation in the following subjects hostility to his penis:

> When I met June she was a virgin....and my feelings towards my penis were less hostile (this was short lived)When she turned me down, it all started up again (MF 128).

Success can pertain to non-sexual aspects of life. Where the 'failure' of male assertiveness is less apparent, so transgender feelings may be relieved:

> When I simply get on with the job, which I can do OK, my feelings are shelved for the time being. Only when I have to act dominantly, this goes against the grain and I begin to have my cross-gender feelings again (MF 170).

When confidence and assertion are experienced to a significantly greater degree, a major reversal can occur. The following subject explains why he is dropping out of the sex reassignment programme:

> Since I have changed jobs with the same newspaper I have felt more secure, less low in my spirits. I've met one or two girls I would like to date, and I have had some penile erection at the thought of those girls which was not unwelcome...I may continue to cross-dress in the future, but only as a hobby. I am more open, and less bothered about the idea of making a fool of myself. I do more in the office and outside socially. I am getting more responsibility and more confidence and am becoming more forceful. I have even started to yell. Not bad for

a stammerer! I now stand up to my father and feel I have a mind of my own (MF 82).

This would appear to be the sort of naturally occurring change that psychotherapists have had such a difficult time producing clinically.

Alternate gender modes

'Successful' functioning in an alternate gender mode to transsexualism, can redirect desire and goals away from a final transsexual status, at least temporarily. Again it is mostly males who experience this as a fluctuation. Females, where they do go through an alternate gender mode, *e.g.* lesbianism, tend to do so on their way progressively to a final transsexual status. In fact none of the females in this study having reached their transsexual commitment (and the gender identity clinic) backtracked, or significantly fluctuated in their gender mode of functioning. The following male subject is not untypical of those whose deviant gender desires is oriented by the gay scene:

> In my teenage years I thought all the time about a sex change. Then in my early twenties, gender reassignment went straight from my mind. I was on the gay scene, and I totally accepted the whole thing as I was young then. Only one or two relationships I had then were really satisfactory. For a while I was happy (MF 31).

Sometimes there are gains in formulating a deviant gender desire in an alternate gender frame. The following subject dropped out from the sex reassignment programme and explained:

> I am swimming away from transsexualism to marriage now with my new friend Jackie. I realised if I carried on developing I would forgo my relationship with Jackie, and also my children...I will continue to be a transvestite, so at least we can still have a relationship...There is a sense of loss of what I might have become...an element of betrayal (MF 84).

Mixed and conflictful gender identities

Where individuals have not reached a final transsexual status, they may find themselves fluctuating back and forth in desires and plans which reflect a highly mixed and conflictful sense of gender. The following individual reports a very mixed picture:

> Last December I would have wanted to live as a female full time. I was obsessed then, now I'm not sure. I variate a bit...My masturbatory fantasies include a bit of everything, it all depends how I feel at the time. Occasionally I revert and imagine I am a male making love to a woman...I am bi-sexual and whether I am passive or not depends on who my partner is (MF 24).

If the above subject has some difficulty deciding what he is, than the following individual is more stuck as regards the problem of defining what he is, stuck as he says in 'a no-woman's land':

> I feel very much neuter between what a man and a woman is. My identity should be a woman's but really I am in a no-woman's land. People don't see me the way I see women. I have tried to become feminised, but that made me feel pressurised to be a stereotype...I have been through a strong period of constructive doubt....and I have wondered if I can be happy to accept my transsexualism and not live as a woman....There is conflict between my male erections and need for orgasms, and my physical libidinal desires as a female (MF 63).

These mixed and conflicted gender identities can exist between individuals in exceptional circumstances. In 1982, two females, identical twins aged 22 years presented themselves at Charing Cross Hospital. The first sister, we shall call her 'Rachel' expressed absolute certainty that she wanted reassignment surgery so she could live a life as a male. Her twin 'Robin' was not so sure this was right for her, but on the first visit used an unequivocal male name 'Robert' to refer to herself. Until the age of six, the twins did not speak English properly, but communicated with each other in idiosyncratic 'twinspeak'. Not surprisingly in their early school years they were behind in their attainments, but in later life they did quite well academically.

Rachel's childhood recollections were atypical for a female transsexual. She felt odd and a negative object 'as a whole'. At times she had experiences of being separated from her body and personality. Sexual desire during adolescence was low, although there were periodic unsatisfying contacts with boys. Her strongest fantasies involved active doing of sexual things to an unrecognisable girl. Beyond this her emotional life was pervaded with a comprehensive sense of insecurity and self hatred. This included the attribute of being an identical twin, wherein she felt that her own identity was dissolved by people treating each twin as an 'extension' of the other. At age 19 she was diagnosed diabetic, three years after her sister.

Using a repertory grid-like procedure, the Identity Structure Analysis, developed by Peter Weinreich at Ulster Polytechnic, Rachel's negative sustained self-image was confirmed. This twin was ego involved in her gender and attributed the source of her identification conflicts and her misery to 'herself as a female'. From being the weaker or following twin, she became the leader in seeking sex reassignment:

> I am aggressive, stupid, leading a false life. I think I feel I am what I am not, I am double faced, nothing good...I feel too grotesque, I do not feel like looking after my body. And my personality as well. I have rejected myself to a great extent. I have no idea why otherwise I would be OK (Rachel).

Rachel's reference models identified by the ISA were mixed except that authority and ability she recognised primarily in males. In her own words:

> I am confused....I have a deep hatred for my gender. I have to conform to idiotic roles...I get confused and reject it (my gender) because it is part of the confusion (Rachel).

The ISA evaluation of 'self as a male' was a precarious fantasy. Indeed she withdrew from her demand for reassignment when, extraordinarily, a relationship with a male friend began to go well and threw her back on reworking the implications of her construction of herself. No ready made construction of gendered self could be provided to give her a sense of direction she craved, but which eluded her. The ISA indicated evaluative uncertainties in the use of such attributes as 'female' and 'being concerned with sexual arousal'. Rachel experienced a classic sense of threat (in personal construct theory terms) when the possibilities of change waxed or waned. The first psychiatrist she saw gave her a clear interpretive diagnosis:

> I went to a doctor, a psychiatrist, and she knew all the truth, interpretations and so on, she degraded me. I was all in tears and she made me feel more confused, giving me connotations of lesbianism and homosexuality. It was the labels not lesbianism or homosexuality as such (Rachel).

At the Gender Identity Clinic, Rachel's personality was explored in a painstaking experimental way which, of course, maintained the uncertainties of change. She didn't like that either:

> I am angry of you pinpointing false assumptions, false interpretations. You get the computations which make you right...I question everybody...My perceptions could be wrong, I cannot pinpoint...this mystification goes on...I expect to be sorted out, have a prescription, be on a trial period, and have the operation, or be pushed back to recognise I am a woman....I am going to vegetate if I take steps back (Rachel).

Robin was also reserved as a child, but sought heroic identifications in western films (much as female transhomosexuals). She had sought great admiration and recognition, in the face of completely contradictory emotional feelings. During adolescence, she didn't feel much sexual desire at all, but began to despise females as 'thick' and not interested in serious things. Their make-believe world had heroes falling for beautiful heroines, and she extended her feelings of desire this far. She did not ever see a real girl she was attracted to. Masturbatory images were of her own body and a generalised unrecognisable 'other'. This 'other' would however be receptive to her advances. She found the idea of female homosexuality revolting and increasingly felt the same about her own body. She saw the male role offering contentment and self-assurance as an alternative to her present experience of 'insecurity and blackness'. She learned about transsexualism from her sister, but was very sensitive to the acceptability or otherwise of this in society.

The ISA indicated that Robin was low in her attribution of self-misery to her gender. Indeed she had very few evaluative dimensions of her own identity at all. She had never accomplished a meaningful notion of personhood, and from time to time her sister's transsexual exclamations would be rendered into a 'considered' alternative:

> I have lived basically in my imagination. I did not know what was wrong until my sister wanted to change (sex) role....I don't know what is myself....it's all a contradiction, ideas come and go (Robin).

Masculinity, along with 'awareness' and 'confidence' was associated with gender identity only as far as her weakly evaluatively defined dimensions (on the ISA) went. In her own words:

> One could say I dislike the idea of being passive and following expectations...it's a contradiction for there are many successful women....I was backward and one part of my mind says I am capable and the other side contradicts this...it sounds absolutely absurd...in the middle of male and female. I want to get rid of my female body, to be normal and respected, I cannot get it by being as I am now...I would be more free as a man, to do what I do not know (Robin).

Both Rachel and Robin were referred for psychotherapy.

Finally, even a completely stable, well established full time transsexual about to have reassignment surgery can suddenly have surprise fluctuations in the sense of gender:

> Although I live and work full time as a female, and have done so for many years now, there are certain days when I feel like being a male. This happens about every couple of months. When pressure mounts up concerning my finances, my business and dealing with the staff, I find the old 'Jack' comes back briefly and acts and sorts things out in a way a man would (MF 122).

Insight into practical problems

One of the major impressions clinicians obtain from many transsexuals is the overwhelming compulsiveness of their desire and demand. Come hell or high water, these individuals, victims of their 'condition', can do no other than press on and brook no obstacle to their final goal of sex reassignment surgery. However there are not an insignificant number of individuals who have presented in order to achieve reassignment surgery, but whose compulsiveness is not at such a strong and final stage that the rational appraisal of practical problems does not have a major impact on their feelings and plans. The following subject has not found it easy to manage himself as a female and is not oblivious to how these difficulties are perceived. This gives rise to various doubts:

> I have given a lot of thought over the past years over whether I should be cured. My desires are amplified when I am with other transvestites and transsexuals, but I am treated as 'cold' by the public...I increasingly believe I could succeed as a woman but this desire fills a space and the more successful you are the more the desire grows. When I fail, *e.g.* getting called names by children, progress stops, and the option of being a withdrawn and celibate male has more appeal....I am unsure about whether I really find men attractive. If offered the operation right now, I would delay it (MF 150).

The following subject sees a problem in the future:

I am worried about the quality of my voice and therefore whether I should be a bloke or a woman. People say I am such a good looking boy but in ten or 20 years I shall be an old queen and that makes me think twice. Old queens are all heavy, look unshaven, and have many problems (MF 88).

This next individual has wrestled with his gender dysphoria and gone through several fluctuating stages as he brings his significant intellect to consider his problem:

I do wonder if my ideas of transsexualism are misguided and a delusion that you can change sex. This has got something to do with squeamishness over (surgery to) my body, but also political ideas about sexism...I have seen transsexuals call themselves 'she' but clearly they are not. I also don't fancy a life of hormonal fixes...I think I might feel like a disguised male, after all I have not had the physical experiences of women, pregnancy, menstruation, abortion and so on...After a further time I can see no way to resolve my anguish but to take the necessary course of reassignment. I've been through an extraordinary series of mental reversals, and this time my rejection of transsexuality is stronger. My real problem is self-expression and confidence. I don't want to be trapped moving from being a neurotic man to a neurotic woman. Buddhism teaches us to go beyond such dualism to find wholeness beyond conflict . I have idealised women. Yes, if I had all the resources and money and social support as Jan Morris did, I might have gone through with the operation. Since I don't I have learned to realise the possibilities of being male and have expectations of some success (MF 109).

The belief then that other modes of gender adjustment are possible provides the subject with a much more critical and careful view of the problems he would be taking on if he presses down the road to full reassignment. The next subject has some of these characteristics in common with the one quoted immediately above:

When I see other transsexuals, I think they must be desperate, and indeed I envy their desperation to continue, in spite of such poor bodes...I have experienced confusion but there is potential for various directions...I am not ugly and pathetic as they are, and I think of all the surgical difficulties, taking pills for ever, and all the social problems changing over, it has put me through so many doubts. I have chickened out of changing for now, and am clinging to my present to try to find some contentment, rather than pursuing something so hard, though I firmly believe in it (MF 31).

Rejection of 'maleness' not leading completely to adoption of full 'femaleness'

The accounts of subjects whose gender identity has developed away from maleness but has not fully adopted a complete sense of femaleness offer important insights in the development and strains of gender dysphoria. It is the confusion and pain which comes across most immediately:

I would like to be treated as a female, but if I wear a skirt I will give off a signal that I am a girl, which I am not. Only my mother is female in our family, and I don't wish to be blunt like her... it is hard to say why I have wanted to be treated as a female, and I think it's just that I don't want to be treated as a male, and no-one really believes me. I am at the crossroads, lonely and alienated from all (MF 83).

So is the following subject alienated from his masculinity, but a final residual attachment co-exists with a strong apprehension about what a complete transsexual commitment means:

I am not sure if I have done the right things. I really do feel I want reassignment surgery now, but something holds me back. I find it hard to distinguish between what I want, what I need, and what I believe...I cannot commit myself to the female role, but I cannot go back, I want to continue hormones, electrolysis, *etc.*, but I need help to say I want to lose all of it (male genitals). The prospect terrifies me. I would like to lose my testes, but not the other yet. My dilemma must be made clear to you. Confusion, depression and worry are with me constantly. I cannot go on. It is such a waste of life (MF 34).

In the light of such testimony it does seem that Gender Identity Clinics, who act only as restrictive gateways to sex reassignment surgery, are rendering less of a service than is genuinely needed.

Mood swings

Usually it is difficult to disentangle mood swings from gender dysphoria and determine which is the dependent variable so to speak. In a few individuals, however, a gender dysphoric development and remission seem to have followed significant mood changes:

Although I've been a lifelong transvestite, in my life's work, I've been at pains to stress the masculine side of my nature. Last year I felt I couldn't go on. I was severely depressed and put on medicine. I felt there was something wrong with my body...I couldn't say exactly what...and the only answer was to become as much female as possible...Now I've recovered a lot of my composure, and I'm clear that (sex reassignment surgery) is not the answer for me (MF 141).

I cross-dressed in my teens. I drank heavily and my attraction to the opposite sex declined. Two years ago I had a serious motor cycle accident. I was concussed and had amnesia for a day and a half. I became very depressed after that and drank a lot. I feared being alive. That's when I came to the gender clinic for a sex change. Now I have stopped drinking and I have some tranquillisers. I've begun to see girls more attractive now. I want to be 'Mr. Average' (MF 89).

Exceptional circumstances

Occasionally there may be dramatic fluctuations or reversals in proclaimed gender identity associated with very unusual circumstances. Spontaneous reversals are rare. The following subject reported this in a letter and it wasn't possible in this case to explore this any further:

> Following my attendance at the Gender Identity Clinic, and the breakup of my marriage, I have been miraculously purged of my transsexual inclinations (MF 9).

Some people report dramatic reversals as a result of strong and suggestible emotional experiences. Faith healing has been reported as a cure in the literature, and one of our subjects reported exorcism which worked for a while. This quotation also highlights the importance of the attributions of feelings, to their management:

> My desire for gender reassignment was in conflict with the evangelistic religious group I joined 12 years ago. I have to recognise that to have a sex change would mean eternal damnation. However, if the condition is something beyond my power, then it's not my fault...I went to a casting out of the spirit, and I felt free. I broke down and cried and was free from deception. Thereafter I laid hands myself on a girl who was suicidal, and I felt the (healing) power flooding back. After that she was not suicidal (MF 126).

One individual who has been already referred to before, tried to treat another transvestite/transsexual with hypnosis. This is what happened to the 'hypnotist':

> After I treated this other transsexual and he had given up his transvestic desires, I found I had to make a tape myself to keep my transsexualism from unwinding. It was a big emotional drain and I cried a lot...I could see what transsexualism was in him and me...I had played him my 'loud confidence' tape and overall I found my feminine feelings gone...Therefore I made a special tape to keep me with my transsexual feelings...I was aware of the identity that I had built up recently and the environmental pressures not to give it up already (MF 40).

Now the transvestite/transsexual, this 'hypnotist' cured temporarily, was obviously a 'good' subject *i.e.* could and would use the suggestions made to overcome his feelings. Although not an original subject in the Charing Cross study, he did agree to be interviewed and co-operate in the making of a video demonstrating our transsexual hypnotist's methods. The 'institute', which recruited and trained the hypnotist, was a highly dubious organisation whose activities were not only unprofessional but unethical and illegal as well. Anyhow, Alan's account below is of interest in describing a fluctuating gender identity, and the attributional problems he had to explain that change:

> The treatment I had by Joanne was brilliant, worked 100 per cent...It had all to do with my lacking confidence as a man. I felt powerful enough also to give up smoking and get my wife and children back...I can assert myself now and I can prove I can succeed in every avenue.

Later:

> Since I was originally cured by Joanne I relapsed in a couple of months. You see I still had these feelings in the background and had tried to block and ignore them. That's why I said I had such faith in what I told you. Later when we did the video demonstration those feelings remitted again, and I felt guilty about my last excuses. I know I might be kidding myself as I did last time, but now I believe I can take pressure and I am stronger than I have ever been over the past 18 months. I can say this in a more relaxed way than when I said it to you last time....Anyway, the hypnosis wears off, but talking to someone about your life helps. Also, being associated with a true transsexual like Joanne helps me see that is not me. I could never accept giving up my kids, Joanne can (MF 40A).

CHAPTER FIVE

TRANSSEXUAL ACCOUNTS: OUTLOOKS AND OUTCOMES

Social Life: Personal Relationships

Limited social support

Among all transsexual subjects, only a few had managed to maintain what might be called an adequate or even ordinary social support system. Having at least a small circle of friends and/or relatives who offer genuine affection, support, understanding and companionship is important in maintaining those social support systems necessary to basic mental well-being. Among the majority of subjects a certain number have no social support at all:

> My social life is absolutely dead. I live at home with my parents but all they do is to continually complain about the length of my hair and nails. They don't understand the significance (MF 47).

For other subjects, they often claim friends enough, but on careful inquiry it becomes clear that those they call friends may deal with them in one special role only *e.g.* as a shopkeeper, or they see the subject in one place *e.g.* a pub or workplace. Generally in these cases evidence of genuine affection, understanding, companionship in any arranged social occasion *etc.* is missing. This issue is often glossed over:

> I knit during the day so I will not have thoughts of changing my mind. My prospects of work are nil. I have got plenty of friends who I see in the street, or I see and drink with in the pub (MF 140).

This unfortunate subject of limited intelligence had not a single person in his life who he could name as being willing to offer help with his many difficulties. The following subject had the advantage of a job where women worked. He construed occasional remarks as follows:

> These girls at work sometimes talk to me. They have mentioned intimate and personal things, you know like women's clothing, and new fashions. You could call this girl talk, it makes us friends (MF 34).

Depending on a consort

As long as individuals have at least one close companion in life this can function as just about enough of a social support system to keep them going. A single source of emotional interpersonal life can be precarious however. The following subject falls into this category and is fortunate that his wife maintains a strong emotional bond with him:

> I have no close friends, not close. However, I am extremely close to my wife. Both emotionally and financially we are completely dependent on each other, although there is no sexual relationship (MF 96).

Such a person as this finds it hard that sex reassignment surgery will require he be divorced. Some subjects find other people from the cross-gender or homosexual 'world' who are equally in need of someone. This mutual need can result in stable liaisons, but the chances of problems, if there is not considerable goodwill and understanding, are high:

> Since the break up of my marriage, I have had this relationship with Vicky, a lesbian lady with a six year old daughter. Now I do have sex feelings towards her - not males - but I don't want my genitals touched. Vicky doesn't want to know about this anyhow. It's all worked out (MF 137).

The following male subject lives with a male transvestite, really his only friend. A respectful consideration of each other has contributed to this being a happy long term relationship:

> My close male friend is a transvestite. We do sleep together
> but there is no anal intercourse. He takes the male role with
> me, hugging me like a female. He never cross-dresses when we
> are together. However, I won't let him sacrifice himself this
> way for too long. He is not a boyfriend or husband really, but
> an inseparable companion. We are happier than many
> married couple because we don't fight or get drunk. We share
> everything and it's a nice comfortable existence (MF 70).

The next subject, whose consort is classified by him in a way
not currently found in psychiatric textbooks, does have
difficulties relying on this companion:

> I haven't been able to find a straight boyfriend with who I can
> express my female sexual needs. My present boyfriend is a
> non-active transsexual, a biological male who is not seeking a
> gender change. He says he is like a woman inside, but has a
> male name because his female name doesn't apply to any of his
> moods and a one name person is easier to deal with. Actually,
> he's not easy to deal with. We are always fighting over my
> sexual feelings and his moods. I don't know if I can take it, but
> he's all I've got (MF 63).

The continual need to keep up a pretence to gloss over a
consort's suspected homosexual motivation can also be a
strain:

> We kiss and cuddle in bed. I have no reason to think he has
> had any previous homosexual experience. He does
> occasionally try to play with my penis but I won't let him. He
> has been in prison and the merchant navy, but I haven't asked
> him directly if he has had any homosexual experience (MF
> 122).

Special social scenes

Many transsexuals, males especially, join what has become
known as the 'gay scene' or the 'transvestite scene', mixing
with people with similar orientations to themselves. When this
is the exclusive 'scene' in which they can feel tolerated, this can

be a serious social handicap, especially if it is more than a temporary phenomenon:

> Between '76 and '77, I did a lot of drug taking with motor bikers. I was a bit of an outsider and I was accepted up to a point in this group which was made up of outsiders ...Later I moved to the TV/drag ball scene, but I have always felt an outsider, even there (MF 62).

Of course there are more conventional 'scenes' too:

> My friends from the past have gone. I have dropped out from the gay scene now I am a normal woman. I spend most of my social life going to evening classes now, I am getting better and really my hairdresser has helped me the most (MF 48).

Acquiring new friends

There is no doubt this is a major problem for 'advanced' transsexuals who may have disassociated themselves from past acquaintances to control information dissemination about their biographies. Even individuals who are gifted, resourceful, stable, and who have opportunity, find social life narrows rather than develops. The following female to male musician is a case in point:

> Since surgery I have been to several large social occasions like parties, and it has been fantastic. I've spoken to lots of people...My public concert in Scotland was successful, and I even managed the press quite well...I have taken up swimming and tennis for the first time, and I am communicating better when I'm teaching. I have learned to be self sufficient and now I socialise only once a week or so. There is plenty of time to let relationships and friendships develop naturally (FM-PR 56).

Where subjects continue to feel inhibited and uncertain about the meaning of basic social displays of companionship, then this experience tends to encourage them to curtail the development of new liaisons. Another female transsexual provides an example:

> I don't mix much, and therefore I don't have any good friends...Adult mixing causes problems. Two lads I got to know recently, knew about me, and we went on pub crawls together. I feel like a fool with them, especially when they had their arms around me...I feel embarrassed if I am brought a drink, or if we are all talking to girls. Course I know not all talk is chatting up, it can be light and loose, and friendly. As I get psychologically stronger I will be able to share the joke...if my friends had put their arms around me too much over the last year and a half, I would have been mentally crippled (FM 21).

It is true that some transsexuals find a new zest for socialising when they make a complete life and gender change, but still these tend to concern initial encounters rather than long term relationships:

> Since moving to Derbyshire I have acquired more friends than I did years before. I go to dances and get invited to dances. I can easily divert sexual advances, there are lots of womanly excuses...Actually, there is only one close person in my life. We have kissed and I was really straining inside to go further but it's stagnating now because I have told him I can't go further sexually because I got off men as a result of former relationships (MF 38).

Given that these problems exist for full time transsexuals it is not surprising that when an opportunity seems to arise for an intimate friendship, then it is grasped with a hasty desperation which does not necessarily auger well for the future:

> I have met a real gentleman Arnold, and we are negotiating to buy a house in Birmingham. He is the same age as I, but does not have a clue about my history. I have told him I have to have a lady's operation. I don't know hardly anything about

him to be honest...He is not really all that fanciable, but I like him as a person, I feel secure with him (MF 62).

The following subject who refers to his *femme* role in the third person has discovered the price of these instant desperate lunges of love:

Virginia is always in love with someone. She falls immediately when someone else touches her heart. Unfortunately her love is always unrequited and she is in a constant state of unhappiness, and this is also due to her almost complete lack of friends (MF 33).

On the same theme, when a subject does achieve a relationship this dependence and desperation can undermine it:

I have been having problems with my current boyfriend. He doesn't want me to be a subservient female, but he has threatened to walk out on me if I don't stop being so dependent and clingy (MF 54).

Personal relationships after sex reassignment surgery

Contrary to what most transsexuals believe, personal relationships after surgery do not appear to develop dramatically. The more idealistic and grandiose have been the fantasies, the more disappointment, disillusion, and depression may set in. However, a degree of psychological comfort and satisfaction does contribute to confidence and competence in managing relationships. Male transsexuals are freed from the dilemma of either stalling their sex hungry partners or gradually informing them about their condition early in the relationship. This skill at managing information is a critical one which will be considered in the next section. Few consorts of post reassignment transsexuals are fully taken in, but a few are. If later they are told the truth this can be a crisis for the relationship:

I finally told my boyfriend about myself last month. He felt tricked and said that he would never be able to take anything at face value again. Afterwards we did make-up, although he stopped cunnilingus and I was a bit hurt over that. He did leave me for someone else but later he took up with me again. His responsivity was restored and he was even more adventurous than he was before he knew about my operation (MF-PR 1).

Females seem to be more successful at finding stable mates than males, and many partnerships remain stable through the whole reassignment programme. Whilst most female transsexuals refuse to consider their partners as 'lesbian', those who do recognise that their partner liked something about their pre-reassignment status require a degree of sensitivity and flexibility to maintain the relationship through progressive stages of masculinisation:

My girlfriend was married to a man but came to understand she was a lesbian. She hasn't been sure she would like me going through with this because, sexually, she liked me as Patricia. Our future looks good because we are compatible and have learned not to label things too much as masculine or feminine (FM-PR 50).

Another problem long term for female transsexuals is that they cannot provide a family. They often look for women who do have children from a previous marriage, for example. In the following case, things seem to have turned out quite happily after the transsexual's wife 'acquired' a family:

Myself and my lady, my wife, have been together for eight years. We split up because she wanted children, a real marriage. This break up didn't work for either of us, and when we decided to get back together she was pregnant. I have really enjoyed the bonus of having a child in the home. We are a proper family and I am a cabinet maker (FM-PR 85).

It is not so common for male transsexuals to maintain their sexual relationships with men through the whole reassignment process. It is even less common for them to continue a sexual relationship with a female through these stages. The following subject achieved reassignment later in life, and accepted that external genital reconstruction would be adequate as full sexual relations with men were not envisaged in the future. However, reassignment surgery triggered a sudden surge of sexual desire which created unpredicted problems:

> Until my operation my relationships with men were platonic. I had little desire, I was a sexual cabbage. Following the operation I found this was far from the case. It's been like a renewed adolescence. I've been to bed with several men, and I can't get enough. I'm in agony that I don't have a vagina and enraged the doctors didn't anticipate this...I remain very close to Anita with whom I have a gentle lesbian relationship. Anita's previous experiences have been with men, including me as a man (MF-PR 39).

Social Life: Passing

To 'pass' as a member of the opposite sex to which one was biologically born is the central practical social task of transsexuals. It also constitutes a 'passage' from the status of one originally assigned sex to that of the transsex. Full time, successful acceptance by virtually all who deal with the individual in his or her life is the conventional prerequisite for sex reassignment surgery. There is no doubt that some individuals manage extraordinary and highly 'successful' transformations. By natural endowment, craft, or a little help from hormones, such success, when it comes about, contributes to a strong sense that this is the demonstration that the subject was truly born or destined for this role in life, notwithstanding the incongruent and inconvenient insignia of their genital anatomy. Understandably, when confronted with such apparitions, medical practitioners generally have far less reservations at removing the incongruent genitalia, to 'complete' the picture, than when the apparition is grotesque and ineffective and it is the physical cross-gender presentation itself which looks in-congruent. Now among our subjects ideal transformations that would 'pass' reliably were not that common. Females were more fortunate in that male hormones have a far greater effect on them, than female hormones have on males. Females can expect a breaking of the voice, the growth of facial hair, and some build up of their musculature. Even if they still look a little 'rounded', they can still pass as little rounded men. Large men on the other hand have great difficulties. Bodily hair is difficult to remove effectively even with electrolysis. Their voices cannot return to a pre-adolescent unbroken stage. Whilst many practice hard to 'acquire' female gestures and small movements, it is easy to overdo this creating an image of a drag queen or tart. It is less easy to 'drop' masculine body language, and a bad actor may end up looking like a poor drag queen. For this reason many gender clinics run special groom-ing and social skill programmes to help men who do not natu-rally pass as women when they are dressed in female clothes.

Now, apart from managing a passable presentation *i.e.* appearance and voice, transsexuals of both sexes have another crucial matter to deal with in order to achieve acceptance in their social community. This is the matter of information. A true biography will not sustain a claim to be a normal member of the opposite sex. Thus a man achieving a change of status in his twenties will not have had an adolescence as a girl. He will not have experienced *menarche*, or teenage heterosexual dating and recreational activities. On the contrary, childhood memories as a boy remain forever as potentially discrediting should they be referred to unguardedly during a perfectly ordinary conversation concerning childhood. Our transsexual subject has got not only himself or herself to consider when attempting to control the dissemination of information about a life. There are all those persons who knew the subject in his or her original role. They are possible sources of discrediting information to others who may have accepted the transsexual's new persona, or having met him or her after the change. For those important persons who do know about the change, the transsexual still has a problem of persuading them to accept a version of this extraordinary happening that will permit a degree of comfort and reliability in future dealings, and reduce potential horror and hostility. Certain relations such as parents or the transsexual's own children may present special difficulties in this regard. Then there are others such as potential sex partners and long term consorts who may have accepted the transsexual at face value at an initial stage of courtship, but will need to be briefed in the 'right' way and at the 'right' time so that their 'discovery' does not come as such a shock as to jeopardise the relationship.

Many transsexuals lacking confidence to manage this, may have to create passable excuses and stalling manoeuvres to inhibit the development of intimacy, without losing their partner. This can be a strain.

It turns out that for males especially, full and unequivocal passing is hard indeed to achieve. What is achieved is often something less, which poses its own special problems and remedies.

The management of ambiguities in passing

It appears that for many individuals there is a margin of equivocability in their tolerance of achieved passing. In many circumstances their 'acceptance' may be only skin deep, and the ability of transsexuals to manage this may in turn depend on how thick skinned they are, what they chose to attend to and reflect on. At a most rudimentary stage, a passing effort may be simply to pass as one who is not an ordinary member of their assigned or perceived sex, *i.e.* equivocation is introduced:

> I can't pass as a woman at the present although I would dearly like to. My present appearance is effeminate in order to suit my personality. I want people to see that it cannot be expected of me that I will drink beer, mend things, be confident, and leer at women. I still suffer some nasty comments but I feel better than when I tried to pass as a real man, grow a beard and do all those things (MF 96).

198

A female subject looking moderately masculine felt she could cope with 'observations' on this point so long as she wasn't taken for the kind of sexual female who was expected to respond appropriately in that role:

> I don't tell anyone anything unless they ask. It is up to their observation. I can cope with questions, I can respond to that. It's when they want responses I haven't got that, I am terrified (FM 21).

Many masculinised lesbians also adopt such an appearance as much to put off male suitors as to enhance their attractiveness to the women they like. Most transsexuals who feel they are making 'progress', will utilise several passing strategies and tolerate an equivocal status until they judge that a less equivocal assertion of their desired status will work.

The following female subject carefully and determinedly planned her progress on a number of fronts:

> My voice is getting deeper thanks to the hormones...I am somewhat overheated at having to wear so many clothes to hide my breasts, but for all this time I will win...I am not male enough to relax my guard completely with female friends. I let one girl throw her arms around my neck and it became obvious there were things on both our chests...You have to learn to stay on the bottom rung of the ladder of masculinity until you can go further. I don't want to broadcast my masculinity to a level which will confuse people. In my job, I am just a 'uniform'. I don't think I am taken for an explicit female. I am sexless to the public, a kind of middle step. If my female name is used, that is harsh, it's like crawling back into the rubbish bag. I have a nickname that's kind of neutral and even people who have known me a long time use that now, and I can join the men making dirty jokes and so on...I spent time weight training to build up my physique...and I try not to go with people who would misread me (FM-PR 51).

Sometimes however this step by step progress is not easy especially when work colleagues are antagonistic:

I was not permitted to use the male toilet at work, and now I have had the first operation, I am banned from both sets of toilets. I have had difficulty getting a male uniform too. It's not the management, it's the union which has insisted. However, I am strong, the management have dropped using 'Miss' on my documents and some men talk to me in a masculine way about girls...I enjoy being treated as a male *e.g.* when people let a door slam back in my face instead of holding it open for me (FM-PR 81).

It may seem strange that having a door let slam in the face should make one's day, but imagine the dilemma of the following subject who wasn't sure what to make of her experience:

I'm not sure that I can pass as a man yet completely. I went to the gents toilets and somebody held the door open for me! (FM 121).

Another intermediate passing manoeuvre which helps bridge a change of status is to develop an eccentric reputation. If successful, it affords a degree of acceptance by others of some extraordinary characteristics:

For most of my adult life I have kept a low profile. I have adopted a more masculine name and now I am much more definite about asking *e.g.* for a male locker key at the swimming pool. I've been told I come over as quite an eccentric character (FM-PR 52).

The trouble with an intermediate status is that it might not be possible to move others on from that level of acceptance:

Those supportive friends of mine, who I've known through all this, don't find it easy to completely accept me in my new gender. Some of them treat me as a female to male transsexual rather than a male, *e.g.* when they lift things for me, or curtail themselves making male chauvinist remarks in my presence (FM 23).

For some individuals, in spite of many difficulties, they operate a threshold of passing achievement which is so low they can rely on considering themselves a success:

> I have been more masculine looking than I wanted, but I'm not bothered by nudges and winks and whispers as to whether I'm a man or a woman. If there is a doubt that you are a man you are almost there...I can't project myself as entirely normal, but the harder the struggle up the hill, the better the view when you get there (MF-PR 135).

Another way to manage ambiguities is through 'covering' by others. Most transsexuals hold the not unreasonable view that a few incongruities in an individual in a group of normals is far more likely to be overlooked than if two or more transsexuals with all their incongruities gather together. They generally avoid this latter circumstance in public anyhow. Passive or, better still, active acceptance or sex appropriate treatment by others in a social group is believed to assist the endeavour of passing enormously. The subject above gives an another example:

> I went to a dance at work and the husband of a friend of mine danced with me. That was marvellous and convinced all the others that I was okay (MF-PR 135).

'Reading', avoidance, and conversational skills in calculating passable exposure to others

The business of managing especially equivocal or precarious passing statuses requires a number of skills. Initially, some individuals choose particular social domains in which the exercise of these skills is not too demanding. They may expect a degree of understanding and acceptance not so available in more conventional settings. This then is an attraction to *e.g.* the gay scene and the hope that suitable tolerant partners or like minded friends may be found. Outside these unconventional scenes, transsexuals may have to exercise discriminative judgement as to whether those they are dealing with can

be expected to accept them, and at what level. Thus, as transsexuals try to avoid being 'read', *i.e.* seen as masqueraders, so
they too try to read those they encounter to judge if they will
embarrass or reject them. Transsexuals whose presentations
are not reliable and unequivocal will learn to avoid potentially
damaging social situations and people. The success of this
restrictive policy may lead such individuals to overestimate
their progress to an unequivocal passing presentation and
universal acceptance. The following male transsexual func-
tioned well in his safe domain but this could not be transferred
when he left it:

> At Art school I mixed with arty people who took my female
> side. Even when they found out I was really male, they were
> not shocked. I have to tell men who fancy me my situation
> because early rejection is easier to handle, than later horror
> and disbelief...After leaving art school I have had to keep
> separate lives between colleagues at work, who I speak to
> minimally, and my art friends. As my old art friends leave and
> go off and do different things, I think this will cause me
> problems for the future (MF 34).

Being 'read' is transsexual argot for the failure of a
transgender presentation to convince some other person or
persons. It is 'seen through' and the subject is read as a
member of his or her biological sex. The more polarised their
presentation the more obvious and problematic is it's failure.
Many transsexuals hedge their bets by presenting a kind of
bisexual persona in the early days so that if 'taken' as a
member of the opposite sex, they are delighted, but if not, then
this will not lead to an embarrassing discrediting of their
presentation. Since reassignment surgery is not likely to be
granted to individuals who can only function at this
intermediate level of gender expression, this leads some
would-be candidates to feel they are being 'forced' by the
gender clinic staff to be more explicit than they dare. It is
something of an irony to listen to a male transsexual *e.g.*
complain that requiring a woman to wear a skirt is stereotyped

and sexist. However, in these tentative stages, a transsexual must judge and manage his or her vulnerability to being 'read':

> I didn't wear a skirt when I was mending juke boxes. It's usually a male job and so I tended to get read by the female staff in a pub...I used to wear bi-sexual blouse type shirts and have my hair made up. I would have to work out fast which way I was taken, especially by the men in the pub. They need to identify the sex of someone to know how to act, you know wolf whistle or whatever. If they subsequently think they have got it wrong, they feel fooled and very angry. I can tell if I'm identified as a female by the way conversation topics go. Also if I am handed over to the wife, that's a good sign (MF 40).

Even subjects, whose presentations are highly passable in ordinary social situations, may have to elicit clues from others as to how accepting they might be to potentially discrediting information. The problem of 'information control' *per se* is dealt with in the next section, but the following subject here indicates the special vigilance required, even when ordinary passing is not a problem:

> Whenever I meet new people who might potentially become closer, I realise I may need to tell them something about myself later. I listen and try to encourage them to speak in such a way that I can assess their liberality and whether they have come across transsexualism before (MF-PR 37).

On the other hand, conversations which threaten to get out of control may require other skills:

> Although I tend not to hide too much now, initially I was always very wary about talking too much and I developed a whole repertoire of conversation closers (FM-PR 125).

Information control

Visual and aural presentations are not all there is to the business of passing. Individuals have biographies and the deeper their engagement with others, the more facts about them will be communicated, or else it will seem very odd if not. Transsexuals are faced with a variety of decisions and problems in controlling potentially discrediting information about themselves. They must decide what to disclose, when to disclose, to whom to disclose, and so on. A certain degree of creativity may be employed (*i.e.* telling falsehoods), and since these are not anchored in real memories this will impose it's own burden of rehearsal and monitoring. In addition, of course, the transsexual subject is not the only source of information about himself or herself. A variety of others, from family to former employers, will know things the transsexual will wish to keep from certain other people. Managing their information flow can be very difficult.

When passing is not perfect, some kind of warranting is required and in formulating an explanation of 'what' he or she is, then plausible stories more or less near the truth may be told:

> At work I am treated as a woman gone wrong. People class me as a pituitary case rather than a lesbian. I would rather demonstrate myself to be a freak of nature, but female...There was a television programme about hermaphrodites in Africa. I exploited that and got all my colleagues to watch so now there can be no lingering doubts as to there being no such thing as a woman gone wrong genetically (MF-PR 135).

Explaining this sort of thing to an intimate friend is not so easy:

> I have recently met someone very suitable for me, who believes he is in love with me...I have told him I had been a transsexual and I let him think I might have had ovaries. I told him, biologically I was a female and I gave him a book to read by Money and Green...Initially he was floored (MF 171).

Different subjects have different attitudes to the disclosures of history. For some the whole business of control of information is not something they want to engage in:

> I can put up with people knowing about my past, and if I can't handle it I will have to leave. I don't want to start my life all over again. Somebody will always blow it, and it might as well be myself telling them (FM 121).

Sometimes there doesn't seem to be a problem:

> Managing information is not a problem for me because those who knew me through the past are accepting of my condition, and those who know nothing are not in a position to be antagonistic (FM-PR 56).

For others only a complete separation of former from present life is seen as viable:

> I have changed my job and lost contact with all people who knew about my history. No-one has any idea about my past and this works out very well (FM-PR 50).

Not everyone can manage such a social and practical separation but a psychological separation can also be strived for:

> I have changed both my names because my old surname was part of my past and I am starting a new life...I am also using my studies as a way of putting off the past and thinking of the future (FM-PR 179).

For special reasons, a transsexual may 'tolerate' a non-recognition of a transgender status:

> I have one friend who calls me 'she', but since she hates all men, I let her get away with it, as she is just signifying that she likes me (FM-PR 197).

Occasionally an unusual problem will call for extraordinary passing skill:

> Once we visited Paris, and we met up with a man who had been a confidant of 'John' my previous self. We got through a conversation somehow, and I indicated that I had been working for John, he was boss. I must have had a completely

altered ego for I was entirely unrecognised...I have to occasionally go and 'consult' with John (in Africa) as he had so many international contacts, it was not politic to kill him off altogether (MF-PR 39).

An incongruent history requires mental control and provides practical advantages:

If I see an old Elvis movie which I first saw in the Forces, I have to shut off and shut out my previous life...In the world of entertainment many people believe I have had the operation or else I wouldn't be allowed to use the (female) toilets (MF 122).

The timing of what is told is just as important as the content. This is especially important in regard to intimate relationships. The following male to female subject makes this point:

This is still a sticky area, I have to manage the timing just right so that a man can love me and be attracted to my personality, want me physically, and then not be put off when I tell him about myself. I need to test his reaction (MF-PR 73).

Some individuals become extraordinarily adroit at this and manage their partners' potential or real shock very capably. The following female to male transsexual is an example:

I would tell girlfriends that I cared for them and nothing else mattered. Now when they felt like that towards me, that was the time to tell them the details. I have never miscalculated this. I remember Laura put her arms around my neck and expressed her admiration...Recently I told Cathy, my present girlfriend about myself. I hadn't told her that I have a problem with my genitals as I used to cover those parts. I used a false penis which I wore all the time. I told her this was me but it had a lot of scars and it wasn't quite as it should be...Cathy didn't know about my prosthesis even when it was used for sex over a couple of years. She was very embarrassed but she wasn't really very angry, rather, hurt (FM-PR 125).

Transsexuals have to generate sets of excuses for many situations. For example, the following male transsexual, after leaving his family for the purpose of a full time change and fearing this transformation would disturb his young children, keeps in touch by telephone:

> The original story I told to the children was that I was very ill and I had to go away. Then they were told my wife and I had parted and that I was too far away from them to visit. (MF 12)

Not very satisfactory! Sometimes it is necessary to generate excuses which are not really needed, but should be:

> I have had to read up on what menstrual complaints are, and all the pains and swellings and concocted stories women use to get out of situations. They are always telling me that I am always so well! (MF-PR 37).

Avoiding sex involves excuses hardly restricted to transsexuals. The following Irish male transsexual seems pretty good at this and was only too willing to help out fellow transsexuals and other females:

> I am able to help a fellow transsexual...because of my experience. I can give advice on how to use excuses such as the time of the month or how to take a fellow off his track of thinking and not give straight answers, so she keeps control...Sometimes me and my friend will hop into Sara's flat several times until it is time for her boyfriend to go.
>
> It's all facial language, we can help each other...She can indicate with a glance that she needs help when her boyfriend is full of Guinness...English girls are slower in real life dealing with the attitude of the male (MF-PR 96).

Most transsexuals try to maintain a degree of separation between their past and future relationships. Those from the past which are maintained are usually trusted ones, and they may mix with new friends acquired in the new transgender role. Even then care must be exercised:

It's only on a few occasions that groups who know my history meet with those who don't. I do remind those who do, to be careful. Those I can't trust, I am cut off from (MF 150).

There are differences, too, in the minds of transsexuals between those who know of the past but only obtained that knowledge after the reassignment surgery, and those who knew of the past through a pre-reassignment relationship:

Those who know you before the operation would never completely consider you a woman, except as a word which has too many meanings. Those who learn about it afterwards become extremely fascinated and you can feel their eyes following you (MF-PR 1).

Preparation for passing in a full time transgender role is given a lot of weight by transsexuals with foresight. This might involve, as in the case below, some special help by a friend to manage what had not been managed before, so that in future the individual would not seem completely inexperienced:

I had an elderly consort who initiated me into intercourse after my operation. This was very useful as otherwise I might have been ridiculously anxious with a man and would have been forced to tell him about myself if I was going to sleep with him (MF-PR 73).

Otherwise, preparation may concern a whole attitude to experimenting and planning for the transgender role change. The following subject describes the differences found in transsexuals, in an original way:

It's a bit like going to another country, to become a naturalised citizen. You don't know how you will blend in but you must plan to provide yourself with all the accoutrements from the land you are coming from, or else you will end up in a defective state...Rather than being an immigrant, one is returning home like a Jew...You can divide up transsexuals into the immigrants who see the new world ahead rather like El Dorado, the refugees who get bundled into that new state without good preparations, and the defectors who have tried very hard to be good citizens, even pretend that they are, but deep inside they are yearning and waiting for a bolt-hole opportunity (MF 131).

Some individuals create trouble for themselves by insisting that their subjective state will accomplish passing for them, rather than develop the necessary skills. The following individual of limited intelligence, holds what is not untypical for this group of transsexuals:

I have all the twitches and movements that come from the certainty of being a woman. My reactions would be more successful if only I knew emotionally I didn't have a penis...I would have full expression of the emotional twitches and twitters if I knew I didn't have a penis (MF 14).

When things go well, passing behaviours become increasingly automatic - or as transsexuals say 'natural'. Artificial and stereotyped gestures tend to be dropped:

These days, I don't think I'm acting. I don't think about what I'm doing. I'm not uncomfortable and I don't have to resort to trivial gestures...I used to be careful even in the way I picked up a beer glass before (MF-PR 97).

Passing failure

Sometimes an individual, desperate for surgery, will 'pass' as a successful candidate at the Gender Identity Clinic, but will only admit to real problems, afterwards, after surgery. This should be a warning to transsexuals who see Gender Clinic criteria simply as obstacles to overcome. The following quote is from a post reassignment female to male transsexual:

I am less self conscious than I used to be, but I still cannot fabricate a history when I need to. Some work mates come to the toilet and, knowing my problem, wait outside. I worry a lot about heavy petting with a girl. I am so afraid I leave girls frustrated rather than go on, and it is getting so that people talk and I am getting well known. I could go to another town and change my surname. On one occasion, a girl said to me, 'You are a sex change!'. This completely threw me off balance and I had a sickening feeling as if I had been caught stealing red handed or masturbating in public (FM-PR 79).

Attending the Gender Identity Clinic

Attending a gender identity clinic with the idea that there is a possibility of sex reassignment, is full of psychological significance as a fact, *i.e.* beyond the process or content of the psychiatric interview *per se*. It means a number of things to the attending patient, and it comes to mean much to significant others, such as relatives, employers, colleagues *etc*. This alone can have a major immediate impact on a patient's 'response' quite apart from any prescribed treatment by a doctor or other practitioner. Since this attendance is not an ordinary clinical interview, patients do sometimes prepare for it rather as candidates for examinations. They do not passively surrender the right to draw conclusions to the clinic professional, although they do perceive their power in this regard. Consequently manipulation or negotiation of histories and impressions may be entered into with various degrees of preparation. The expectations of patients are not always met and this can lead to complaints and problems.

The psychological significance of an appointment at the Gender Identity Clinic

Perhaps the most simple response of patients is relief that at last their difficulties will be attended to by practitioners who are specialists:

> At last I felt everything would be understood. Everyone is in the same boat at Charing Cross, and this has made me feel more calm and relaxed (MF 43).

An important dimension of this relief is the feeling that this problem has been duly recognised:

I am not so depressed now or suicidal...The most helpful thing about the clinic is the recognition that there is something here that matters, we are not just pretending (FM-PR 125).

This attendance extends recognition beyond the patient, himself or herself, to significant others:

My fellow workers used to mock me, but when they heard I was attending the clinic and getting treatment and might possibly accomplish a sex change, they have admired me...and realized how strong a character I must have (MF 34).

Major employers too can be suitably influenced:

The airline is willing to let me work on the ground and then after the operation I will get a full female uniform. Basically Charing Cross is a bastion of defence and the corporation has been convinced I am doing the right thing (MF-PR 10).

As times goes by, an initial impact may be revised:

Having such a detailed assessment and everyone knowing I was being dealt with at the hospital gave me the incentive and challenge to live full time in the cross-gender role.

Five years later:

I have recanted the desire to have sex reassignment surgery...You never see a happy transsexual in the Gender Clinic waiting rooms (MF 14).

For some individuals their registration at a gender clinic becomes their 'secret path', not to be proclaimed to others:

I was considered an unstable lesbian, vulnerable to suicide. My parents even moved closer to London to keep an eye on me...Later when I was referred to Charing Cross I was thrilled and I was determined from then on to reveal as little as possible to my parents (FM-PR 56).

For not a few individuals, an appointment, especially the first, consolidated their commitment to a transgender role:

On the first day I set out to come to Charing Cross I still wasn't altogether certain. However, I travelled completely cross-dressed and even spoke to people on the bus and train. My mind became completely made up...It was so important that I had my decision made in time. The interview confirmed that I had made the right decision, and I became so much more relaxed.

Significantly, this same subject added at a later time:

I am very frightened indeed of medical complications and risks. Sometimes I wish the whole operation was completely unavailable and so it wouldn't have forced me to decide (MF 31).

Subsequent attendance can help bring individuals along the transgender road, even when this is not the clinic's intention:

Initially when I first attended the clinic, I didn't want surgery, just a few hormones to give me a more masculine image. I have become more aggressive since then, especially before my periods, when I used to just get depressed. I am wondering if I should go the whole way now, like the others (FM-PR 35).

This subject did eventually do so. For other subjects the moral strength available from the hospital is a *sine qua non* of progress even though this again was not intentional clinic policy. Clinic policy was one of benevolent disinterest. This means no-one was officially encouraged in a cross-gender direction. When certain stages were reached or criteria fulfilled, then the clinic would recognise the fact with appropriate hormonal and surgical recommendations. A few subjects got some help, counselling, social skills training *etc*., if they insisted on progressing to a full time cross- gender role and had marked difficulties. What some subjects wanted however was the authority and legitimacy of the hospital rather than just hormones *etc*:

I am not taking any further steps to change my work role and gender role until I get more help from the hospital. I need the moral help of Charing Cross, to begin the 'championship training' of getting my life together...I feel like a sinner or a hypocrite, and I will be bankrupt spiritually, unless I can get an acceptable assessment at Charing Cross Hospital. I can imagine myself crying and crying if I don't get that because it would mean I wouldn't have changed my life....I have had a spiritual baptism in church and now I seek from the hospital a physical baptism to be reborn (FM 21).

And in much more concrete vein:

Even the appointment card you get in your chosen name from the hospital is important, because the doctors are an authority (MF 12).

Immediate changes which follow an appointment at the Gender Identity Clinic

Given the psychological significance of attending a gender identity clinic, it is not surprising to find that some subjects report almost immediate changes in their mental states:

Since I came to the clinic for the first time there had been a definite change. I feel I am definitely doing something to bring me to a new life. My repressed transvestism has become not a compulsion but it has become something about me. I am lighter and lighter than ever (MF 64).

I used to have depression very seriously and used to stay indoors a lot. Once I attended the clinic, just being on the books helped enormously (FM-PR 113).

I have just been prescribed hormones and I think some of my feelings have changed. I don't feel so flat and all this has occurred in 18 hours. My male sex drive has disappeared completely, and now I recognise which males are sexy to me (MF 47).

Preparation for assessment

Given transsexuals' views of the importance of 'assessment' interviews, it is not surprising that many prepare themselves emotionally and informationally in order to increase the probability that they will be recognised or diagnosed as trans-sexuals, and thus be considered for elective sex reassignment surgery:

> I used to come to London regularly but I only found doctors who knew less about transsexualism than I did. Eventually I was referred to Charing Cross. In dealing with doctors you have to learn to manipulate them. This is hypocrisy but you have to play the system. They like to diagnose transsexualism, so you have to time your reference to yourself as a woman just right or they will pounce on you. You may have to allow them to try prescribing female hormones to reduce your sex drive and relieve the discomfort of your condition. Of course they could do that with non-oestrogens, but so long as you get oestrogens you can present your enhanced feminine curves and behaviour next time as evidence that transsexualism is the right diagnosis. We cannot really be honest with doctors and doctors cannot be honest with the rest of the world (MF 131).

Another subject summarises this stance neatly:

> I didn't disclose everything in all my interviews for I treated them as a series of obstacles which I had to negotiate and survive (MF-PR 97).

Occasionally conflicts may occur between different doctors' assessments and the importance of the private market in medicine, where a patient can find a practitioner to suit his desires, becomes apparent:

> My doctor in charge of my paraplegia has been furious at my getting hormones and is extremely conservative about reassignment surgery. The National Health Service clinic requires you to reassemble your life without any guarantee on

their part that surgery will be granted. People get strung along for years and it's a rotten position. Now I've switched to private practitioners, everything is happening much faster...We've run a review of what can be expected from various private and national health clinics in the newsletter of our self-help association for transsexuals (MF-PR 66).

Sometimes transsexuals' attempts to 'manage' the impressions at interview can have unfortunate results. The following is one example:

I was very wary about asking questions because I thought the doctor would misinterpret this as a sign of caution or reserve on my part. I was actually given very little information and I wish the Gender Clinic had not made the operation the be all and end all. Subsequently, I have experienced the shock of the loss of pleasure from my penis more than I thought (MF-PR 97).

Clearly a lesson here for both parties!

Complaints about the Gender Identity Clinic

Interestingly, the closer patients came to reassignment surgery, the more understanding and tolerant they became of the strains associated with attending the Gender Identity Clinic. The trial by ordeal makes more sense when an individual has passed through successfully. Apart from complaints of practitioners not taking the same view as themselves, transsexuals' frequent complaints fell into a few categories. The following quotations reflect the chief ones:

I think referrals to the clinic should be easier. I waited many years, then when I satisfied all the criteria I still had years to wait on the surgical waiting list. I've had to muddle through all my problems myself, and I think social work help should be made available to all of us (MF 101).

Many of the pills I am prescribed make me constipated and give me problems like biliousness in my bowels. I don't like to complain because I am afraid all medicines will be withdrawn. I am made to feel I have to beg Charing Cross for permission to live. I have become much more astute, even cynical now. It seems odd to make such a long journey from Scotland for a three minute interview (MF 122).

Divided and Reconstructed Consciousness

As transsexuals commit themselves to a full time transgender role (with or without sex reassignment surgery), so their reconstructed lives give rise to memories and ways of seeing which may be more compatible with their transformed life directions, but which, by definition, are different from their personal life experiences. It is a measure of the plasticity of self-constituted consciousness that such reconstructions are viable, but sometimes a divided consciousness remains which may require a very considerable bias in an individual's perceptual system to overcome.

Being open to biased and self-suggested interpretations

If transsexuals have anything in common at all, it is that they are willing to accept suggestive interpretations that things are the way they would like them to be. The following female transsexual, having progressed a long way to a transgender masculine role with mastectomy and long standing male hormone administration, is still actively at work, holding on to and reporting interpretations of experience which fit the over-all way she sees things:

> If Beryl touches me, she tells me I am being stimulated in the same place as a man. Hormones began working on me in a couple of days and I felt more sexy and felt I was getting looks from women as if I were a male. Beryl always refers to me as him now, and our dog responds to me now as his master and only to Beryl as a mistress (FM-PR 135).

Sometimes a very intelligent individual, especially an intellectual, finds that a thought can be translated into a 'decision' to feel in a particularly suggested way:

> I had to meet a friend in this unwholesome part of town. A drunk guy came lumbering up to my car, then asked me if I was a boy or a girl. I realised I had done wrong. It was quite wrong for me as a female to sit in a car at night. If you operate your life according to rules you can see that is a mistake. I was not actually afraid and I should have been. It is necessary to actually feel like a female, and now I have decided to feel afraid (MF-PR 66).

Reconstructive explanations

The meaning that events may have had at one time may be reversed in the hindsight of a revised view of self and life. These all go to support this reconstruction. The following is a typical example:

> I understand my feelings better and certain things that were unexplained are now all falling into place. My small hands make me look feminine, and suggest this is how it should have been. My outlook on life, feeling threatened by men, finding sex pictures vulgar, and not wanting to smoke and drink in pubs makes sense to me now. It explains why I have a greater appreciation of small delicate and pretty things like clothes (MF 111).

Some subjects find a way of explaining away what might have been expected, but wasn't. The following individual evidenced very little in the way of anything during childhood, adolescence, or early adulthood that fitted his idea of what would be expected for a transsexual-to-be. This 'explanation', a desperately brief and impoverished account, served his purpose, but would not be an adequate objective aetiology:

> I was shocked to be put into breeches at the age of four. The pressure was so great that I broke out and declared that I was going to be a girl when I was between eight and ten. My family descended on me in full Victorian and Edwardian manner and

beat such shame into me that it didn't emerge again for 20 years (MF 80).

The tendency to operate a biased and simplistic way of thinking is often mostly sadly evident in mentally handicapped individuals. In these cases the grossest features of self-delusion stand out:

I have friends and they are at the Samaritans. My mother doesn't understand why I have to have sanitary towels. But they are part of feminine wear and if a female has them then I must treat myself like that. People say I look younger. I think I would be letting people down if I don't go through with this, and other people want me to have the operation because they think I look better (MF 130).

Divided memories

The reconstructive process creates divisions in consciousness and the overriding of older aspects by the newly reconstructed ones does not always work satisfactorily. The following subject has to manage co-existing alternate dimensions of consciousness even though she had passed through the entire sex reassignment programme some years previously:

I am pleased all the time about my operation....However I have not changed completely and have to accept the residue of history...I have grown into the male role from the female and the female is still there...Psychologically I feel like a hermaphrodite, which is why I don't have relations with others...I am conscious of being two people without that being a morbid state. So I rarely feel alone. I feel between the two sexes (FM-PR 114).

Then again when an individual has come to terms with two sides of personality for over a quarter of a century, as the next subject did, a major 'progression' such as sex reassignment surgery can unhinge the arrangement, so to speak, of divided memories so that the division becomes a separation giving rise to practical problems in thinking, and emotional disorders:

> Surgery made a total difference to my life and attitude to everything. It resulted in my total acceptance of the female role versus the male and the gulf is enormous. I am so far removed from my pre-operational person that I cannot even recall data I was responsible for. I don't understand even my own mathematics of four years ago, it's a sort of amnesia... I became withdrawn and curled into a tight ball naked on the floor, barely conscious...I couldn't recognise Alice and she had to slap my face because I was hysterical...Apart from that my general motor behaviour has changed *e.g.* my writing style, my driving and so on. Prior to the operation I had tried to live as two persons for 30 years (MF-PR 39).

New feelings may arise from historical physiology, creating a little problem of classification:

> For the first time since surgery, I get orgasms. I wonder if the feeling I get is a result of a small amount of tissue left from my penis following the operation. I wonder if that makes it a male orgasm because if it was I wouldn't like it. I would feel much better if I believed it was not part of a male penile orgasm (MF-PR 181).

Outlooks and Outcomes: Post-Reassignment

Clinical approaches to outcomes of treatment are usually couched in the language of problems. It is the relief, the reduction or the prevention of further discomfort, distress or deterioration which are the usual objectives of clinical treatment. The language of enhancement of the quality of life, or 'happiness' is far less precise and difficult to agree on. Most successful transsexuals, declare themselves 'satisfied' with having had reassignment surgery. They will usually have already lived 'successfully' in the cross-gender role as a pre-requisite to surgery, so in effect there is a 'ceiling effect' *i.e.* there is not much more 'success' to be had. Although clinicians would like to be able to show some objective improvements to justify their interventions, most spontaneous accounts emphasise subjective satisfaction.

This is even the case when there is some objective gain to point to *e.g.* per vaginam sexual intercourse for males, a more stable relationship, improved job prospects, or less reliance on psychiatric treatment.

The feeling of being a stronger personality

Objective improvements tend to support and confirm subjective feelings rather than be the basis for them:

> Since the operation I have been really enjoying life socially. I have reached out for the golden apple and now I feel I no longer have one arm tied behind my back so to speak. I am no longer an animal on an elastic leash. My other ambitions have been fulfilled. I became a qualified nurse this year. That just confirmed my ambition and confidence (MF-PR 134).

Not untypically, happiness grows without any objective 'gain'. In the following case, the absence of any knowledge that the constructed vagina might be not ideal, helps contribute to a long lasting happiness:

> Following surgery there hasn't been any difference in practical ways. But everything is better. I have never seen a real vagina, only drawings, but I am happy with mine...I still live with my mother and I have day dreams of going on holiday with my family and a cine camera. I am just happier, have put on weight and am eating well. I just know the operation was the best thing that ever happened. Just knowing that I have had it makes an enormous difference as I walk down the road. I am more as I should be (MF-R 78).

Apart from colleagues at work, this individual had no social life outside family at all, three years after surgery. There can be a sense of loss after genitals are removed, but in successful or satisfied cases, this does not spoil the 'spiritual harmony':

I am very happy about my surgery although I had to have an additional operation because I had trouble passing urine...It was a psychological shock having the surgery and finding one's penis gone. There was a sense of loss, but I was psychologically happy. Sometimes I have wanted the intensity of sexual sensation I used to get with penile orgasm, but I have not wanted the penis back. The gain of spiritual harmony far outweighs that (MF-PR 97).

There are often still problems after surgery, but successful transsexuals (in their own judgement) are those who face up to them and deal with them:

I have benefited from the operation, and am more confident now. Immediately after the hysterectomy, I felt strange and somehow asexual, in a way, neither male or female, and that was un-nerving. At the same time I lost my girlfriend and that really didn't help. Also my ovaries were potential testes, so my potential testes were now gone. After some weeks my idea of my maleness were not so dependent on these biological potentials...Now incongruities are just that. Sometimes I think of myself as a boy in childhood, but since the dominating memory was wanting to change sex, that isn't all that helpful. Everyday I became stronger (FM-PR 27).

Another dimension to this sense of psychological 'strength' is that problems may be put into a better perspective:

Being transsexual has made me realise just how trivial ordinary problems are. Being transsexual has given me so much in the way of rewarding experiences, that I am naturally optimistic (FM-PF 95).

On the successful side of psychological functioning this could be considered one of the best examples, so too could the following male to female transsexual:

I have been selected for two Conservative wards as a candidate for the local council, and also for the Social

Democratic Party-Liberal Alliance in another place. My business is going well, and I have a nice boyfriend (MF-PR 13).

It is always possible, perhaps to chase too much success after so any years of subjective disadvantage. It is understood that individuals who go through with the whole reassignment programme must want the surgery very much, and it's accomplishment must be an intrinsic gain. However, occasionally, post-surgical evaluations by subjects throw this open to question:

> I had the hysterectomy recently, and since then I have had hot flushes and sweating and our little girl notices these...if the operation had not been available I would have carried on as I was. I would have got by, but I wanted the peace of mind of the op. I don't feel that much different now from not having periods. Previously, my periods didn't really bother me, they are a damn inconvenience (FM-PR 185).

Surgical problems: post-reassignment

It is very understandable that transsexuals' satisfaction with reassignment surgery will be very significantly impaired if their dream operation turns into a nightmare *i.e.* serious medical complications arise:

> I have tried to escape from my past but that has been unsuccessful. I have had persistent problems over being unable to pass urine. I must have been back in hospital half a dozen times. I have suffered a lot of bleeding and my vagina tended to close up. Although it was very painful I have tried to keep it open by using a dilator vigorously. Whether it was my fault or not I don't know but then the whole thing prolapsed in my knickers when I was at work. I thought my problems before were due to people treating me as a pre-operative transsexual. Now I know that isn't so (MF-PR 30).

Some individuals somehow maintain an extraordinary robust cheerfulness:

After my operation in Belfast I went with a taxi driver. I told him to go easy but we both had had a lot to drink. He just went ahead and caused a lot of damage. Never mind, I've come to your hospital for a sort of re-bore if you see what I mean (MF-PR 29).

Another post-surgical complication is a desire to have more and more surgical tailoring to make the physical appearance more passable and attractive. The following subject has taken this path to considerable lengths, and then reflects on a reservation rather late in the day:

I had my gender reassignment in July 1978. I had mammoplasty in February 1979. I had an alteration on my jaw in May 1980. I have had a nose job in September 1981. In the main I have been satisfied with all these operations. I am supposed to have another one on my chin. I also want a skin peel to get rid of hair because electrolysis hasn't worked after nine years. I don't want to become a surgery junkie (MF-PR 1).

Continuing problems after surgery

Even among 'satisfied' post-surgical transsexuals, it is clear that a considerable number are unhappy because of difficulties with social problems. It is not uncommon for these to have been endured pre-operatively with the belief that they would disappear once post-reassignment status was achieved:

I have found it unexpectedly difficult to expand social life and really I don't know where or how to meet people. Eighteen months after surgery I have experienced extreme depression and floods of tears, and have a pessimistic outlook. I realise what all this has cost, eight years without any social life and that was preceded by a very distorted social life. I have lost opportunities to be a lawyer or get married and have children. I joined a dating agency and that was a failure. I am a normal woman now but utterly isolated. I don't want the support of the transsexual clique at this stage (MF-PR 131).

Existing social relationships may have unexpected developments:

> I would have been shattered if I had not been allowed to have the operation, but as it is, the outcome has not been as expected. My relationship with my girlfriend is very shaky. She has decided she might want children and this conversation makes us both very miserable. I have become more conscious now of how she keeps me away, a bit of a secret, from many people she knows. This all plays on my mind now (FM-PR 85).

A few transsexuals find an increase in sexual drive which they had not anticipated, and that can be a problem:

> My operation did not involve a construction of an artificial vagina as I was advised that this was not necessary nor a good idea as I was in my fifties. After surgery I suddenly rediscovered a huge increase in my sexual desires, and since I have had to lie to my boyfriend about my inabilities we have had so many rows, and I am exceedingly depressed. I blame the hospital entirely for not warning me about this (MF-PR 39).

A very few transsexuals developed major psychiatric disorders some time after reassignment surgery. Whilst these did not seem to be related to the reassignment surgery itself, this creates special problems for the patient and for those managing his treatment:

> This patient developed paranoid schizophrenia some five years after sex reassignment surgery. There is a family history of schizophrenia, in his mother...This patient has been extremely difficult to assess and manage because many of his delusions refer in content to cross-gender themes and social conflicts associated with his transsexualism. It is difficult to disentangle what is psychotic and what is part of his personality disorder (letter from psychiatrist treating MF-PA 42).

Serious deterioration and tragedies after sex reassignment surgery

Nine subjects in this research study suffered serious deterioration in their lives following reassignment surgery. Physical problems arising from surgery impair satisfaction as mentioned above, but usually strong efforts are made to repair damage by the surgeons. For one individual the number of problems and their duration overwhelmed him:

> I've had several operations because of the tendency of my vagina to prolapse. I've also had problems of urgency (of urine) and incontinence. I've felt very anxious as a result and I've constantly failed to find a job. I've overdosed once and was admitted to hospital. I had a phantom penis experience for weeks after the operation, and although that has gone I get uncomfortable feelings when I sleep on my stomach. This feeling is a kind of rawness, a stumpiness as if something was cut off. Because I used a dildo so much as I mentioned before, I got another prolapse and cystitis. Hormone implants put into me have come away. My blood pressure is very high and I have just undergone tests for kidney functions. I've been desperately unhappy for years now (MF-PR 30).

The realisation that one is really failing to pass can be traumatic for the post-operative transsexual. This can lead to alcohol abuse or desperate violence as the following two cases illustrate:

> Came to interview extremely angry and upset. He demanded an explanation that the law would not allow marriage. Accused the hospital of treating him as a guinea pig, not a person with feelings. Was drunk having consumed a bottle of spirits, which he claimed was his daily intake. Has been diagnosed alcoholic. Claims he lied about having homosexual relations in order to get the operation. In fact he has never been able to have sex with anyone. Was in tears about all his discrediting rejection outside. Claimed he was going to set up

a pirate radio station to give transsexuals a voice. He stated that it wasn't so much that he wanted to be a woman as that he wanted what would feel right. Now nothing is right (hospital notes on MF-PR 174).

A large grotesque transsexual with deep voice who stripped off in the Charing Cross reception area and smashed a window in an office door. Screamed demands to have his face changed by cosmetic surgery. Was assaulted recently by skin heads and had his nose broken. Reset unsatisfactory. Has been on a grooming course but now believes 'she' looks like a freak. Has given up looking for work and overdosed twice. Since this appearance she has been depressed and feels inadequate in the female role to the point where she dresses in unisex style and has renounced every kind of social life (hospital notes of PR 72).

For some individuals, outside social circumstances are difficult to overcome. The following subject is a Chinese male to female transsexual from Singapore:

My vagina is a bit tight and I have to use constant dilation. My boyfriend cannot get all his penis in and I'm worried this might not get resolved. I have no friends even my Chinese acquaintances tend to stay away because my boyfriend is a white Australian. I am very shy and would be absolutely lonely if I lost him. I am very sad and hopeless. I have been in the UK for 15 years and I am always a stranger. I have lost my Singapore citizenship so I am stateless. My life is in limbo (MF-PR 152).

If there is one personality attribute which will serve post-operative transsexuals badly, it is an obsessional approach to 'correct' all incongruities and inconsistencies in appearance, legal documentation or social life. This is often overlooked as being simply part of the transsexual compulsive desire for reassignment in the first place. The following two individuals have lived lives of constant misery and recurring serious depressions because of this:

This patient is still bothered by small breasts and the presence of facial hair, and has a constant feeling of inferiority. She is distressed by the fact she will not bear children or be properly married. She is isolated and alone and fearful that someone will find out about her. She is now a chronically unhappy person, especially when she hears other women talk of marriage and children...She does not have the resources to deal with the difficulties of a sex change. She has found hairs growing inside her vagina. She expresses pervasive doubts about almost every aspect of her life and declares any possible remedy impossible and totally rejects all advice (psychiatric letter concerning (MF-PR 98).

The following individual was illiterate and considered mentally backward when he came out of the army. After the operation he demanded a reversion of surgery and said his life had been ruined because his birth certificate could not be changed. He never worked, had no social life and lived in poverty relieved only by hospital admissions for depression. It was considered to have been a mistake to have operated on him, and indeed the surgeon who did so refused to carry out any further operations. The referring psychiatrist however took responsibility:

I must take responsibility for this because I thought his depression was due to his frustration as a transsexual. It is clear now that I made a misassessment of his personality for he is woefully inadequate and a chronically miserable person (medical notes on MF-PR 69).

What is interesting in this case is that as is so often found in borderline mentally handicapped individuals, an unglossed despair over not 'being right' is communicated as being 'behind' the demand for a transformed gender identity. As can be seen from this unfortunate man's own words, he is virtually ready to settle for either gender so long as it can be 'right':

I wanted to change back and I have been entirely miserable because they didn't change my birth certificate. I regret I am neither one thing or another. I have been misled. How can I live as a male without male sex organs? I can't come to terms with my present situation and they should change my birth certificate or reverse the operation. I know certificates are changed and if mine was I would be in work in a week...If you had seen me before the operation you would know a lot of females were not as feminine as I was. I had hardly anything between my legs and it was very embarrassing. I tried not to let anyone see I was not right. Everything you know has to be complete and right. Not having this done means I don't feel part of the human race. I feel like another creature (MF-PR 69).

Problems of finding work, companionship and financial security can contribute to some transsexuals drifting into the world of petty crime and prostitution:

Complains of headaches, pounding in the head and breathlessness. Heavy smoker and regular heavy consumer of spirits especially vodka. When finances run out resorts to petty crime. Known to police for criminal associations and as a recidivist. Police not pursuing her marriage to a biological female. History of being drunk and neglecting child. Known to local social services (referral letter of family doctor of FM-PR 36).

I can't get work so I'm on the game. I have three regular punters a week, and I have been doing this for about nine months now. Even so, it gets me down and I don't want to do this all my life (MF-PR 11).

Perhaps the worst tragedy befell a male to female transsexual patient we shall call 'Jackie'. Jackie lived outside of London and her history of deception, anxiety and sense of dislocation from the Gender Clinic contributed to her deterioration, the nature and degree of which was not recognised at the Gender Clinic. At one of her last presentations she stated:

I have no regrets whatsoever about my decision to have this

operation and I am happy to be able to function sexually as a female...I shall settle for obscurity and enjoy life at last. I am still waiting for an operation to raise the pitch of my voice, and I get a little more depressed every time someone addresses me as 'sir' on the CB radio...I am under the care of Dr. R (a psychologist) because of my suicidal frame of mind due to the complete lack of follow-up which would complete my life style as a woman. I feel I have been neglected....by Charing Cross (MF-PR 136).

Shortly after, the following letter was received from Dr. R, Jackie's psychologist:

On Christmas day, Jackie blew herself up in her caravan. She has suffered from serious burns and it is predicted she will die. (She did.) She was recently arrested and charged with shoplifting and has had the habit of buying expensive articles and then taking them back to the shop because she doesn't really need them. She has been terrified of having to go to Court on the charge of shop-lifting and having her male identity exposed. She took a number of pills to make her go to sleep and then re-directed the gas from her gas cylinder into her sleeping quarters in the caravan. It seems she must have woken up during the course of the night and in a dazed state, tried to light something and the result was a horrible explosion. Jackie was never employed. She was worried about the fact that her vagina was closing and there was labial infection. She was very disappointed about her attempted masturbation with a dildo. Jackie got depressed after surgery because of all the difficulties and the hope that future surgery would solve all her problems could no longer be seen in that light. She refused to go into a psychiatric hospital because she feared that would make her lose the operation.

Special Problems: Low Intelligence/Mental Handicap

Fourteen people out of our overall cohort samples were assessed as of low intelligence or borderline mentally handicapped. This classification was not meant to be psychometrically precise; intelligence tests were not administered. Rather this categorisation is a clinical judgement based on the intellectual resources these subjects brought to their interviews and had available to them to deal with everyday problems. Almost all these subjects, it was ascertained, had had special educational provision in their childhood. This was usually because of their backwardness, sometimes it was for their 'maladjustment'.

Social relationships

As with many transsexuals, social relationships are limited and superficial. For those of limited mental ability, there is a tendency to classify almost anyone normally encountered as 'friends'. This can lead to inappropriate expectations, and a lack of real emotional support when it is needed:

> I have friends, a sort of friendly relationship with my mother, the rent collector, the landlady, her son-in-law, and some shop keepers (MF-PR 136).

Petty crime

Poor judgement, and a willingness of others to exploit those with below average intelligence, can result in many breaks with the law:

> I am always getting into trouble with the law, because someone tells me to do something. I signed for something in the registered post when it was for someone else. I always get caught when someone tells me to go and fetch something from warehouses (MF 140).

Poor judgement

> If I get the operation, there will be a vast difference. There would be no long face and if a person spoke to me they would recognise me as a female, there is a different (female) outline within me. Now children take the micky. I don't think I have

any problems with the cross gender-role. I know some people think I don't look good (MF 187).

This quotation is from an individual with a very poor appearance. His lack of judgement prevents him being sensitive to people 'reading' him if they don't make it obvious. 'Some people' and children do, and he tried to deal with that problem by avoiding them.

Unfulfillable fantasies

This is linked to poor judgements. Low intelligence subjects tend to believe everything will be just fine and transformed once they have the powerful operation:

Being a new person has helped overcome my past history, When it's all finished, I'll have friends around every night (MF 140).

This male had not any visiting friends at this time. Below a comment by a borderline mentally handicapped female illustrates a comparable simplicity:

In ten years time I would like to have a lot of money, and live abroad. Perhaps I could be a policeman, or a villain in films, or I could sell things (FM 195).

This young lady lives with Mum and has never earned a penny in her life. Sometimes however a childlike creation, such as an imaginary companion, can be helpful:

I have conversations with this other person within me and that's why I don't need to go out with anyone. Paul and Sally look after each other....Sally is happy and a pleasing good person. There is no struggle and she has taken over my body (MF 140).

Fearfulness

Fearfulness can itself be considered to be an anxiety based version of inappropriate fantasies. They are more raw and primitive than those elaborated and glossed by transsexuals of normal intelligence:

> I am afraid of the dark...of being raped...I am so frightened I run. It's of the violence and sex. I don't have any real sexual feelings myself....I hate men looking at me, especially coloured men. I wouldn't want to be a prostitute and thought of as easy (FM 195).

Disinhibition and maladjustment

Disinhibited, poorly socialised and maladjusted behaviour is marked in a significant proportion of mildly mentally handicapped subjects. With the complications of transsexualism, their management can be enormously difficult:

> An individual who attended child guidance because of backwardness and who has made wild approaches to other men who have rejected his sexual overtures. Wants to have anal intercourse and be passive, and have a baby and experience pregnancy. Didn't get on well with anyone at school and was teased (medical referral letter concerning MF 57).

The following case was simply unmanageable by the doctors and social workers involved with him:

> Man of low intelligence associated in this case with childhood history of severe maladjustment, aggressive behaviour, speech problems, later, homosexuality, a variety of serious traffic accidents on his motorbike which have included his being unconscious twice. His attempts to obtain homosexual boyfriends has resulted in violence being used against him. He has been violent himself against all members of his family, he has lot all jobs because of his demeanour and hostility when people make remarks concerning his appearance, which is usually considered to be grotesque. Has hardly any friends, but calls friends, people he might speak to in shops *etc*...Suffers from depression and has required medication on and off for many years (medical referral letter concerning MF 130).

This kind of frustrated rigidity can lead to unsatisfying obsessionality of the type mentioned in the previous section on serious social deterioration. There is little evidence that reassignment surgery relieves psychic distress and disturbance of such magnitude.

Multiple mental impairments

When low intelligence is coupled with other kinds of brain damage then the transsexual picture is compounded or even dominated by the package of problems arising out of this. The following individual suffered brain damage at birth along with a moderate number of musculo-skelital abnormalities:

I can't spell but can read some parts of a newspaper. I'm always getting depressed and I can't understand being alive. Sometimes I feel I am outside my body...I would kill all people if I had a gun, and myself...I have killed cats and birds in my time when I was young (MF 102).

The following individual's problems began after a serious road traffic accident in his teens:

Man with history of brain damage and epilepsy, and physical disfigurement following a road traffic accident in his teens, Has been involved in many violent homosexual encounters with young boys. He has had a variety of psychiatric treatments for depression. Has indulged in cross dressing from time to time and has come to believe that transsexualism is the answer to his perpetual unhappiness and has begun to hate his male body (medical referral concerning MF 59).

Although only a small proportion of the overall number of individuals presenting with severe gender dysphoria, these multiply handicapped desperate people clearly need and deserve more from a specialist gender identity clinic than a screening test for sex reassignment surgery.

CHAPTER SIX

CONCLUSIONS

Diagnostic Difficulties Concerning Transsexualism

Chapter one provided a review of the problems associated with treating transsexualism as a specific psychiatric syndrome, particularly so called 'primary' transsexualism. These are briefly recapitulated.

Adults come to express a strong cross-gender identity following various histories. A few have had unequivocal and undisregardable childhood cross-gender identity. Many more develop their gender dysphoria through adolescence and young adulthood. Some have been long standing transvestites with fetishistic and heterosexual components to their sexuality. Some may have been diagnosed in another gender dysphoric category *e.g.* effeminate homosexuality. No matter how they reach a strong and successful adult cross-gender status, so long as they have the resourcefulness required, then their lives and responses to sex reassignment surgery (the course or outcome of their condition) is independent of any syndrome label pinned on them due to their histories, or their initial presentation.

Children express striking cross-gender identities rarely, but when they do there is a varied permutation of cross-gender role expression and strength of cross gender-identity. Such children grow up expressing a variety of gender identities and sexual orientations. Only a small minority become transsexual. Cross-gendered boys often have other constitutional or neurotic problems, and other boys who attract diagnoses of various other neuroses have been shown to exhibit opposite sex typed behaviour, depending on the severity of their psychopathology. This supports an alternative view that childhood cross-gender behaviour - in boys anyway -

is associated with general neurotic maladjustment and, under certain circumstances, this may lead to a spoiled sense of gendered self. Transgenderisation then develops as a course towards restoration.

The idea of 'true', early transsexualism is derived from psychoanalytic ideas of the 'bedrock' of gender identity being forged during the first couple of years of life, the so called oedipal period. Later, extreme cross-gender presentation cannot be accommodated in this theory, so the majority of transsexuals are classified as 'secondary'. In fact, the review of the cognitive developmental studies of gender identity acquisition and socialisation reveals a much more prolonged, staggered process. It is not bedrock, it is clay.

The concept of a syndrome would carry more weight if some biological fault (or 'force' as some workers think of it) could be identified. For the majority of transsexuals nothing has been found. The general finding that individuals of the same hermaphroditic diagnosis differentiate gender identities in accordance with their biography, irrespective of chromasomal, gonadal and hormonal sex indicates that the idea of a 'biological force' as a dynamic tendency is too simple. Where incongruities exist (hermaphroditic or otherwise) concerning behaviour, bodily functioning and the treatment of the individual by others, then experience of these anomalies may indeed disturb the sense of gender identity. The efforts to manage biologically grounded experience by the individual alone, or together with physicians and therapists, in a psychologically meaningful way, is central to the story or career of becoming transsexual. Nowadays a transsexual assessment at a Gender Clinic is confounded by the presentation of the individual as a victim of a condition rather than the true author of his or her actions. This surrender of responsibility can be a self-fulfilling prophecy, for as the late Don Bannister (1975) once commented:

> Man is not a victim of his biography, although he may enslave himself by adhering to an unalterable view of what his past means. He thereby fixates his present.

236

Accounting for Transsexualism: Gender Dysphoric Careers as Enterprises of Imaginative Involvement and the Experimental Construction of Meanings

Early life

Very few young children are reported with marked cross-gender dysphoria. Adult transsexuals however often emphasise a cross-gendered childhood which is not usually confirmed. Pre-transsexual meanings of early distress are recoverable in spite of this tendency. Many boys reported marked emotional reactions to physical defects, appearances, poor physique and stuttering for example. Childhood nervous timidity and fears were marked in 80 per cent of boys. A minority exhibited atypical aggressive and disturbed childhoods.

Where such pre-transsexual meanings could be recovered, it was possible to see how these became linked to gender, at critical turning points, often around seven or eight years. A 'sense of failure as a male' is then a precursor to a fully fledged transgender identity. Now this fits the cognitive developmental approach to gender identity and constancy. Much gender role behaviour is normative, and very young children follow rules without understanding them fully. The intellectual grasping of gender stability (boys become men, girls women) following reliable self-reference in the correct or assigned gender is almost universal. Gender socialisation is a continuing process, and failure to meet assigned norms may lead to a reworking (or in Piagetian terms an 'accommodation') of the gender constancy rule, if problems are genderised, and gender appropriate behaviour cannot be sustained. The raw experiences of early failure in males take many forms, and are not reliably distinguishable from general childhood neuroticism. Sreenivason's (1981) study showing high cross-gendered behaviour naturally occuring in neurotic boys - whose problems were not genderised - is very supportive of this position. Even in later childhood, boy transsexuals-to-be may exhibit a far from fully fledged cross-gendered identity *e.g.*

involving 'qualities' of femininity or being 'different' from other boys.

For girls, early childhoods are usually less disturbed, and it is almost unheard of for little girls to be brought to attention for cross-gender identity 'disorder'. Their tomboy propensities seem to be accepted when they are young. As the normative constraints of gender socialisation are imposed with greater strictness, around puberty, then the genderised attribution that they are being robbed of the status of being 'one of the boys' emerges, together with a hatred for the feminine fate. This fits Archer's (1984) sketch of the divergent gender developmental pathways for boys and girls. Most tomboys become gender role conformists at puberty, but it would seem that the coexistence of early lesbian feelings in our transsexual subjects makes this conformity unbearable. The male role model is often diffused and many female transsexuals realise at some level that their task is to learn to become an acceptable male and rival other males for the affections of women.

Adolescence then is a time of major distress for both sexes. Sexual feelings and potential relationships present huge management difficulties to those whose gender role rehearsals are half transformed muddles, or totally inadequate to fit both private desires and public expectations. Females are more dramatically ambushed by the complexity of the roles of appropriate sexual conduct, and at that age do not have a ready made source of meanings at hand, from *e.g.* the 'gay scene'. The salvation promised by the discovery of transsexualism (often from books) is that it provides a supposed aetiology from childhood, a bridge between past and future. It provides a source of meanings which permits an individual to live in relation to a biography that looks fundamentally fractured 'first woman, then man'. This is probably one reason why transsexuals write autobiographies so often to demonstrate coherence where there is apparently only incoherence. Early life is a tragic story of a great error of nature, and post-reassignment life awaits as the final putting right. The development of workable legends for both sexes, ('I should have been a girl' to 'I have always been a girl trapped in a male body') is difficult if sexual and other response habits do not really fit the newly discovered 'transsexual phenomenon'. The continuing task to reach or maintain a workable transgender identity in adulthood is set out in detail in chapter four: 'Manhood and Womanhood, Doubts and Destinies'.

Dissociative aspects and imaginative involvements

High levels of imaginative involvement are frequently reported by transsexual subjects. Green and Money's (1966) study of extraordinary role play capabilities and imaginary companions in childhood has been mentioned. Through adolescence and adulthood too, this tendency seems to have been abetted by periods of lonely isolation.

The dissociation of gender roles or personas is perhaps a central mechanism to successful transgender performance. The effort involved goes far beyond the same self dressed up in the clothes of the opposite sex. Divergence occurs in food and drink preferences, motor skills, temperamental 'traits', and placebo reactions to hormones. Amnestic barriers develop to control early memories, but control over these barriers exists to different degrees. In a few cases, imaginary companions or bereaved loved ones have been enacted almost completely. Many experiences were reported as 'psychic' or concerned with reincarnation. It is of interest in this regard that many cases of reincarnation, reported from cultures where this is a central belief, involve cross-gendered rebirth and make legitimate marked cross-gender lifestyles which would otherwise be taboo. The salience of these experiences was varied and not always directly related to gender identity. Those subjects whose transsexual commitments crystallised after important losses provided good testimony of how their plan for living-in-the-world was transformed during the bereavement period, with heightened suggestibility and even hallucinatory sensitivity contributing to the final transgender leap of the imagination. There were striking parallels to the attributional theorists' reformulation of learned helplessness as a substrate for depression, following a major loss *e.g.* a marital breakdown (Abrahamson, Seligman and Teasdale 1978). Distressing feelings tended to be attributed as due wholly to an internal disposition, that disposition was stable, not due to circumstances and was global, *i.e.* affected everything. For depressed people this internal disposition was their sense of failed self-worth. For male transsexuals it was their sense of failed masculinity.

Extreme capacity for strong imaginative involvements can work against a new stable persona being finally sustained. One individual was cited whose propensity for hypnotic change was such that 'her' transsexualism began to 'unwind' when she treated someone else with hypnosis. Transhomosexuals reported such shifting transforming imaginative involvements, but although these often constituted a form of transsexual identity, they were not fixed there. Sexual aspects often dominated the shifting mosaic of gender identity, but other social aspects of gender role could be quite stable. Such people lived fairly ordinary lives, with a dissociated, secret extraordinary sense of sex role in fantasy, or arranged under special conditions.

The dissociative control over what is attended to in sexual behaviour especially is necessary for glossing over a great many incongruities of transsexual life. Those few who could not tolerate more than a tiny amount of slippage between 'reality' and attributional discrepancies, found themselves leading obsessional and depressingly failing lives trying to coerce everyone to 'put things right'.

Some imaginative involvements developed very gradually over a lifetime of fantasy rehearsal and a slowly evolving transvestite compulsion. The eventual outcome of this dissociation process was one role, finally unbearable, and another, finally 'craved' as irresistable, full time.

Sex and gender

Kenneth Plummer (1975, 1981), in his various studies of unconventional sexuality, has concluded that persons interpret their sexual selves situationally. By scanning past life in terms of emotions, bodily reactions, group membership and the implications of behaviour for significant others, so a symbolic enterprise of building a sexual identity is achieved. The day-to-day experiences of those whose sexuality is problematic are diffuse and do not provide a neat fit between public categories and private meanings. Historically for example, the use of the term 'homosexual' to describe a type of person, only became current in the last century. The act of buggery in Christian societies was viewed as unnatural whether carried out on a man, woman or animal. Some individuals 'know' they are homosexual, having never engaged in such acts, others think they could be. Rice's study on young male prostitutes found that 'peers' were distinguished from 'queers' by a number of rules which meant one was not the other.

The accounts gathered on transsexuals' constructions in the area of sex and gender reveal the complexity involved concerning the implications gender identity has for sexual behaviour and *vice versa*. There were personal differences in behavioural style reflecting perhaps basic sexual dimorphism in sexuality. Initiative, dominance, and manner of using parts of the body reflected this. However, sometimes minor differences in certain acts led to them being distinguished as 'male', 'female', 'homosexual' *etc.* Many transsexuals of both sexes had early encounters with other people of the same biological sex. However, a homosexual construction placed on these activities, became increasingly intolerable as a cross-gender identity developed, because such an act 'should' be heterosexual. The acceptance of a particular partner, the desire for a particular touch or kiss or bodily penetration was affected as much by how those acts were classified as by the objective nature of the stimulation. This varied between individuals, but also within one person's gender career development. Some males tried sexual role reversals with their wives and only later became attracted to men who they imagined could more fully treat them the way they wanted. Others with a clear homosexual identity - on the gay scene for example - came to dislike other gay men who didn't treat them in a feminine enough manner. Their gender style shift carried identity with it, as they sought the reciprocal sexual response they desired.

The attribution of an act as arising out of a homosexual or heterosexual nature might be based on an imaginative implication that it could lead on to something unequivocally noxious. These implications could be far fetched or remote, for example the belief of one middle aged female transsexual that any friendly conversation with a male would lead to unbearable sexual intercourse. Like other (non-sexual) deep phobic conditioned emotional reactions, such implications affected cues and circumstances not themselves intrinsically noxious. Like these other types of phobic reactions, they were attended by excessively strict vigilance and obsessive control to maintain gender propriety. Thus underneath a rigid and demanding cross-gender presentation could often be found an anxiety concerning a fundamental matter, which was associated and genderised as a major implication of being in the original assigned gender. Many examples have been cited, but one instance for female transsexuals was the fear of being sexually overwhelmed (whether by penetrating men or masculine lesbian women) which was the implied fate for women. Many males and females reported noxiousness to 'normal' sexual arousal in their genitals. These were generally prohibited areas until the tissues were reformed by surgery or hormones. The disorder of transsexualism has so many layers of effort and construction constituting the final crystalised cross-gender identity, that reaching, let alone treating the original 'disorders of desire',is rarely embarked upon. This is a pity, for some males experienced orgasms and post-orgasmic auras which were depressive, draining, raw and panicky. In some cases this seemed to definitely precede strongly labelled gender dysphoria, and perhaps alternative help might have been more appropriate at that earlier stage.

Not all subjects seen in the study manifested unduly tight implicative structures mediating gender and sexual behaviour. Androgynous presenters and some transhomosexuals seemed turned on by the imaginative power of ranging over any restrictions or implications. Social gender identity might be stable and dissociated from this secret world, but if not, there were special problems of gender confusion arising out of the arbitrariness of gender expression and sexual responsiveness. Such individuals' dysphoria was diffuse, and generally they didn't have specific demands to make at the Gender Clinic. Their general complaint was that they honestly didn't know where their sexual identity should be anchored, and therefore what it meant. This is a practical problem in relationships where more conventional partners did want to know what they meant by wanting to carry out this or that strange act. Subjects who lacked sexual desire at all were not common. Those few subjects, who were so identified, seemed to have other personality difficulties which led them to a point of quiet desperation. There was a diffuse and vague focus to their cross-gender aspirations, and they generally didn't stay with the clinic very long.

Progressions and fluctuations

The detailed accounts of progressive transgender identity developments reveal the importance of many turning points in transsexual career commitments. It is clear, for example, that for most males the surrender of masculinity does not happen in one go. Stressful life events such as illness or relationship breakdowns can push an individual to a transformation of male 'deficiency'. For females, this seems usually a less staggered process. In both sexes, however, accounts are rendered about 'progress' to heroically resolve the mental burden of operating through two sets of co-existing labelled feelings.

The scanning of past life is part of the 'symbolic enterprise' of constructing an emergent sexual identity (*cf* Plummer and Farraday 1979), but the discovery of 'transsexualism' as a diagnosis crystalises unanchored feelings and tends to petrify the 'presentation of self' as a case of transsexualism. From the moment of first attendance at the Gender Clinic, this may marshall and motivate various elements of experience to eventually sustain success as a post-operative person. However, where this petrification does not fit aberrant emotions or failed social experiments well enough, a crisis may occur. There are many accounts of individuals floundering for a period, and also tragedies which follow serious deterioration after sex reassignment surgery. A major area of experience preceding progress to a final transsexual status is alternative modes of gender functioning. Where these fail, this is seen to make sense in a new light of transsexual commitment. Equally, relative success diverts individuals from the portals of sex reassignment. Detailed accounts from individuals who fail to develop any commanding meaning to unhappy and unconsumated feelings reveal the full power of the longing for the heroic career of transsexual salvation, and the scrambled retreats from it.

Mood variation, sometimes coupled with addictive aspects of transvestism, is a major element of meaningful experience. Only occasionally could accounts uncover a clear order of a mood crisis preceding a major identity change. More often transgender feelings of despair, hostility and depression were interwoven in the demand for reassignment. Accounts of the expected gains from sex reassignment reveal that salvation from this despair is not a matter of achieving a few practical gains. What emerges in so many individual forms of expression is a desire that a subjectively satisfying and legitimately acknowledged definition of gendered self be imposed on a precarious sense of 'being right', which is pervasively threatened by external invalidation and internal doubt. This contrasts markedly with the fluid and floating transgender imaginative progressions of transhomosexuals. For them, their attributional systems concerning sexual experience and behaviour, were such, that their sense of self was not at stake.

Where a sense of self is at stake, successes and failures in other areas of life may carry more important implications than those concerning sexual activity *per se*. Some individuals claimed almost no erotic interests at all. Reflective individuals who operate shifting modes of behaviour and fantasy as they search for a meaningful and stable construction of their gendered self appear to be more 'steady' in their progress and reversals than their fellow 'compulsive' gender clinic attenders. Exceptional circumstances which abet dissociative mood attributions, *e.g.* faith healing or hypnosis have provided special opportunities for studying the task of accounting for changes in gender identity perceptions, renouncings and relapses.

Practical issues

For transsexuals, every day is a test and retest of matching meanings to outcomes of action. A close look at the business of 'passing' has been reported in chapter five. What is a practical problem is not only a practical task requiring more groomng classes and so on. Success is evidence of the rightness of transgender commitment. An undercurrent commentary (often biased or even self-deceptive) monitors this activity. Biographical stories are woven into the transsexual legend, and this both requires a certain masquerade, and excuses what cannot be glossed over.

Once the transsexual condition is 'recognised' at the Gender Identity Clinic, an orchestrated set of manoeuvres are set in motion, which if successful - and the candidate knows exactly what that means - will result in a formal status passage from one gender to the other. In spite of claims of 'benevolent disinterest', Gender Identity Clinics have the scheduling, regularising and prescriptive functions of a status passage management agency (Glaser and Strauss 1971). Again, notwithstanding good intentions to the contrary, clinical practice can be perceived as a selection and monitoring process for sex reassignment surgery, and this as 'the be all and end all'. This can blind both passagees and managers of their passages to the dislocation of this one passage from various other more integrated passages in society *i.e.* achieving new status related to family life, professional qualifications, political and recreational roles, and so on. Intense involvement, investment and isolation in one passage not only imposes unwisely a monolithic meaning on what life is all about, but it tends to obscure future negative consequences. If the desired end point or graduation fails to be achieved this is highly painful and problematical.

The successful passagees, those who develop feelings of being a stronger personality, manage incongruities and objective losses as a price, an affordable psychic cost, for the prize of great value which their achievement represents. Those expecting solutions and reliefs to fall into place in a bright sparkling tapestry of a new life face cruel disappointment. Their very efforts, obsessionally to mend the fabric of what life-should-have-been, make a travesty of the whole endeavour of a sex reassignment passage. For none is this more evident in extreme form than for the mentally handicapped. Unlikely as they are to be granted surgery, their 'unmanageability' is a compelling sign of our need to give more attention to the non-surgical component of treatment.

Transgender Prospects and Destinies

The limitations of the transsexual passage to sex reassignment

In their discussions of passages which come to occupy excessive commitments of time and effort, Glaser and Strauss (1971) considered Budd Schulberg's report of a dedicated marathon runner, 'What makes Sammy Run?'. In striving to reach the top, Sammy committed himself to unceasing total effort. He was driven round the clock to using any time, even when with others, as a means to help him win his ultimate prize. He was perceived to be excessively manipulative, calculating and self-centred. Even apparently successful transsexuals are often judged in this vein. The functions and fantasies of the passage come to take up such a huge proportion of life-time and effort, that other personal roles and developments are neglected.

Many practical social and sexual restrictions exist, and although they are accepted as the price of reassignment, still only around 10 per cent of initial presenters reach that stage, perhaps after many years. Now social life with only a few 'principal attachment figures' *i.e.* family and close friends can be enough to protect against mental distress and disorder, so long as those figures can be relied upon for trustworthy support and affection (Henderson, Duncan-Jones, McAuley and Ritchie 1978). Although reluctant to admit it, transsexuals often have impoverished and emotionally unpleasant times with even their principal attachment figures.

Medical policies can themselves gloss these uncomfortable issues by the fiction, generally certified in writing by a psychiatrist, that surgery is justified to 'prevent further mental health deterioration'. However patients, who exhibit any significant mental health problems to a degree where an intervention for further prevention of deterioration would undoubtedly be justified, are just those patients who would be excluded from the programme as not being sufficiently psychologically robust. The language of mental health deterioration is not adequate, and other ideas about human purposes need to be explored.

Dysphoria as demoralisation

Frank (1986) has argued that psychotherapy is akin to the discipline of rhetoric not only because of common methods of persuasion, the use of vivifying metaphors and images and so on, but also because of the recognition that psychopathological symptoms have demoralising meanings in the context of modern social life. New concepts and information are provided to make new and meaningful connections with experience. Despairing implications are replaced with hope and feelings of incompetence are transformed into a 'progress' towards self-efficacy. Frank's objection to excessively deterministic aetiologies is that various life stories can be compatible with various symptoms presented. Personal histories are selected and reconstructed into more or less disabling apologias.

In contrast to the above, much of the 'management' of transsexuals can be seen having a technical basis - hormonal, behavioural or surgical as the case may be. This, according to Janice Raymond (1980), requires the individual to be cooperatively acquiescent and manipulable. Social and moral possibilities of a patient's individuality become neglected, as the artifacts of genital reconstruction and desired grooming become a fetish, a portion of psychological reality being substituted for the whole. Transsexuals latch on to, and credit the other sexual half of humanity with a redeeming sense of adequacy, and this distracts from any deeper inquiry into their own unredeemable gendered self. It is possible to search the detailed accounts of over 200 transsexuals, and to find little material concerning genuine self-fulfilment. This finding supports Raymond's call for meeting the problem on 'deeper ground' which would not:

> replace gender suffering with an artificially prolonged and synthetic maintenance of the problem, so that the transsexual becomes an uncritical and dependent spectator of deeply decaying self...transsexualism's greatest weakness is its deflection of the courage to be, and its short circuiting of existential risk, creativity,...and social healing.

This line of consideration can be taken further by going backwards in time to Aristotle (*Nichomachean Ethics*) and his discussion of 'dysdaimonia', or the disorder of not living in accordance with one's true self. For the Greeks, every person had an ideal possibility, a destiny and therefore a 'course' they could follow. A life could only be justified and intelligent if it was truly an alternative among other possibilities. There could be no point to undertake a life course which was either impossible or inevitable (Norton 1976). The Dysdaimonic individual was seen as at variance with himself through an incommensurable disparity between actuality and possibility. Such an individual can only move lamely. The future robs the present when the means to attain a new good are not fulfilling and all that's at hand is hated for it's dissatisfactoriness. The Greeks obviously recognised something of the neurotic or compulsive in the dysdaimonic individual, seeing how attainments, promising so long to transform life, turn to ashes once reached.

The converse condition 'eudaimonia' is expressed in individuals who accept heroically certain discomforts and pains as part of the value of existence, rightfully belonging to the individual. These are avoided or medically excised only at a cost of acting untruths to oneself. 'Noble suffering' thus understood does not gainsay the authentic role of medicine, ancient or modern. However, its affirmation can be considered to underlie some of the extraordinary powers of men and women in overcoming many human limitations or living within them fully. This kind of philosophy and the imperative derived from it to exercise courage, which, in Bertrand Russell's (1930) words: '...enable people to face up to unpleasant matters...admit facts without flinching, and be free from the "empire of fear" ' can be considered one underpining of contemporary attributional style cognitive therapies.

What kind of problem is transsexualism?

The examination of the evidence thus far has compelled the production of a different kind of theory for transsexualism to that assumed in current conventional psychiatric classification systems. The career model posits the transsexual course as a special case of forging and repairing of personal identity. The important twist in the 'mobius strip' of transsexual identity is that problems and crises of personal identity (how an individual is different from other people) are solved by attempting to transcend a social identity (the reference of self to group categories). Generally, very early 'disorders' in the acquisition of gender identity, gender stability and gender constancy are simply not to be found in individuals whose general cognitive development is unimpaired. Indeed even people with quite serious handicaps, if they are aware at all of the gendered division of human society, are themselves not 'disordered' in respect of their own. The final stages of gender socialisation, however, are significantly normative, and it is the failure to meet the standard of gender appropriate conduct that leads to a crisis. Crises may be resolved or survived in a great variety of ways. Transsexualism appears to constitute one special course.

What sets the scene for this special course, rather than any other, are the nature and development of pre-transsexual meanings and conflicts initially. Whether these comprise male neurotic failures or female tomboy active mastery, they do not fix a transsexual destiny. However, as the child dwells on the gender significant aspects of its experiences, and contributes active imaginative reworkings of gender relevant cognitive structures, the foundation is laid for a final rejection of 'assigned' gender.

Gender schema (Bem 1981) constitute in the growing person a network of associations which organise and guide perceptions. Much evidence has been adduced by Bem and her associates showing how people actively search for, and assimilate, incoming information in gender relevant terms. Now this varies considerably across individuals, as in the course of development, their self-concepts are assimilated into gender schema, by evaluations of their perceived adequacy to match attitudes and activities to gender prototypes. For some, the matching is highly normative producing 'sex typed' persons. Individuals, who develop strongly sex typed standards of behaviour and judge they fail them clearly, are candidates for some kind of major reworking. Standards may be physical as well as behavioural, and when identified at the time when those discrepancies are emerging into experience, treatment may help sustain one gender course. This opportunity did not arise for the transsexuals in this study, but Money and Ehrhardt (1972) describe how this can be done, with a male who had a micropenis. The following is from his doctor's file:

> At age ten he began to retreat from play with boys, a change which he explained away as inconsequential. I was not satisfied. Therefore, I resorted to a personalised projective test in the form of a narrated parable.... The parable was of a boy with a micropenis who had dreamed that perhaps God had intended him to be a girl. In fact he had actually dreamed of changing to be a girl.

> With all the calm of a ten year old who has just learned that his talking doctor had non-explosive ears,...he responded that he had often thought about changing his sex. He knew something of Christine Jorgensen's case through the media. He had already made up his mind, however, that he would not bother with a change of sex unless he could be guaranteed to have children by his own pregnancies. The upshot of this interview was that the boy elected to try local application of an androgenic ointment to the penis, in order to induce it's pubertal growth ahead of time...The penis enlarged...The morale enlarged even more.

> In early teenage years I arranged a program of sex education... the subject of sex change fell by the wayside. At the age of 19, I specifically referred to it again in inquiring about masturbatory imagery. Approximately 25 per cent of the time the fantasy would be of having sex as a girl; and 75 per cent of having sex as a boy with a normal sized penis.

> At around the same time the boy began writing feminine French verse and English masculine short stories...Two options of language were being opened so to speak to match two options of gender identity. Meanwhile the boy's sex life resembles that of a college teenager except that he gets severely depressed and is more diffident than most boys.

According to Harré (1983), an 'identity project' may be undertaken when a view of oneself is not matched by the beliefs others have about one's history. Given that the individual realises what social attributes must be required, there is a major task of convincing others that they belong to one identity, or should belong to one identity as of right. This involves the construction of an appropriate and commanding autobiographical legend, and the development of full good faith in it. This task, the forging of the self, is to reach an experience of one's personal life as a unity. The rules, which permit diverse events and roles to be so marshalled, may be stretched under conditions of special threat. These include undisregardable failure in core gender standards, the loss of intimate partners (Duck and Lea 1985), and situations where one group reference is polarised in conflict with, or ambiguous in relation to, another, *e.g.* gender, race, parenthood *etc.* (Weinrich 1983).

Following the transsexual path rather than others

Crises and difficulties in personal identity and functioning are not new, or limited, to the small minority of people who become transsexual. This small minority is growing in number every year. Why is it then this path rather than others gets followed? The results of this study are not supportive of a model that so many predisposing or precipitating variables 'cause' transsexualism. Rather, whether the transgender path is followed, and how far, and if it is left at some point, all seem to depend on idiosyncratic autobiographies of events and experiences and the success of imaginative reworking of gender related themes. The capacity and need to do so are ground conditions but that is not enough. Progressions and fluctuations in the emergent expressive and symbolic task of marshalling meanings play a highly individualistic role, bringing some people to the serious question of their gender identity, and taking them beyond. These have been examined in some detail and summarised in the previous section. The research study monitored the filtering of transgender career commitments, picking up those whose commitment became fullest. The long and winding pathways of some individuals' careers, and the lateness of their final commitment provided one view of what they 'might-have been'. Many had long histories of transvestism or homosexuality. Some simply as inadequate males, who for a while anyway, achieved a recognition of being a proper married person.

The corrollary to the retrospective review of various routes to a transsexual status is the examination of individuals, who at an early stage, looked pointed towards transsexualism. The study of Zucker (1985) has already been cited as evidence against the 'early disorder unfolding through life' theory. His review of the outcomes of the long term follow up of 94 strongly cross-gendered identified boys is revealing of the alternative paths which are possible. Five became adult transsexuals; 43 became homosexuals or bisexual; one was a heterosexual transvestite,; 21 were heterosexual; and 24 were uncertain at the time of the follow up. These individuals were known about in childhood because of their contact with the mental health profession, and that experience may have been an important turning point for some. However, Zucker identified many individuals who did not become transsexual, when therapeutic contact was minimal. However, apart from the therapy itself, is the fact that parents brought their child for therapy. This is an important difference between them and most adult transsexuals.

Transsexualism is a final common pathway for those who reach this point, and one additional influence on those approaching it nowadays is that this final way is now well trodden and well marked in current times. Increasing numbers of gender doubting people make their first contact with self-help groups of transsexual veterans who offer advice, hope, solidarity and 'understanding' of this one path. Autobiographies of people, who are finally committed to a transsexual status, are freely available, and, according to subjects in this research study, freely read. Contrasting autobiographies of those who might have been transsexuals, but did not become so, are not usually written. Finally there is the recognition of transsexualism as a real medical disorder which can happen to a person. Gender Identity Clinics are particularly concerned with those who fit the criteria of transsexualism, and people with gender dysphoria try to fit those criteria because a major 'saving from distress' intervention appears to be available for that diagnostic group. Under the circumstances it is not surprising that the number presenting as transsexual increases every year.

Symbolic issues

The kind of developments towards transsexual commitment which have been hitherto discussed are essentially symbolic. Attributes of behaviour or appearance or even intra-psychic orientations of desire, all depend for their significance on their relationship to those perceived or judged attributes of some category or other, which socially will be deemed more or less worthy. Where such attributes have a discrediting effect, they constitute failings, shortcomings, handicaps, 'disorders'. Such stigmata refer to a spoiled identity, and result in an individual being discounted as fully worthy, good or what would normally be expected (Goffman 1968). There are three major kinds of stigma according to Goffman. There are the physical deformities, the blemishes of character *i.e.* the morally valued aspects of personality, and tribal or group marks. In all these cases, obtrusive or unanticipated and undesired differentnesses impose or are feared will impose themselves on social intercourse. In the case of young male transsexuals to be, their accounts clearly relate to shortcomings in physical and behavioural prowess as boys and, in a different way, young female transsexuals-to-be are made to feel deeply shamed or marked at being 'only girls', a group stigma in the context of their special experience and judgement. Consistent with Goffman's observations, such stigmatised individuals accept the conventional criteria of what it takes to be accepted on 'equal grounds', and are therefore intimately alive to what others see as their failing. He or she knows how shameful it is not to meet socially demanded standards and like many other crippled people can imagine and even lapse into believing they do meet those standards.

Many stigmatised people will seek out merchants who offer some repair - restorers of youth, hair, public speaking composure and so on. Another move is to join circles of those 'like us'. Moral support and comfort will be available albeit in the context of a marginal or half world. In the case of transsexuals, contact at a distance through books or letters may accomplish similar goals. The fullest 'sad tale' accounting for possession of the stigma is likely to be elaborated, together with atrocity tales, group superiority and how various tricks can successfully be played on normals. In the case of transsexuals, many 'atrocity' tales of grief have been documented in this study and elsewhere. Group superiority may seem a little less obvious, but it can be found in the correspondence of self-help organisations. A theme of superiority over transvestites exists in the attribute that transvestites are just 'playing at it'. Transvestites in turn try to reduce this superior view by claims that transsexuals are simply transvestites with 'big ideas'. Some transsexuals maintain a special experience line of being exquisitely informed about what it is like to be both genders. One organisation offers assistance to novices to help them 'on the greatest journey of a lifetime'.

In going through the stages of realising that a person is stigmatised, what the consequences are, and what significance that has for one's self-concept, such an individual is said by Goffman to have a moral career. There are likely to be a whole sequence of personal adjustments, not least because the attribute in question may have a different chronological history to that of an individual's overall lifetime.

Thus there will be different patterns of self-concept development as a stigmatised or unstigmatised individual.

The young female transsexual-to-be is like someone who acquires a disability or disfigurement suddenly. There is a shocked reaction that assumptions and what was taken for granted about one's place suddenly no longer apply. Young male transsexuals-to-be are more like handicapped children who, protected by their family, only gradually realise the significance of their deficits at key points such as their first day at school, or at the onset of dating at adolescence. Where individuals of either sex make transgender moves the problems develop beyond being seen simply as a 'faulted' person. Close family and friends, attached to a conception of what the person once was, may be unable comfortably to treat him or her with either formal tact or familiar acceptance. However, new in-group alignments offer a 'heroic' role with packaged fantasies of humiliation and triumph. Alternative pathways and less dramatic adjustments do not match sex reassignment surgery for its capability to be symbolically commensurate in its promise of salvation to the depth of despair and confusion which severe gender dysphoria involves.

The potential contribution of cognitive attributional style psychological therapies

The accounts of committed and crystalised transsexuals concerning their gender dysphoria and identity seem to involve similar dimensions to those of people suffering chronic depressive states. First of all, the dysphoria itself is attributed to a wholly internal disposition, something about the individual's nature. It is not therefore fundamentally a problem of other people's gender role stereotypes or behaviour. Secondly, this disposition is highly stable or, if anything, has got stronger over time. It is not a problem of getting upset under certain circumstances, or a feeling which can be overcome with effort or ingenuity. Thirdly, it is global. The whole of life is affected, not just certain activities or relationships. The change which is sought is commensurately global. The personal matter which is wrong is pretty idiosyncratic. It is not something like the feelings of discomfort or oppression of anxiety felt by other ordinary people when they have to deal with gender related or sexual problems. Transsexuals at this committed stage generally believe the problem is psychologically uncontrollable. Therefore, they want their bodies altered to fit their dysphoric state.

At the same time, accounts of most transsexuals reveal that at some time, and often for prolonged periods of time, important life experiences and situations have served as crucial attributional turning points concerning how they see how they can live and in what category they will put themselves. Attributional theories and therapies therefore not only provide one kind of descriptive framework but are suitable for describing real life-change effective conditions, which can then be enhanced and developed in therapy. This would be difficult if the clinical population remains as it is, *i.e.* comprising people who have reached the terminal finally committed stage of transsexualism. So in the first place, gender identity services have to attribute to themselves something more than being simply the gateway to sex reassignment surgery.

Most attribution and attribution style therapy is currently aimed at helping individuals to see that their failures and low self-esteem are not due to internal, stable, global and uncontrollable faults. Borrowing and adapting from this, many therapeutic strategies and practical learning tasks could be evolved to demonstrate that many important outcomes in social life do not depend on dimorphic gender roles which are often invoked to explain a lack of satisfaction. Norms and assumptions about acceptable, puzzling or sex typed behaviour can be challenged and made open to change by information and experiences of others, to which transsexuals often pay little attention. Many transsexuals hold a strong belief that they are following a major destiny to which they are fated. There may be difficulty or confusion in finding the path at times, but that may just make them more desperate and ready for a terminal solution than ever. In the light of this comparative study it should be possible to facilitate informed cognitive reappraisals of the variability and corrigibility of gender careers. This would be a healthy antidote to the petrification of gender identity which becomes increasingly untreatable over time. This involves teaching individuals to scan experience for various explanations as a matter of habit rather than fixing on the automatic preoccupation of the time. Future possibilities, too, need to be shown to be less fixed, uncontrollable and creative than was hitherto imagined. The use of a diary is common in this type of therapy and it helps identify indisputable erroneous attributions. In a controlled group setting, for example, attributions of how others perceive or value an individual can be checked out and experimented with. Many male transsexuals cannot bear to be expected to be dominant or aggressive.

Simple assertive exercises can help them to discover this does not violate their sense of gentle respect for others, nor will playing the female role help them to escape from this in any better way. We have a much better idea now of how it is to be transsexual and what such people are doing to cope with their desperate dysphoria. Strategically it should be possible to enjoin at an earlier stage and help such people to work out a satisfying sense of gendered self which works.

APPENDIX 1

NOTE ON TRANSHOMOSEXUALITY

The term 'transhomosexuality' has been coined by Dorothy Clare (1984) to refer to an undocumented dimension of human psychosexuality. Clare's work turned on the discovery that sexual orientation was not always defined by the choice of sex of a sexual partner, but also the type of relationship. Transhomosexuality centres around firstly a 'psychosexual arousal value' and a 'positive emotional valence' *i.e.* an approval, admiration and idealisation for homosexual relations of the opposite sex to the subject. Together these two aspects have been considered the subject's special penchant for homosexual relations with the opposite sex. Identification may exist with homosexual actors of the opposite sex with the subject's own self seen as one of those actors. This desire to be of the opposite gender would put the individual in a transsexual subcategory. Bridging constructs proposed by Clare include the wish to take part in homosexual activities and relations with opposite sex homosexuals, and what can be considered a special empathy or in-feeling (Einfuhlung).

Clare has assessed over 100 subjects, obtained mostly from advertisements, as these individuals generally do not attend clinics. The majority were highly intelligent educated and articulate. 'Core' subjects presented a transhomosexual picture strongly and virtually exclusively. 'Peripheral subjects' had a weaker and more diverse sexual orientation.

As mentioned above, subjects strong on identification were classed in a transsexual subcategory. In the predominantly empathic group, there is an overwhelming desire on the part of females to experience all male homosexuality from the inside (*vice versa* for males). There is obviously a practical problem if such persons do not wish to change their sex, but ingenuity, determination, and the existence of tolerant or marginal homosexuals can make almost anything possible. Subjects tend to idealise romantic relationships of opposite sex homosexuality as *e.g.* 'the supreme relationship' or 'the ultimate poetry of life'.

A small and overlapping category is transpositional. A direct homosexual disposition in a subject gets transposed onto the homosexuality of the opposite sex, often because of a significant degree of the empathy referred above. Male subjects for example may have decided that male homosexual behaviour is too aggressive, whereas lesbian relationships may be described as tender, loving, blissful and lasting. Some subjects may conduct their own same sex homosexual relationship whilst idealising the opposite. Thus one female had a female lover at school, and instead of being 'lesbians' their fantasy and identity centered on the superb male lovers of ancient Greece. Many of these women would be avid readers of the late Mary Renault's detailed and in depth novels involving the homosexual love of classical Greece.

A further subcategory identified by Clare was that called androgynous. Here the bisexuality or androgynous aspects of the love object are of predominant importance. Some females especially sought out transvestite/transsexual/highly effeminate men. One female subject had become so specialised that she was on the look out only for males who were Klinefelter syndromes! A submissive dominant subgroup comprised almost all males seeking a domatrix who would be a lesbian, and who would feminise or symbolically castrate them for a lesbian relationship. For these subjects such fantasies and activities were restricted to the sub-dom scene. A final mixed bag group of multiple paraphilias were again almost all male, willing to try almost anything and with only a tenuous and peripheral link to core transhomosexuality.

A number of these subjects were seen at the Charing Cross Gender Identity clinics and participated in the research programme.

APPENDIX 2

STATISTICAL TABLES

PROPORTION OF RESEARCH SUBJECTS ACHIEVING REASSIGNMENT SURGERY

Table 1

Contingency table of M-F and F-M subjects who achieved or did not achieve sex reassignment surgery out of all the cohort samples

	Achieved Surgery	Did not Achieve Surgery	Total
M-F	34 (24%)	109	143
F-M	26 (43%)	35	61
	60 (29%)	144	204

OCCUPATIONAL ACCOMPLISHMENTS OF THE RESEARCH POPULATION

Occupations were classified in a simple upper (I), middle (II), and lower (III) category of accomplishment.

THE UPPER CATEGORY (I) -was defined as higher professional, post-graduate occupations.

THE MIDDLE CATEGORY (II) -was defined as middle management or skilled work vocations or their equivalents.

THE LOWER CATEGORY (III) was defined as generally working class occupations not requiring any extended training or qualifications.

Occupations of transsexual subjects, categorized according to levels of accomplishment

Table 2

I UPPER CATEGORY

Lawyer	Senior Social Worker	Chemist	Mathematician
Concert Pianist	Civil Engineer	Biochemist	Historian
Medical Practitioner	Clinical Psychologist		
Senior Civil Servant	Electronic Engineer	Naval Architect	

II MIDDLE CATEGORY

Librarian   Artist Photographer   Draftsman Horticulturalist
Cabaret Artiste   Racing Car Driver   Witch   Insurance Broker
Safety Officer (Industrial)   Actor Secretary   Shipwright
Journalist   Farm Manager   Supermarket Manager
Theatre Design Technician   Cabinet Maker   Computer Programmer
Civil Servant (mid-level)   Superintendent of Children's Home
Registered Nurse School Teacher

III LOWER CATEGORY

Salesperson   Railwayman Clerk Soldier   Labourer   Seaman
Domestic Appliance Repairman   Restaurant Worker   Bus Driver
Window Cleaner   Computer Operator
Air Steward   Domestic Worker   Swimming Pool Attendant
Prostitute   Van Driver   Bookseller Factory Worker
Nursing Attendant   Garage Mechanic

A breakdown of our research subjects across these occupational classifications is provided at Table 3

Table 3

Occupational categories of subjects
Number of subjects in each category

	(I)	(II)	(III)
M-F achieved surgery	8	12	14
M-F did not achieve surgery	21	51	37
F-M achieved surgery	7	12	7
F-M did not achieve surgery	7	7	21

Percentage of subjects in each category

	(I)	(II)	(III)	Total
M-F achieved surgery	24%	35%	41%	100%
M-F did not achieve surgery	19%	47%	34%	100%
F-M achieved surgery	27%	46%	7%	100%
F-M did not achieve surgery	20%	20%	60%	100%
Total M-F	20%	44%	36%	100%
Total F-M	23%	31%	46%	100%

TRANSSEXUAL SUBJECTS WHO HAD BEEN MARRIED

Table 4

Number of subjects who had been married when they first attended the Gender Identity Clinic, Charing Cross Hospital (Fulham).

	Number of subjects married	% of total
M-F achieved surgery	11 (2)	32% (6%)
M-F not achieved surgery	55 (7)	50% (6%)
F-M achieved surgery	3 (-)	12% (-)
F-M not achieved surgery	2 (-)	6% (-)

Figures in brackets indicate subjects married more than once.

TRANSSEXUAL SUBJECTS WHO HAVE HAD CHILDREN

Table 5

Number of subjects who had children when they first attended the Gender Identity Clinic, Charing Cross Hospital, (Fulham)

	Number of subjects who had children	% of total
M-F achieved surgery	6	18%
M-F did not achieve surgery	42	39%
F-M achieved surgery	5	19%
F-M did not achieve surgery	2	6%

PSYCHIATRIC TREATMENT HISTORY OF TRANSSEXUAL SUBJECTS

Table 6

Incidence of consultations for psychiatric treatment.

	Number of subjects with history of psychiatric consultations	% of total
M-F achieved surgery	16 (2)	47 (6)
M-F not achieved surgery	75 (23)	69 (21)
F-M achieved surgery	9 (-)	35 (-)
F-M not achieved surgery	20 (2)	57 (6)

Figures for inpatient treatment are in brackets.

SEVERE FAMILY PROBLEMS

Table 7

Subjects with a history of severe family problems

	Number with history	% of total
M-F achieved surgery	5	15%
M-F not achieved surgery	49	45%
F-M achieved surgery	6	23%
F-M not achieved surgery	12	34%
Total M-F	54	38%
Total F-M	18	30%

APPEARANCE OR DISABILITY WHICH GAVE RISE TO A SIGNIFICANT DEGREE OF SELF CONSCIOUSNESS DURING CHILDHOOD OR ADOLESCENCE

Table 8

Categories of appearances or disabilities which gave rise to a significant degree of self-consciousness during childhood or adolescence:

MALE TO FEMALE TRANSSEXUALS

Small/atrophied testes   Low body weight/size   Small size penis
Delayed puberty   Podgy fat nose ("queer looking bugger")   Psoriasis
Deaf and dumb   Puny strength   Meningitis   Lack of foreskin
Gynaecomastia   Sleeping sickness Undescended testicles   Acne
Ugliness/Physical Disfigurement   Facial scars from accident
Mental handicap   Epilepsy   Diabetes   Stuttering   Fat
Strangulated testicle   Congenital abnormalities of knee and lip
Protruding teeth   Broken nose   Small hands   Baby face
Fat legs   Eczma   Inflamed nipples   "Crooked body"
Lack of hair   "Sensitive body"   High/unbroken voice
Childhood cerebral convulsions   Chronic priapism
Rheumatic joints   Spastic paraplegia   Nervous asthma
Ulcerative colitus   Dark skin   Clumsiness
Chinese looking   Viral infective paraplegia

Table 9

Categories of appearance or disabilities which gave rise to a significant degree of self-consciousness during childhood and adolescence

FEMALE TO MALE TRANSSEXUALS

Mental handicap   Bronchitis   Stammer
Hirsute on face ("billy goat appearance")

Table 10

Incidence of conditions or appearances in childhood about which subjects were significantly anxious and self-conscious

	No of cases	% of total
M-F achieved surgery	14	41%
M-F not achieved surgery	72	66%
F-M achieved surgery	3	12%
F-M not achieved surgery	4	11%
Total M-F	86	60%
Total F-M	7	11%

TRANSSEXUAL SUBJECTS WITH A HISTORY OF HAVING BEEN A VICTIM OF VIOLENCE

Table 11

Subjects with a history of having been a victim of violence

	Number with history	% of total
M-F achieved surgery	15	44%
M-F not achieved surgery	59	54%
F-M achieved surgery	9	35%
F-M not achieved surgery	17	49%
Total M-F	74	52%
Total F-M	26	43%

TRANSSEXUAL SUBJECTS WITH A HISTORY
OF CRIMINAL ACTIVITY

Table 12

Subjects with a history of criminal activity

	Number with history	**% of total**
M-F achieved surgery	14	41%
M-F not achieved surgery	63	58%
F-M achieved surgery	10	38%
F-M not achieved surgery	9	26%
Total M-F	77	54%
Total F-M	19	31%

TRANSSEXUAL SUBJECTS WITH A SIGNIFICANT HISTORY OF
CHILDHOOD NERVOUS TIMIDITY

Table 13

Subjects with a significant history of childhood 'nervous timidity'

	Number with history	**% of total**
M-F achieved surgery	28	82%
M-F not achieved surgery	87	80%
F-M achieved surgery	0	0%
F-M not achieved surgery	6	17%
Total M-F	15	80%
Total F-M	6	10%

AGES AT WHICH TRANSSEXUAL SUBJECTS FIRST ATTENDED THE GENDER IDENTITY CLINIC, CHARING CROSS HOSPITAL (FULHAM)

Table 14a

Ages at which subjects first attended Gender Identity Clinic, Charing Cross Hospital, (Fulham)

	Under 20	20 -29	30 -39	40 -49	50 -59	60 -69	70 -79
M-F achieved surgery	1	16	14	3	-	-	-
M-F not achieved surgery	5	34	31	25	11	2	1
F-M achieved surgery	8	11	5	1	1	-	-
F-M not achieved surgery	12	15	8	-	-	-	-

Table 14b

Percentage of subjects in each age group when first attended Gender Identity Clinic, Charing Cross Hospital, (Fulham)

	Under 20	20 -29	30 -39	40 -49	50 -59	60 -69	70 -79
M-F achieved surgery	3	47	41	9	-	-	-
M-F not achieved surgery	5	31	28	23	10	2	1
F-M achieved surgery	31	42	19	4	4	-	-
F-M not achieved surgery	34	43	23	-	-	-	-

TIME THAT TRANSSEXUAL SUBJECTS CONTINUED TO ATTEND THE GENDER IDENTITY CLINIC, CHARING CROSS HOSPITAL, (FULHAM)

Table 15

Time (in years) from first attendance at Gender Identity Clinic, Charing Cross Hospital (Fulham) to achievement of sex-reassignment surgery, or last recorded attendance for those who had not achieved reassignment surgery

	1	2	3	4	5	6	7	8	9	10
M-F achieved surgery	2	12	13	3	3	-	-	-	1	-
M-F not achieved surgery	48	20	16	9	9	3	2	1	1	-
F-M achieved surgery	16	8	1	-	1	-	-	-	-	-
F-M not achieved surgery	17	15	2	-	-	1	-	-	-	-

Bryan Tully

TRANSSEXUAL AUTOBIOGRAPHIES

Listed chronologically by date of publication

Lind, Earl (Ralph Werther - Jennie June) (1918) *The Autobiography of an Androgyne*. The Medico-Legal Journal, New York.

Elbe, Lili (1933) *Man Into Woman*: An Authentic Record of a Change of Sex: The true story of a miraculous transformation of the Danish Painter Einer Wegener (Andreas Sparre), (Ed) Neils Hoyer, translated from the German. E.P. Sulton, New York.

Cowell, R. (1954) *Roberta Cowell's Story by Herself*. Heinemann, London.

Reese, Tamara (1955) *'Reborn': A Factual Life Story of a Transition from Male to Female*. Irene Lipman, Los Angeles.

Costa, M. (1960) *Reverse Sex* (translated by J. Block). Challenge Publications London.

Sevile, Latina (1965) *I Want to be a Male Again*. Novel Books, Chicago.

Sinclair, Abby (1965) *I was Male*. Novel Books, Chicago.

Jorgensen, C. (1967) *A Personal Autobiography*. Paul S. Eriksson Inc., New York.

Dianna (1972) *Behold I am a Woman* (as told to Felicity Cochrane). Pyramid Communications Inc., New York.

Morgan, Patricia (1973) *The Man-Maid Doll* (as told to Paul Hoffman). Secaucus, New Jersey.

Fry, J. (1974) *The Autobiography of Jane Fry*. Wiley, New York.

Canary, C. (1974) *Canary: The Story of a Transsexual*. Nash, Los Angeles.

Morris, J. (1974) *Conundrum*. Faber and Faber, London.

Jan of Skegress (1980) 'To be Reborn'. *Self Help Association for Transsexuals*, (UK), Newsletter 2.

Cheryl of Kennington (1980) 'Counsellors, Experts and Know-Alls'. *Self Help Association for Transsexuals*, (UK), Newsletter 3.

Cheryl of Kennington (1981) 'Are Transsexuals Human?'. *Self Help Association for Transsexuals*, (UK), Newsletter 10.

Johnson, C., and Brown C. with Nelson, W. (1982) *The Gender Trap*. Proteus, London.

Grant, J. (1983) *George and Julia*. Pan Books, London.

BIBLIOGRAPHY

Abrahamson, L., Seligman M. and Teasdale J. (1978) 'Learned Helplessness in Humans'. *Journal of Abnormal Psychology 87* pp.49-74.

Abrams, D. and Condor S. (1984) 'A Social Identity Approach to the Development of Sex Identification in Adolescence'. Unpublished manuscript. *University of Bristol*.

Ackroyd, P. (1979) *Dressing Up,* Transvestism and Drag: The History of An Obsession. Thames and Hudson, London.

Archer, J. (1984) 'Gender Roles as Developmental Pathways'. *British Journal of Social Psychology 23* pp.245-256.

Ajzen, I. and Fishbein, M., (1977) 'A Bayesian Analysis of Attribution Processes'. *Psychological Bulletin 82 (2)* pp.261-277.

Antaki, C. and Brewin, C. (Eds) (1982) *Attributions and Psychological Change*. Academic Press, London.

Apter, M. (1983) 'Negativism and the Sense of Identity'. In *Threatened Identities* (Ed) Breakwell G. John Wiley and Sons, London.

Bancroft, J. (1972) 'The Relationship between Gender Identity and Sexual Behaviour" Some Clinical Aspects'. Chap.4 in *Gender Differences: Their Ontogeny and Significance* (Eds) Ounsted C. and Taylor D. Churchill Livingstone, London.

Bancroft, J. (1974) *Deviant Sexual Behaviour*. Clarendon Press, Oxford.

Bannister, D. (1975) 'Biographies as a source in Psychology'. Paper presented at *Psychology and Psychotherapy Association Conference* UK.

Bannister, D. and Agnew J. (1977) 'The Child's Construing of Self. In *Nebraska Symposium on Motivation* (1976). University of Nebraska Press, Nebraska.

Bannister, D. and Fransella, F. (1971) *Inquiring Man*. Penquin Books. Harmondsworth.

Barlow, D., Abel, G. and Blanchand, E. (1977) 'Gender Identity Change in a Transsexual: An exorcism'. *Archives of Sexual Behavior 6 (5)* pp.387-395.

Barlow, D., Abel G. and Blanchard E. (1979) 'Gender Identity Changes in Transsexuals'. *Archives of General Psychiatry 33* pp.1001-1007.

Barlow D., Mills, J., Agras, W. and Steinman, D. (1980) 'Comparison of Sex-Typed Motor Behavior in Male to Female Transsexuals and Women.' *Archives of Sexual Behavior 9 (3)* pp.245-253.

Barlow, D., Reynolds, J., Agras, S. and Jackson, M. (1973) 'Gender Identity Change in a Transsexual'. *Archives of General Psychiatry 28* pp.569-576.

Barr, R. (1973) 'Responses to Erotic Stimuli of Transsexual and Homosexual Males'. *British Journal of Psychiatry 123* pp.579-585.

Bates, J., Bentler, P. and Thompson, S. (1973) 'Measurement of Deviant Gender Development in Boys'. *Child Development 44* pp.592-593.

Bates, J., Bentler, P. and Thompson, S. (1979) 'Gender Deviant Boys Compared with Normal and Clinical Control Boys'. *Journal of Abnormal Child Psychology 7 (3)* pp.243-259.

Bates, J., Skilbeck, W., Smith, K. and Bentler, P. (1975) 'Interventions with Families of Gender Disturbed Boys'. *American Journal of Orthopsychiatry 45 (1)* pp.150-157.

Bell, A., Weinberg, M. and Kiefer-Hammersmith S. (1981) *Sexual Preference; It's Development in Men and Women*. Indiana University Press, Bloomington.

Bem, D. (1966) 'Inducing Belief in False Confessions', *Journal of Personality and Social Psychology 3* pp.707-710.

271

Bem, D. (1967) 'Self Perception: An Alternative Interpretation of Cognitive Dissonance Phenomena'. *Psychological Review 74* pp.183-200.

Bem, D. (1972) 'Self Perception Theory'. In *Advances in Experimental Social
Psychology 6* (Ed) L. Berkowitz. Academic Press, New York.

Bem, D. and Allen A. (1974) 'On predicting some of the People some of the Time: The
search for Cross Situational Consistencies in Behaviour'. *Psychological Review 81*
pp.506-520.

Bem, S. (1981) 'Gender Schema Theory: A Cognitive Account of Sex Typing' *Psychological Review 82* (4) pp.354-364.

Benjamin, H. (1953) 'Transvestism and Transsexualism' *International Journal of
Sexology 7* pp.12-14.

Benjamin, H. (1966) *The Transsexual Phenomenon.* Julian Press, New York.

Benjamin, H. (1967) 'Transvestism and Transsexualism in the Male and Female'.
Journal of Sex Research 3 (2) pp.107-127.

Benjamin H., Gutheil E., Deutsch D. and Sherwin R. (1954) 'Transsexualism and
Transvestism: Symposium'. *American Journal of Psychotheraphy 8* p.219.

Bentler, P., Rekers G. and Rosen A. (1979) 'Congruence of Childhood Sex-Role
Identity and Behaviour Disturbances'. *Child Care, Health and Development 5*
pp.267-283.

Berkowitz, L. and Turner, C. (1972) 'Perceived Anger Level, Instigating Agent and
Aggression'. In *Cognitive Alteration of Feeling States* (Eds) London H. and Nisbett
R. Aldine, Chicago.

Bernard, D. (1979) 'A Psychological Profile of Male to Female Transsexuals'. Unpublished Manuscript, Queen Victoria Medical Centre, Melbourne, Australia.

Bolin, A. (1983) 'Transsexuals and the Helping Professions'. *Outreach Newsletter
(USA) 7* (2).

Bower, G. (1981) 'Mood and Memory'. *American Psychologist 36* (2) pp.129-148.

Brautigam, W. (1964) 'Korperliche Seelische und Soziale Einflusse auf die Gesch-
lechtszugehorigkeit des Menschen'. *Der Internist 5* pp.171-182.

Brown, J. and Sime, J. (1977) 'Accounts as a General Methodology'. Paper presented
to the *British Psychological Society Annual Conference*, Exeter.

Buhrich, N. (1981) 'Psychological Adjustment in Transvestism and
Transsexualism'. *Behaviour Research and Therapy 19* pp.407-411.

Buhrich, N. and McConaghy, N. (1977) 'The Discrete Syndromes of Transvestism
and Transsexualism'. *Archives of Sexual Behavior 6* (6) pp.483-496.

Buhrich, N. and McConaghy, N. (1978) 'Two clinically descrete syndromes of
Transsexualism'. *British Journal of Psychiatry* 133 pp.73-76.

Buhrich, N. and McConaghy, N. (1978) 'Parental Relationships during Childhood in
Homosexuality, Transvestism and Transsexualism'. *Australia and New Zealand
Journal of Psychiatry 12* p.103-108.

Buhrich, N. and McConaghy, N. (1979) 'Three clinically descrete categories of
fetishistic transvestism'. *Archives of Sexual Behavior 8* pp.151-157.

Buhrich, N. and McConaghy, N. (1985) Preadult Feminine Behaviours of Male
Transvestites. *Archives of Sexual Behavior 14* pp.413-419.

Button, E. (1982) 'Personal Construct Theory and Psychological Well-being'. Paper
presented to *British Conference on Personal Construct Psychology* Manchester
(UK).

Butts, J. (1981) 'Growing up Black, "Gay", and Gender Dysphoric: An analysis of 10
Transsexuals and 3 Transvestites'. Paper presented to the *7th International
Gender Dysphoria Symposium*, Lake Tahoe, Nevada.

Canter, D. and Brown, J. (1981) 'Explanatory Roles'. In *Ordinary Explanations of*

Social Behaviour (Ed) Antaki, C. Academic Press, London.

Cantor, J., Zillmann, D. and Bryant, J. (1975), 'Enhancement of Experienced Sexual Arousal in Response to Erotic Stimuli through Misattribution of Unrelated Residual Excitation'. *Journal of Personality and Social Psychology, 32* (1) pp.69-75.

Carlsson, M. and Jaderquist, P. (1983) 'Note on Sex-Role Opinions as Conceptual Schema'. *British Journal of Social Psychology 22*, pp.65-68.

Cauldwell, D. (1949) 'Psychopathia Transsexualis'. *Sexology 16* pp.274-280.

Ciccarese, S., Massari, S. and Guanti, G. (1982) 'Sexual Behaviour is Independent of H-Y Anitgen Constitution'. *Human Genetics 60* (4) pp.371-372.

Clare, D. (1984) 'Transhomosexuality'. Paper presented to the *Annual Conference of the British Psychological Society* Warwick, UK.

Cogan, S., Becker, R. and Hossman, A. (1975) 'Adolescent Males with Urogenital Anomalies: Their Body Image and Psychosexual Development'. *Journal of Youth and Adolescence 4* (4) pp.359-374.

Conolly, F. and Gibson, M. (1978) 'Dysmorphophobia - A long term study'. *British Journal of Psychiatry 132* pp.568-570.

Corbett v. Corbett (Otherwise Ashley) (1970) *All England Law Reports.* 33-51 Probate, Divorce and Admiralty Division, London. Before Mr. Justice Ormrod.

Cox, T. and Araoz, D. (1977) 'Sexual Excitement and Response by Imagery Production'. *Journal of the American Society of Psychosomatic Dentistry and Medicine 24* (3) pp.82-92.

Davenport, W. (1976) 'Sex in Cross-Cultural Perspective'. In *Human Sexuality in Four Perspectives* (Ed) Beach F. Johns Hopkins Press, Baltimore.

Dawes, A. (1981) 'Becoming Drug Dependent - An Exercise in Construct Elaboration'. Paper presented to the *4th International Congress on Personal Construct Psychology,* Brock University, Ontario.

Devereux, G. (1937) 'Institutionalized Homosexuality of the Mohave Indians'. *Human Biology 9* pp.508-527.

De Waele, J.P. and Harré, R. (1976) 'The Personality of Individuals' in *Personality* Ed. R. Harré. Blackwell, Oxford.

De Waele, J.P. and Harré, R. (1979) 'Autobiography as a Psychological Method'. *In Emerging Strategies in Social Psychological Research* (Ed) Ginsbury, G. Wiley, London.

Diamond, M. (1965), 'A Critical Evaluation of the Ontogeny of Human Sexual Behaviour'. *Quarterly Review of Biology 40* pp.147-175.

Diamond, M. (1975), 'Sexual Anatomy and Physiology: Clinical Aspects'. In *Human Sexuality" A Health Practitioner's Text* (Ed) Green, R. Williams and Wilkins, Baltimore.

Diamond, M. (1982) 'Sexual Identity, Monozygotic Twins Reared in Discordant Sex Roles and a BBC follow-up'. *Archives of Sexual Behavior 11* pp.181-186.

Doobar, R. (1969) 'Psychological Testing of Male Transsexuals: A brief report on results from the Wechsler Adult Intelligence Scale, the Thematic Apperception Test and the House-Tree-Person Test'. In *Transsexualism and Sex Reassignment* (Ed) Green, R. and Money, J. John Hopkins Press, Baltimore.

Dorner, G. (1976) *Hormones and Brain Differentiation.* Elsevier Scientific Publishing Co., Amsterdam.

Dorner, G., Rohde, W. and Krell L. (1972) 'Auslosung Eines Positiven Ostrogenfeedback Effekts kei Homosexuellen Mannern'. *Endokrinologie 60* pp.297-301.

Dorner, G., Rohde, W., Stahl, F., Krell, L. and Masius W-G (1975) 'A Neuroendocrine predisposition for Homosexuality in Men'. *Archives of Sexual Behavior 4* pp.1-8.

Duck, S. and Lea, M. (1983) 'Breakdown of Personal Relatioships and the Threat to Personal Identity'. In *Threatened Identities* (Ed) Breakwell, G. John Wiley and Sons, London.

Eber, M. (1982) 'Primary Transsexualism: A critique of a Theory'. *Bulletin of the Menninger Clinic 46* (2) pp.168-182.

Ehrhardt, A., Evers, K. and Money, J. (1968) 'Influence of Androgen and some aspects of Sexually Dimorphic Behavior in Women with the late treated Adreno-genital Syndrome'. *Johns Hopkins Medical Journal 123* pp.115-122.

Ehrhardt, A., Meyer-Bahlburg, H., Rosen, L., Feldmen, J., Veridiano, N., Zimmerman, I., and McEwan, B., (1985) 'Sexual Orientation after Prenatal Exposure to exogenous Estrogen'. *Archives of Sexual Behavior 14* (1) pp.57-75.

Eicher, W., Spolijar, M., Cleve, H., Richter, K., Murken, J-D., and Stengal-Rutkowski, S. (1979) 'Transsexuality and the H-Y Antigen'. Paper presented to *4th world congress of sexology,* Mexico.

Ellis, A. (1945) 'The Sexual Psychology of Human Hermaphrodites'. *Psychosomatic Medicine 7* pp.108-125.

Ellis, A. (1975) 'Rational-Emotive Approach to Sex Therapy'. *The Counselling Psychologist 5* pp.14-21.

Ellis, A. (1977) 'Rational-Emotive Therapy: Research Data that supports the Clinical and Personality Hypotheses of RET and other modes of Cognitive-Behaviour therapy'. *The Counselling Psychologist 7* (1) pp.2-42.

Ellis, H. (1928) "Eonism and other studies', vol.7: *Studies in the Psychology of Sex,* F.A. Davies, Philadelphia.

Emmerich, W., Goldman, K., Kirsch, B. and Sharabany, R., (1977) 'Evidence for a Transitional Phase in the Development of Gender Constancy'. *Child Development 48* pp.930-936.

Epstein, A. (1973) 'The Relatioship of Altered Brain States to Sexual Psychopathology'. In *Contemporary Sexual Behaviour:* Critical Issues in the 1970s. (Ed) J. Zubin and J. Money. Johns Hopkins University Press, Baltimore.

Evans, F. (1982) 'The Accessiblity of Dissociated States: Hypnotizability, Control of Sleep, and Absorbtion'. Paper presented at *9th International Congress of Hypnosis and Psychosomatic Medicine*, Glasgow, Scotland.

Festinger, L. (1957) *A theory of Cognitive Dissonance.* Stanford University Press, Stanford Ca.

Ford., C. (1931) *University of California Publications in American Archaeology and Ethnology 28.*

Frank, J. (1986) 'Psychotherapy - the transformation of meanings: discussion paper. *Journal of the Royal Society of Medicine 79* pp.341-346.

Freund, K., Langevin, R., Zajac, Y., Steiner, B. and Zajac, A. (1974) 'Parent-Child Relatins in Transsexual and Non-Transsexual Homosexual Males'. *British Journal of Psychiatry 124* pp.22-23.

Freund, K., Steiner, B. and Chan, S. (1982) 'Two Types of Cross Gender Identity'. *Archives of Sexual Behavior 2* (1) pp.49-63.

Garfinkel, H. (1956) 'Conditions of Successful Degradation Ceremonies'. *American Journal of Sociology 61* pp.420-424.

Garfinkel, H. (1967) *Studies in Ethnomethodology.* Prentice Hall, Englewood Cliffs, N.J.

Glaser, B. and Strauss, A. (1967) *The Discovery of Grounded Theory: Strategies for Qualitative Research.* Aldine, Chicago.

Glaser, B. and Strauss, A. (1971) *Status Passage.* Routledge and Keegan Paul, London.

Goffman, E. (1958) *The Presentation of Self in Everyday Life*. University of Edinburgh, Scotland.

Goffman, E. (1968) *Stigma: Notes on the Management of Spoiled Identity*. Penguin Books, Harmondworth.

Goffman, E. (1970) *Strategic Interaction*. Blackwell, Oxford.

Goode, E. and Haber, L. (1977) 'Sexual Correlates of Homosexual Experience: An Exploratory Study of College Women'. *Journal of Sex Research 13* pp.12-21.

Gooren, L., Rao, B., Van Kessel, H. and Harmsen-Louman, W. (1984) 'Estrogen Positive Feedback on LH Secretion in Transsexuality'. *Psychoneuroendocrinology 9* (3) pp.249-259.

Gosslin, C. and Wilson, G. (1980) *Sexual Variations: Fetishism, Transvestism and Sado-masochism*. Faber and Faber, London.

Green, R. (1970) 'Persons Seeking Sex Change: Psychiatric Management of Special Problems'. *American Journal of Psychiatry 126* (11) pp.1596-1603.

Green, R. (1974) *Sexual Identity Conflicts in Children and Adults*. Duckworth, London.

Green, R. (1978) 'Sexual Identity of 37 Children Raised by Homosexual or Transsexual Parents'. *American Journal of Psychiatry 135* (6) pp.692-697.

Green, R. (1979) Discussion In *Male Homosexuality: Perversion, Deviation or Variant?* (Ed) Crown, S. Ciba Foundation Symposium, 62 Excerpta Medica New York.

Green, R. (1985) 'Gender Identity of Childhood and Later Sexual Orientation'. *American Journal of Psychiatry 142* pp.339-341.

Green, R. and Money, J. (1966) 'Stage-Acting, Role-Taking, and Effeminate, Impersonation During Boyhood'. *Archives of General Psychiatry 15* pp.535-538.

Green, R. and Money, J. (1969) (Eds) *Transsexualism and Sex Reassignment*. Johns Hopkins Press, Baltimore.

Green, R., Williams, K. and Harper, J. (1979) 'Cross-Identity: Peer Groiup Integration and the Double Standard of Childhood Sex Typing'. In *Childhood and Sexuality*: Proceedings of the International Symposium held at the Universite du Quebec, Montreal (Ed) Samson. J-M. Edition Edutos Vivantes Montreal.

Halle, E., Schmidt, C. and Meyer, J. (1980); 'The Role of Grandmothers in Transsexualism'. *American Journal iof Psychiatry 137* (4) pp.497-498.

Hampson, J. and Hampson, J. (1961) 'The Ontogenesis of Sexual Behaviour in Man'. In *Sex and Internal Secretions 2* (Ed) W. Young. Williams and Wilkins, Baltimore.

Hargraves, D., Bates, H. and Foot, J. (1985) 'Sex-typed Labelling Affects Task Performance'. *British Journal of Social Psychology 24* pp.153-155.

Harré, R. (Ed) (1976) *Personality*. Blackwell, Oxford.

Harré, R. (1983) 'Identity Projects' In *Threatened Identities* Ed. G. Breakwell. John Wiley and Sons, London.

Harré, R. and DeWaele, J-P (1977) 'The Personality of Individuals' In *Personality* (Ed) Harre, R. Blackwell, Oxford.

Harré, R. and Secord, P. (1972) *The Explanation of Social Behaviour*. Blackwell, Oxford.

Harry, Debbie (1980) 'I always feel like a man trapped in a woman's body'. *The Sun* Newspaper August 27. p.7. UK.

Hazelwood, R. and Douglas, J. (1980) 'The Lust Murderer'. *FBI Law Enforcement Bulletin April,* pp.1-5.

Healy, W. and Healy, M. (1915) *Pathological Lying, Accusation and Swindling; A Study in Forensic Psychology*. Heinemann, London.

Heiman, J., Lopiccolo, L. and Lopiccolo, J. (1976) *Becoming Orgasmic*: *A Sexual Growth Program for Women*. Prentice Hall, Englewood Cliffs, N.J.

Helling, I. (1976) 'Autobiography as Self-Presentation: The Carpenters of Konstanz'. In *Life Sentences: Aspects of the Social Role of Language*. (Ed) Harré, R. John Wiley and Sons, London.

Helman, R., Green, R., Gray, J. and Williams, K. (1981) 'Childhood Sexual Identity, Childhood Religiosity, and 'Homophobia' as Influences in the Development of Transsexualism, Homosexuality and Heterosexuality'. *Archives of General Psychiatry 38* pp.910-915.

Henderson, S., Duncan-Jones, P., McAuly, H. and Ritchie, K. (1978) 'The Patient's Primary Group'. *British Journal of Psychiatry 132* pp.74-86.

Hetherington, E. (1966) 'Effects of Paternal Absence on Sex-Typed Behaviours in Negro and White Preadolescent Males'. *Journal of Personality and Social Psychology 4* pp.87-91.

Hetherington, E. and Frankie, G. (1967) 'Effects of Parental Dominance, Warmth, and Conflict on Imitation in Children'. *Journal of Personality and Social Psychology 6* pp.119-125.

Hilgard, E. (1977) *Divided Consciousness: Multiple Controls in Human Thought and Action*. John Wiley & Sons, New York.

Hilgard, J. (1979) *Personality and Hypnosis: A Study of Imaginative Involvement*, 2nd Edn. University of Chicago Press, Chicago.

Hill, W. (1935) 'The Status of Hermaphrodite and Transvestite in Navaho Culture'. *American Anthropologist 37* pp.273-279.

Hirshfeld, M. (1925) *Die Transvestiten*, 2nd Edn. Wahrheit, Leipzig.

Hoenig, J. (1974) 'Sexual and Other Abnormalities in the Family of a Transsexual'. *Psychiatrica Clinica 7* (6) pp.334-346.

Hoenig, J. (1982) 'Transsexualism'. In *Recent Advances in Clinical Psychiatry* Vol.4 (Ed) Gransville-Grossman K. Churchill Livingstone, London.

Hoenig, J. (1985) 'Etiology of Transsexualism'. In *Gender Dysphoria:* Development, Research, Management (Ed) Steiner, B. Plenum Press London.

Hoenig, J. and Hamilton, C. (1960) 'Epilepsy and Sexual Orgasm'. *Acta Psychiatrica Neurologica Scandinavica 35* pp.448-456.

Hoenig, J. and Kenna, J. (1974) 'The Prevalence of Transsexualism in England and Wales'. *British Journal of Psychiatry 124* pp.181-190

Hoenig, J., Kenna, J. and Youd, L. (1970) 'Social and Economic Aspects of Transsexualism'. *British Journal of Psychiatry 117* pp.163-172.

Hudson, L. (1978) *Human Beings: An Introduction to the Psychology of Human Experience*. Paladin, St. Albans.

Hunt, D., Carr, J. and Hampson, J. (1981) 'Cognitive Correlates of Biological Sex and Gender Identities in Transsexualism'. *Archives of Sexual Behavior 10* pp.65-77.

Hunter, I. (1964) *Memory* .Penquin Books, Middlesex, UK.

Hunter, R. (1967) 'Transvestism, Impotence, and Temporal Lobe Dysfunction'. *Journal of Neurological Science 4* pp.357-360.

Huxley P., Kenna, J., and Brandon, S. (1981) 'Partnership in Transsexualism. Part I: Paired and Unpaired Groups'. *Archives of Sexual Behavior 10* (2) pp.113-141.

Huxley, P., Kenna, J., and Brandon, S. (1981) 'Partnership in Transsexualism. Part II: The Nature of the Partnership'. *Archives of Sexual Behavior 10* (2) pp.143-160.

Imperato-McGinley, J., Peterson, R., Gautier, T. and Sturla, E. (1979) 'Androgens and the Evolution of Male Gender Identity Among Male Pseudohermaphrodites with 5 - Reductase Deficiency'. *New England Journal of Medicine 300* (22) pp.1233-1237.

Ionescu, B., Maximillian, C. and Bucur, A. (1971) 'Two Cases of Transsexualism with Gonadal Dysgenesia'. *British Journal of Psychiatry 119* pp.311-314.

Jaspers, K. (1913-1946) *General Psychopathology*. English Translation by Hoenig, J. and Hamilton, M. Manchester University Press, Manchester.

Johnson, M. and Raye, C. (1981) 'Reality Monitoring'. *Psychological Review 88* (1) pp.67-85.

Jones, E. and Nisbett, R. (1972) 'The Actor and the Observer: Divergent Perceptions of the Causes of Behavior'. In *Attribution: Perceiving the Causes of Behaviour* (Eds) Jones, E., Kanouse, D., Kelley, H., Nisbett, R., Valins, S. and Weiner, B. Learning Press, New York.

Karst, T. (1983) 'On the Relationship Between Personal Construct Theory and Psychotherapeutic Techniques'. In *Personal Construct Approaches to Cognitive Therapy* (Eds) Landfield, A. and Leitner, J. Wiley, J. Interscience, New York.

Kaplan, H. (1979) *Disorders of Sexual Desire and Other Concepts and Techniques in Sex Therapy*. Simon Shuster, New York.

Katz, J. (1982) 'Personal Constructs and Psychiological Responses in a Word Association Task: A Test of the Psychophysiological Correspondence Hypotheses'. Unpublished Manuscript, University of Lancaster.

Keady, M. (1983) 'I Was a Transsexual, Now I'm a Woman'. *Community Care* Feb. 3. pp.18-19.

Kelley, H. (1967) 'Attribution Theory in Social Psychology'. In *Nebraska Symposium on Motivation* 15 (Ed) Levine, D. University of Nebraska.

Kelley, H. (1972) 'Attribution in Social Interaction'. In *Attribution: Perceiving the Causes of Behavior* (Eds) Jones, E., Kanouse, D., Kelley, H., Nisbett, R., Valins, S. and Weiner, B. General Learning Press, Morristown, N.J.

Kelly, G. (1955) The Psychology of Personal Constructs. Norton, New York.

King, D. (1976) 'The Transvestite/Transsexual Community in Britain'. Paper presented to *British Sociological Association Study Group on Sexuality Conference*, Manchester.

King, D. (1981) 'Gender Confusions, Psychological and Psychiatric Conceptions of Transvestism and Transsexualism'. In *The Making of the Modern Homosexual* (Ed) Plummer, K. Hutchinson, London.

King, D. 'Condition, Orientation, Role of False Consciousness: On the Homosexual Role Debate and Its Application to Transsexualism'. Unpublished Manuscript, University of Liverpool.

Kingham, M. (1978) 'The Orgasm: a Sociological Consideration of the Interpretation of Psychologically Derived Response Norms'. *Changing Patterns of Sexual Behaviour*. Academic Press, London.

Kirkpatrick, M. and Friedman, C. (1976) 'Treatments of Requests for Sex Change Surgery with Psychotherapy'. *American Journal of Psychiatry 133* (10) pp.1194-1196.

Klein, A. and Bates, J. (1980) 'Gender Typing of Game Choices and Qualities of Boys' Play Behavior'. *Journal of Abnormal Child Psychology 8* pp.201-212.

Koestler, A. (1954) *Arrow in the Blue: An Autobiography*. Collins & Hamilton, London.

Kohlberg, L. (1966) 'A cognitive-Developmental Analysis of Children's Sex-role Concepts and Attitudes'. In *The Development of Sex Differences* (Ed) Maccoby, E.E. Stanford University Press, California.

Kolarsky, A., Freund, K., Machek, J. and Polak, O. (1967) Male Sexual Deviation: Association with Early Temporal Lobe Damage. *Archives of General Psychiatry*

134 pp.735-743.

Langevin, R. (1985) 'The Meanings of Cross Dressing'. In *Gender Dysphoria:* Development, Research, Management, Ed. Steiner, B. Plenum Press, New York.

Langevin, R. (Ed) (1985) *Erotic Preference, Gender Identity and Aggression in Men:* New Research Studies. Lawrence Erlbaum Associates, New Jersey.

Layden, M. (1982) 'Attribution Style Therapy'. In *Attributions and Psychological Change* (Eds) Antari, C and Brewin, C. Academic Press, London.

Laub, D. and Fisk, N. (1974) 'A Rehabilitative Program For Gender Dysphoria Syndrome by Surgical Sex Change'. *Plastic and Reconstructive Surgery 53* (4) pp.388-403.

Levine, M. (1974) 'Scientific Method and the Adversary Model'. *American Psychologist 29* pp.661-677.

Lewis, M. and Weinraub, M. (1979) 'Origins of Early Sex Role Development'. *Sex Roles 5* (2) pp.135-153.

Lothstein, L. (1977) 'Psychotherapy with Patients with Gender Dysphoria Syndromes'. *Bulletin of the Menninger Clinic 41* (6) pp.563-582.

Lothstein, L. (1979) 'The Ageing Gender Dysphoria (Transsexual) Patient.' *Archives of Sexual Behavior 8* (5) pp.431-444.

Lothstein, L. (1983) 'Sex Reassignment Surgery, Historical, Bio-ethical, and Theoretical Issues'. *American Journal of Psychiatry 139* (4) pp.417-425.

Lothstein, L. (1984) 'Psychological Testing with Transsexuals: A 30-Year Review'. *Journal of Personality Assessment 48* (5) pp.500-507.

Lothstein, L. and Bilowitz, L. (1984) 'Transsexualism and Physical Deformity: A Single Case Study'. *Journal of Nervous and Mental Diseases 172* (10) pp.618-624.

Lothstein, L. and Levine, S. (1981) 'Expressive Psychotherapy With Gender Dysphoric Patients'. *Archives of General Psychiatry 38* pp.924-929.

Lothstein, L. and Roback, H. (1984) 'Black Female Transsexuals and Schizophrania: A Serendipitous Finding?' *Archives of Sexual Behavior 13* (4) pp.371-386.

Lundstrom, B. (1981) 'A Social-Psychiatric Follow Up Study of 31 Cases Not Accepted for Sex Reassignment'. *Reports From the Department of Psychiatry and Neurochemistry, St. Jorgen's Hospital, University of Goteberg*, Sweden.

Luria, A. (1969) 'Speech Development and the Formation of Mental Processes' In *A Handbook of Contemporary Soviet Psychology* (Eds) Cole, M. and Maltzman, I. Basic Books, New York.

Maccoby, E. and Jacklin, C. (1974) *The Psychology of Sex Differences.* Stanford University Press, California.

Margolese, M. and Janiger, O. (1973) 'Androsterone/Etiocholanolone, Ratios in Male Homosexuals'. *British Medical Journal 3* pp.207-210.

Marin, M. (1976) 'Impulsive Sexual Behavior, Masking Insidious Depression'. *Medical Aspects of Human Sexuality 10* (3) pp.45-55.

Marks, I. and Gelder, M. (1967) 'Transvestism and Fetishism: Clinical and Psychological Changes during Faradic Aversion'. *British Journal of Psychiatry 113* pp.711-729.

Marks, I., Gelder, M. and Bancroft, J. (1970) 'Sexual Deviants Two Years after Electric Aversion'. *British Journal of Psychiatry 117* pp.173-185.

Markus, H. and Muruis, P. (1985) 'Possible Selves'. Unpublished Manuscript, University of Michigan.

Marshall, G. (1981) 'Accounting for Deviance'. *The International Journal of Sociology and Social Policy 1* (1) pp.17-45.

Martin, L. (1981) 'Transsexualism and Homosexuality in a Monozygotic Twin Pair'. Paper presented to *7th International Gender Dysphoria Symposium*, Lake Tahoe,

Nevada.

Masters, W. and Johnson, V. (1966) *Human Sexual Response*. Little Brown & Co., Boston.

Meyer, J. and Reter, D. (1979) 'Sex Reassignment: Follow Up'. *Archives of General Psychiatry 36* pp.1010-1015.

Milgram, S. (1974) *Obediance to Authority*. Tavistock, London.

Milliken, A. (1982) 'Homicidal Transsexuals: Three Cases'. *Canadian Journal of Psychiatry 27* (1) pp.43-46.

Mills, C. (1940) 'Situated Actions and Vocabularies of Motive'. *American Sociological Review 5* pp.904-913.

Mixon, D. (1979) 'Understanding Shocking and Puzzling Conduct'. In *Emerging Strategies in Social Psychological Research* (Ed) Ginsbury. J. Wiley, New York.

Money, J. (1974) 'Two Names, Two Wardrobes, Two Personalities'. *Journal of Homosexuality 1* pp.65-70.

Money, J. (1979) 'Cryprotone Acetate and the Paraphilias'. Talk given at the *York Clinic, Guy's Hospital*, London.

Money, J. (1980) *Love and Lovesickness:* The Science of Sex, Gender Difference, and Pair Bonding. The Johns Hopkins University Press, Baltimore.

Money, J. and Eherhardt, A. (1972) *Man and Woman, Boy and Girl*. Johns Hopkins University Press, Baltimore.

Money, J., Hampson, J.G. and Hampson, J.L. (1957) 'Imprinting and Establishment of Gender Role'. *Archives of Neurology and Psychiatry 77* pp.333-336.

Money, J. and Tucker, P. (1977) *Sexual Signatures*. Abacus, London.

Money, J. and Wolffe, G. (1973) 'Sex Reassignment: Male to Female to Male'. *Archives of Sexual Behavior 2* (3) pp.245-250.

Murray-Parkes, C. (1971) 'Psycho-Social Transitions: A Field For Study'. *Social Science and Medicine 5* pp.1901-115.

McCaghy, C. (1970) 'Social Sources of Verbalized Motives for Adult-Child Sexual Contacts'. In *Childhood and Sexuality: Proceedings of the International Symposium held* at the Universite du Quebec, Montreal (Ed) Samson, J-M.. Edition Edutes Vivantes, Montreal.

McConaghy, M. (1979) 'Gender Permanence and the Genital Basis of Gender in the Development of Constancy of Gender Identity'. *Child Development 50* pp.1223-1226.

McConaghy, M. (1983) 'The Gender Understanding of Swedish Children'. *Child Psychiatry and Human Development 2* (1) pp.19-32.

MacCulloch, M. (1981) 'Male Homosexual Behaviour'. *The Practitioner 225* pp.1635-1641.

Macfarlane, D. (1984) 'Transsexual Prostitution in New Zealand: Predominance of Persons of Maori Extraction'. *Archives of Sexual Behaviour, 13* (4) pp.301-309.

McGuire, W. and McGuire, C. (1984) 'Developmental Trends and Gender Differences in the Subjective Experience of the Self'. Paper presented to *Self Identity Conference*. Cardiff, U.K.

McKee., Roback, H. and Hollander, M. (1976) 'Transsexualism in Two Male Triplets'. *American Journal of Psychiatry 133,* (3) pp.334-337.

Newman, L. and Stoller, R. (1974) 'Nontranssexual Men Who Seek Sex Reassignment'. *American Journal of Psychiatry 131* (4) pp.437-441.

Nisbett, R. and Bellows, N. (1977) 'Verbal Reports About Causal Influences on Social Judgements: Private Access versus Public Theories'. *Journal of Personality and Social Psychology 35* (9) pp.613-624.

Nisbett, R. and Ross, L. (1980) *Human Inference: Strategies and Shortcomings of*

Social Judgement. Prentice Hall, Englewood Cliffs, NJ.

Nisbett, R. and Wilson, T. (1977) 'Telling More Than We Can Know: Verbal Reports on Mental Processes'. *Psychological Review 84* pp.231-259.

Norton, D. (1976) *Personal Destinies: A Philosophy of Ethical Individualism.* Princeton University Press, NJ.

Parker, G. and Barr, R. (1981) 'Reported Parental Characteristics of Transsexuals'. Paper presented to *7th International Gender Dysphoria Symposium*, Lake Tahoe, Nevada.

Pauly, I. (1969) 'Adult Manifestations of Male Transsexualism'. In *Transsexualism and Sex Reassignment* (Eds) Green, R. and Money, J. Johns Hopkins University Press, Baltimore.

Pauly, I. (1981) 'Outcome of Sex Reassignment Surgery for Transsexuals'. *Australian and New Zealand Journal of Psychiatry 15* pp.45-51.

Pearce, D., Pauly, I. and Matarazzo, R. (1981) 'The Psychosocial Characteristics of the Wives and Girlfriends of Female to Male Transsexuals'. Paper presented to the *7th International Gender Dusphoria Symposium*, Lake Tahoe, Nevada.

Person, E. and Ovesey, L. (1974a) 'The Transsexual Syndrome in Males: I Primary Transsexualism'. *American Journal of Psychotherapy 28* pp.4-20.

Person, E. and Oversey, L. (1974b) 'The Transsexual Syndrome in Males: II Secondary Transsexualism'. *American Journal of Psychotherapy 28* pp.174-193.

Piaget, J. (1962) *Play, Dreams and Imitation in Childhood.* Norton, W.W., New York.

Plummer, K. (1975) *Sexual Stigma: An Interactinist Account.* Routledge and Kegan Paul, London.

Plummer, K. (Ed) (1981) *The Making of the Modern Homosexual.* Hutchinson, London.

Plummer, K. and Farraday, A. (1979) *Symbolic Interactionism and Sexual Differentiation:* An Empirical Investigation. Final Report of Exploratory Phase to Social Science Research Council (UK).Koestler, A. (1954) *Arrow in the Blue: an Autobiography.* Collins and Hamilton, London.

Powell, G., Gudjonsson, G. and Mullen, P. (1983) 'Application of the Guilty-Knowledge Technique in a Case of Pseudologia Fantastica'. *Personality and Individual Differences 4* (2) pp.141-143.

Prilbram, K. (1967) 'The New Neurology and the Biology of Emotion: A Structural Approach'. *American Psychologist 22* pp.830-838.

Prince, M. (1905) *The Dissociation of a Personality*, Longmans Green, New York.

Prince, V. and Bentler, P. (1977) 'Survey of 504 Cases of Transvestism'. *Psychological Review 31* pp.903-917.

Qualls, P. and Sheehan, P. (1979) 'Capacity for Absorption and Relaxation During Electromyograph Biofeedback and No-Feedback Conditions'. *Journal of Abnormal Psychology 88* (6) pp.652-662.

Ray, M. (1961) 'Abstinence Cycles and Heroin Addicts'. *Social Problems 9* (2) pp.132-140.

Raymond, J. (1980) *The Transsexual Empire.* The Women's Press Ltd., London.

Reiss, A. (1961) 'The Social Integration of Queers and Peers'. *Social Problems 9* pp.102-120.

Rekers, G. (1977) 'Assessment and Treatment of Childhood Gender Problems'. In *Advances in Clinical Psychology* pp.267-306, Plenum, New York.

Rekers, G., Mead, S., Rosen, A. and Brigham, S. (1983) 'Family Correlates of Male Childhood Gender Disturbance'. *Journal of Genetic Psychology 142* pp.31-42.

Riddell, C. (1980) 'Divided Sisterhood: A Critical Review of Janice Raymond's 'The

Transsexual Empire'. *News from Nowhere*, Liverpool (UK).

Roback, H., NcKee, E., Webb, W., Abramowitz, C. and Abramowitz, S. (1976) 'Psychopathology in Female Sex Change Applicants'. *Journal of Abnormal Psychology 85* (4) pp.430-432.

Roeder, F. and Muller, D. (1969) 'The Stereotaxic Treatment of Paedophilic Homosexuality'. *German Medical Monthly 14* (6) pp.265-271.

Rorty, A. (1972) 'Belief and Self Deception'. *Inquiry 15* pp.387-410.

Rosen, A., Rekers, G. and Friar, L. (1977) 'Theoretical and Diagnostic Issues in Child Gender Disturbances'. *Journal of Sex Research 13* pp.89-103.

Rosen, R. and Kobel, S. (1977) 'Penile Plethysmography and Biofeedback in the Treatment of a Transvestite-Exhibitionist'. *Journal of Consulting and Clinical Psychology, 45* (5) pp.908-916.

Ross, M. (1976) 'The Self Perception of Intrinsic Motivation'. In *New Directions in Attribution Research* (Eds) Harvey J., Ickes W. and Kidd R. Vol.I. Erlbaum, Hillsdale, New Jersey.

Rotenberg, M. (1974) 'Self-labelling: A Missing Link in the 'Societal Reaction' Theory of Deviance'. *Sociological Review 3* pp.335-354.

Russell, B. (1930) *The Conquest of Happiness*, George Allen and Unwin, London.

Ryle, G. (1949) *The Concept of Mind*. Hutchinson, London.

Sartre, J-P (1962) *Sketch for a Theory of the Emotions*. Methuen, London.

Schacter, S. and Singer, J. (1962) 'Cognitive, Social and Physiological Determinants of Emotional State'. *Psychological Review 69* pp.379-399.

Scheff, T. (1966) *Being Mentally Ill: A Sociological Theory*. Weidenfeld and Nicholson, London.

Schreiner, L. and Kling, A. (1953) 'Behavioral Changes Following Paleocortical Injury in Car'. *Journal of Neurophysiology 16* pp.643-659.

Scott, G. (1983) *Dominant Women, Submissive Men: An Exploration of Erotic Dominance and Submission*. Praeger Publishers, New York.

Scott, M. and Lyman, S. (1968) 'Accounts'. *American Sociological Review 33* pp.46-62.

Scott, M. and Lyman, S. (1968) 'Paranoia, Homosexuality and Game Theory'. *General Health and Social Behavior 9* pp.179-187.

Sears, R., Rau, L. and Albert, R. (1965) *Identification and Child Rearing*. Stanford University Press, California.

Shen, J. and Jones, S. (1981) 'Sociological and Psychological Characteristics of Female to Male Transsexuals: A Review of Four Year Clinical Data on 39 Patients'. Paper presented to the *7th International Gender Dysphoria Symposium*, Lake Tahoe, Nevada.

Shore, E. (1984) 'The Former Transsexual: A Case Study'. *Archives of Sexual Behavior 13* (3) pp.277-285.

Shotter, J. (1978) 'In Criticism of Attribution Theory: Prospective and Retrospective Functions of Self Descriptions'. Paper presented to *British Psychological Society London Conference*.

Shotter, J. (1981) 'Telling and Reporting: Prospective and Retrospective Uses of Self-ascriptions'. In *The Psychology of Ordinary Explanations of Social Behaviour*. Ed. C. Antaki. Academic Press, London.

Siegelman, M. (1972) 'Adjustment of Male Homosexuals and Heterosexuals'. *Archives of Sexual Behavior 2* pp.9-25.

Siegelman, M. (1974) 'Parental Background of Male Homosexuals and Heterosexuals'. *Archives of Sexual Behavior 3* pp.3-18.

Singer, J. (1980) 'Imaginative Play as the Precursor of Adult Imagery and Fantasy:

The Origins of Adult Fantasy'. In *Imagery: Vol.2, Concepts, Results and Applications.* (Ed) E. Klinger. Plenum Press, New York.

Singer, J. (1981) *Daydreaming and Fantasy.* Oxford University Press, Oxford.

Slaby, R. and Frey, K. (1975) 'Development of Gender Constancy and Selective Attention to Same Sex Models'. *Child Development 46* pp.849-856.

Snowdon, J., Solomons, R. and Druce, H. (1978) 'Feigned Bereavement'. *British Journal of Psychiatry 133* pp.15-19.

Sørenson, T. (1981a) 'A follow up study of operated transsexual males'. *Acta Psychiatrica Scandinavica 63* pp.486-503.

Sørenson, T. (1981b) 'A follow up study of operated transsexual females'. *Acta Psychiatrica Scandinavica 64* pp.50-64.

Sørensen, T. and Hertoft, P. (1982) 'Male and Female Transsexualism, The Danish, Experience with 37 Patients'. *Archives of Sexual Behavior 2* pp.133-155.

Sørensen, T. and Hertoft, P. (1980) 'Transsexualism as a Nosological Unity in Men and Women'. *Acta Psychiatrica Scandinavica 61* pp.135-151.

Spence, J. and Helmreich, R. (1981) 'Androgyny Versus Gender Schema: A Comment on Bem's Gender Schema Theory'. *Psychological Review 88* (4) pp.365-368.

Spender, D. (1980) *Man Made Language.* Routledge and Kegan Paul, London.

Sreenivasan, U. (1981) 'The Effeminate Boy in the Psychiatric Clinic'. Paper presented to the *7th Internatinal Gender Dysphoria Symposium*, Lake Tahoe, Nevada.

Steiner, B. (Ed) (1985) *Gender Dysphoria: Development, Research, Management.* Plenum Press, London.

Steiner, B. (1985) 'Transsexuals, Transvestites, and their Partners'. In *Gender Dysphoria: Development, Research, Management.* (Ed) Steiner, B. Plenum Press, London.

Steiner, B., Sanders, R. and Langevin, R. (1985) 'Crossdressing, Erotic Preference and Aggression: A Comparison of Male Transevestites and Transsexuals'. In *Erotic Preference, Gender Identity and Aggression in Men: New Research Studies.* (Ed) R. Langevin. Lawrence Erlbaum Associates, New Jersey.

Steinman, D. and Wincze, J. (1981) 'The Behavioral Treatment of Individuals Presenting Gender Identity Disorders: A Serendipitous Finding'. Paper presented to the *7th International Gender Dysphoria Symposium*, Lake Tahoe, Nevada.

Stoller, R. (1968) *On the Development of Masculinity and Feminity. Vol.1 of Sex and Gender.* Hogarth Press and the Institute of Psychoanalysis, London.

Stoller, R. (1970) 'Pornography and Perversion'. *Archives of General Psychiatry 22* pp.498.

Stoller, R. (1975) *The Transsexual Experiment: Vol.2 of Sex and Gender.* Hogarth Press and the Institute of Psychoanalysis, London.

Stoller, R. (1982) 'Near Miss: "Sex Change" Treatment and its Evaluation'. In *Eating, Sleeping and Sexuality: Treatment of Disorders in Basic Life Functions.* (Ed) M. Zales. Brunner Mazel, New York.

Stoppard, J. and Kolin, R. (1978) 'Can Gender Stereotypes and Sex Role Types be Distinguished?' *British Journal of Social and Clinical Psychology 17* pp.211-217.

Storms, M. (1981) 'A Theory of Erotic Orientation Development'. *Psychological Review 88* (4) pp.340-353.

Storms, M. and Nisbett, R. (1970) 'Insomnia and the Attribution Process'. *Journal of Personality and Social Psychology 2* pp.319-329.

Tellegen, A. and Atkinson, G. (1974) 'Openness to Absorbing and Self-Altering Experiences ('Absorption'), A Trait Related to Hypnotic Susceptibility'. *Journal of Abnormal Psychology 83* (3) pp.268-277.

Thomas, A., Chess, s. and Birch, H. (1968) *Temperament and Behavior Disorders in Children*. New York University Press, New York.

Thompson, S. and Bentler, P. (1971) 'The Priority of Cues in Sex Discrimination by Children and Adults'. *Developmental Psychology 5* (2) pp.181-185.

Timirias, P. (1969) 'Role of Hormones in Development of Seizures'. In *Basic Mechanisms of the Epilepsies* (Eds) Jasper M., Ward A. and Pope A. Little Brown, Boston.

Totman, R. (1982) 'Philosophical Foundations of the Attribution Therapies'. In *Attributions and Psychological Change*: *Applications of Attributional Theories to Clinical and Educational Practice*. (Eds) Antaki C. and Brewin C. Academic Press, London.

Totman, R. (1982) 'Undermining People's Attributions'. Paper presented at *British Psychological Society* London Conference.

Tsoi, W., Kok, L. and Long, F. (1977) 'Male Transsexualism in Singapore: A Description of 56 Cases'. *British Journal of Psychiatry* 131, pp.405-409.

Tsushima, W. and Wedding, D. (1979) "MMPI Results of male Candidates for Transsexual Surgery'. *Journal of Personality Assessment* 43 (4) pp.385-387.

Tully, B.(1981) 'Multiple Identities as Personal Experimentation: A Personal Construct Psychological Approach to Transsexualism'. Paper presented to the *4th International Congress of Personal Construct Psychology*, Brock University, Ontario, Canada.

Tully, B. (1982) 'The Dangers and Unexpected Outcomes of a Lay Transsexual Hypnotherapist Attempting to Cure Severe Gender Dysphoria in Another client'. Paper presented to *9th International Congress of Hypnosis and Pschosomatic Medicine,* Glasgow, Scotland.

Tulving, E. and Thompson, D. (1973) 'Encoding Specificity and Retrieval Processes in Episodic Memory'. *Psychological Review* 80 pp.352-373.

Turtle, G. (1963) *Over the Sex Border. Change of Sex: A Comprehensive Study*. Gollancz, London.

Valins, S. (1966) 'Cognitive Effects of False Heart-Rate Feedback'. *Journal of Personality and Social Psychology* 4 pp.400-408.

Valins, S. and Nisbett, R. (1972) 'Attribution Processes in the Development and Treatment of Emotional Disorders'. In *Attribution: Perceiving the Causes of Behavior* (Eds) Jones E., Kanouse D., Kelley H., Nisbett R., Valins S. and Weiner B. General Learning Press, New Jersey.

Van Kammen, D. and Money, J. (1977) 'Erotic Imagery and Self-Castration in Transvestism/Transsexualism'. *Journal of Homosexuality* 2 (4).

Van Putten, T., Fawzy, I. and Fawzy, M. (1976) 'Sex Conversion Surgery in a Man with Severe Gender Dysphoria, A Tragic Outcome'. *Archives of General Psychiatry, 33* pp.751-753.

Vigotsky, L. (1962) *Thought and Language*. MIT Press, Cambridge, Mass.

Walinder, J. (1969) 'Transsexuals: Physical Characteristics, Parental Age, and Birth Order'. In *Transsexualism and Sex Reassignment* (Eds) Green, R. and Money, J. John Hopkins Press, Baltimore.

Walinder, J. (1981) 'Cross Cultural Approaches to Transsexualism: A Comparison Between Sweden and Australia'. Paper presented to *7th International Gender Dysphoria Symposium*, Lake Tahoe, Nevada.

Walinder, J., Lundstrom, B. and Thawe, I. (1978) 'Prognostic Factors in the Assessment of Male Transsexuals for Sex Reassignment'. *British Journal of Psychiatry 132* pp.16-20.

Walker, P. (1981)'Factitious Presentations of 'Transsexualism' - 35 Cases'. Paper presented to *7th International Gender Dysphoria Symposium,* Lake Tahoe, Nevada.

Walter, K. and Brautigam W. (1958) 'Transvestismus bei Klinefelter Syndrom: Kasuisticher Beitrag zur Problematik von Geschlechtsrolle und Genetischem Geschlect'. *Schweiz. Med. Wschr. 88* pp.357.

Weeks, G. (1981) 'Discourse, Desire and Sexual Deviance, Some Problems in the History of Homosexuality'. In *The Making of the Modern Homosexual* (Ed) K. Plummer. Hutchinson, London.

Weinberg, M. (1978) 'On "Doing" and "Being" Gay: Sexual Behaviour and Homosexual Male Self Identity'. *Journal of Homosexuality* 4 pp.143-156.

Weinreich, P. (1983) 'Emerging from Threatened Identities: Ethnicity and Gender in Redefinitions of Ethnic Identity'. In *Threatened Identities* (Ed) Breakwell, G. John Wiley and Sons, London.

Wilson, S. and Barber, T. (1980) 'Vivid Fantasy and Hallucinatory Abilities in the Life Histories of Excellent Hypnotic Subjects ('Somnabules'): Preliminary Report with Female Subjects. In *Imagery: Vol.2, Concepts, Results and Applications.* (Ed) E. Klinger. Plenum Press, New York.

Winzce, J. and Steinman, D. (1981) 'Physiological and Subjective Evaluation of the Sexual Arousal Patterns of Individuals with Gender Identity Disorders'. Paper presented at the *7th International Gender Dyshporia Symposium*, Lake Tahoe, Nevada.

Wise, T. and Meyer, J. (1980) 'The Border Area Between Transvestism and Gender Dysphoria: Transvestitic Applicants for Sex Reassignment'. *Archives of Sexual Behavior* 9 (4) pp.327-342.

Zucker, K. (1982) 'Childhood Gender Disturbance: Diagnostic Issues'. *Journal of the American Academy of Child Psychiatry* 21 (3) pp.274-280.

Zucker, K. (1985) 'Cross-Gender-Identified Children'. In *Gender Dysphoria: Development, Research, Management* (Ed) Steiner, B. Plenum Press, London.

Zuger, B. (1970) 'Gender Role Determination: A Critical Review of the Evidence from Hermaphroditism'. *Psychosomatic Medicine* 32 pp.449-467.

Zuger, B. (1974) 'Effeminate Behavior in Boys. Parental Age and Other Factors. *Archives of General Psychiatry* 30 pp.173-177.

Zuger, B. (1976) 'Monozygotic Twins Discordant for Homosexuality: Report on a Pair and Significance of the Phenomenon'. *Comprehensive Psychiatry* 17 pp.661-669.

Zuger, B. (1978) 'Effeminate Behavior Present in Boys From Childhood: Ten Additional Years of Follow-Up'. *Comprehensive Psychiatry* 19 pp.363-369.

INDEX